Library of
Davidson College

HUMAN VALUE

A Study in Ancient Philosophical Ethics

PHILOSOPHIA ANTIQUA

A SERIES OF MONOGRAPHS
ON ANCIENT PHILOSOPHY

EDITED BY

W. J. VERDENIUS AND J. C. M. VAN WINDEN

VOLUME XL

JOHN M. RIST

HUMAN VALUE

A Study in Ancient Philosophical Ethics

LEIDEN
E. J. BRILL
1982

HUMAN VALUE

A Study in Ancient Philosophical Ethics

BY

JOHN M. RIST

LEIDEN
E. J. BRILL
1982

Rist, John M. - Human value : a study in ancient
philosophical ethics / by John M. Rist. - Leiden : Brill.
   - (Philosophia antiqua ; vol. 40)

UDC 141

ISBN 90 04 06757 4

Copyright 1982 by E. J. Brill, Leiden, The Netherlands

*All rights reserved. No part of this book may be reproduced or
translated in any form, by print, photoprint, microfilm, microfiche
or any other means without written permission from the publisher*

PRINTED IN THE NETHERLANDS

TABLE OF CONTENTS

Introduction:	1
I. The Gods	6
II. Usefulness	11
III. Plato: Value and Form	16
IV. Aristotle: Mind and Person	42
V. Freedom	59
VI. Divine Sparks	71
VII. Society and the State	84
VIII. Plotinus	99
IX. Social Contracts	114
X. Claiming One's Rights	123
XI. Metaphysics or Sociology?	132
XII. Individuals and Persons	145
XIII. A New Perspective?	153
Notes	164
Select Bibliography	173
Index	175

INTRODUCTION

The Problem of Human Value in Ancient Philosophy

All of us have heard it said, at some time or another, that every man is born with certain inalienable rights. Although the Declaration of Human Rights is substantially flouted in most countries of the world, the majority of governments still feel obliged to pay it at least lipservice. What rights have we in mind? The right to life, to have enough to eat, to live without fear of torture or degrading punishments, the right to work or to withhold one's labour. The view that these, or any other, rights are the universal property of men as such was virtually unknown in classical antiquity. Frequently when it is presented even now, there is little comprehension of the *philosophical* difficulties it entails. It is in many respects an ethical survival whose first espousal depended on a now-abandoned theological belief that man was formed in the image of God. That belief provided the basis for maintaining, at least in theory, that all men are in some important sense equal, and above all, that all men are endowed at birth (or before) with a certain value. Classical antiquity had no such theory of the value of man, though some of its philosophers took certain steps towards a theory with certain resemblances to it. Let us also notice that since the ancients did not possess such a theory, they could not *abandon* it.

Cicero, in the *De Amicitia* (14.13), provides a rare example in antiquity of a distinction with which we ourselves are also very familiar: the distinction between persons and things. What is so absurd, he asks, as to delight in many empty things, like public office, glory, fine buildings, or dress and bodily ornament, and not to delight a little in a sentient being, endowed with virtue and capable of loving, and, to coin a phrase, of "loving back"?[1] Cicero speaks as though everyone would be familiar with the point he makes and the distinction he implies between persons and things. It is persons, he is telling us, who are the objects of love. Naturally one would treat persons and things differently; above all one would feel love for them in a different way. Yet in a famous section of the *Symposium* (208C-212A) Plato, apparently quite deliberately, refuses to draw any such distinction. The ascent of the philosophic lover is from the love of bodies to the love of souls to the love of institutions, forms of government, and finally to the Form of Beauty itself. Certainly these latter love-objects are not, for Plato, "merely abstractions", but he is well aware that they are not persons either. And the thought that the highest form of love, even though it begins with persons, surpasses the love of persons does not disturb him.

Consider two further examples, one from Aristotle, the other from Plotinus. Aristotle devotes a good deal of space in the *Politics* to the question of "natural" slaves, people who to all external appearances are human beings, but who totally lack the power of practical decision-making and are *only* suited to the recognition of the superior status of others and to obedience to their orders. Since these natural slaves contribute only their physical strength to the society to which they belong, it might be supposed that they are no more important in that society than domesticated animals. Indeed Aristotle reminds us that according to Hesiod a primitive community consists of man, wife and ox, though the poor man who cannot afford an ox may have a slave instead (*Pol.* 1252B12). Of course, females and children are less valuable too, and since Aristotle thinks that the minimum requirements for citizenship must include participation in the exercize of government and service in the law-courts, it is clear that all those who cannot share in these activities through lack of leisure, and are therefore in the strict sense not to be classed as citizens, must be afforded a lower value in the eyes of the State. Certainly even in a well-ordered city such as Aristotle envisages, they will not necessarily enjoy what we referred to above as basic human rights. Undoubtedly certain "rights" will be given them, but not as of right.

Our second example, of a quite different kind, is from Plotinus. In the course of his denunciation and refutation of Gnosticism, he says much which most of us would normally applaud. His treatise (*Enn.* 2.9) is regularly described as a great defence of the Greek rationalist tradition and a refusal to compromise with superstition, even when dressed up in those Oriental robes which were often seductive to the Greek mind. But one particular charge that Plotinus brings against the Gnostics we find somewhat strange. They have too exalted a view of man, he says; they place man higher in the scheme of things than the heavenly bodies, the sun and the planets. What outrageous and unhellenic arrogance! Nor should we delude ourselves with the thought that Plotinus' objection is ecological. He is not reacting, as some of our contemporaries might, against any kind of technological abuse of nature. The point he is making is simply that man is not the highest, most valuable being in the physical cosmos. Again we find good evidence of a very different scheme of values from our own.

Let us take one or two more examples, this time dealing with the taking of human life. Socrates, we recall, was condemned to death by a larger number of jurymen than had originally voted him guilty. In other words there were a number of jurymen who first voted him innocent and then chose the death-penalty over the offensively low counterproposal he himself made.[2] But even if Socrates' proposal was insulting, it is worthy of notice that a number of Athenian citizens thought that the added offence warranted the death-penalty. So far as I know, no-one commented on this anomaly in ancient times; certainly no contemporary appears to have done so.

Comparable to this behaviour in a number of ways is the attitude of the Emperor Marcus Aurelius to the regular butcheries of the Roman amphitheatre. Being torn to pieces by the beasts seems part of the ordinary daily round (7.68; 8.51); and indeed Marcus' attitude here merelyhighlights the problem of "cruel and degrading" punishments in general. We mentioned earlier that freedom from fear of such punishments is now a principle to which lip-service is widely paid. Yet Marcus, in common with almost the whole of antiquity, thinks nothing of the most barbarous penalties being inflicted. And Cicero, sometimes hailed by classical scholars as morally sensitive, is only inclined to think gladiatorial shows cruel and brutal, as they are *now* conducted. In the old days when it was only criminals who fought, they were instructive exhibitions of courage.[3] Of course antiquity is full of tirades against "tyrants" who treat their victims, particularly their high-born victims, savagely. But the emphasis on these occasions is that a vicious man is treating the innocent badly. We may sympathize with the view that the innocent should not suffer, but where many of us differ from the ancients is that they—including such "advanced" and "civilized" thinkers as Cicero and Marcus—suppose that there are certain crimes, indeed a large number of crimes, for which cruel and degrading punishments *are* appropriate. It is true that the philosophers play such things down in their ideal constitutions, but what we miss is any outright condemnation. And our inspection of philosophical value systems may lead us to recognize that it is no accident that such condemnations are not forthcoming. But it is impossible to see this until we are able to generalize on the basis of a full-scale survey of the evidence in the philosophers about the value of man, the relation of that value to moral worth, and the way in which each of us should treat his fellows.

Clearly such an enquiry as I propose could be a study in cultural anthropology. It would be possible, and indeed desirable and of considerable interest, to investigate the beliefs of "Homeric" Greeks, of Greeks of the archaic age, of the fifth century, etc., about the problems we have raised. Doubtless some would say that such an investigation is necessary, or even necessary and sufficient, to account for the attitudes of Plato, Aristotle and the rest of the philosophers. In one sense this may be true, for such an enquiry might help explain the motives (as distinct from the intentions), and particularly the subconscious motives, which prepared the minds of the philosophers—set up the context of thought perhaps—in which new and strictly philosophical attitudes could be developed. But in general, I do not intend at the moment to proceed along that road. For one thing it is too long—there is a lot of literary evidence to be covered. Secondly it is not clear that it can be done properly, for the literary evidence helps us to understand only the most influential group, the literary aristocrats, and may tell us little about the general situation. Of course, as Professor Dover has recently shown us, there are ways of approaching the wider scene.[4] We can look at what the orators evoke when they appeal for their causes and clients in language which encapsulates the value assumptions of the average man, or at least the average Athenian or Roman. And we can consider the comic writers, who are always happy to pander for a laugh to popular moral assumptions, particularly when they afford an opportunity to condemn an "outsider" or a foreigner.

But in the main this study is not intended as cultural history, or social anthropology. My own approach is by three routes. I wish in the first instance to look at the ethical and metaphysical systems, and sometimes at the logical assumptions, of a number of philosophers: Socrates and Plato, Aristotle, various Cynics and Stoics, as well as Epicurus and Plotinus. Besides this I shall deal more systematically with a number of recurring themes: the view that man is a fragment of God, the theory of the state as a social contract. And in chapter 11 I shall have something to say on how far hidden, but identifiable assumptions rather than logical necessities govern the final form of some at least of the theories I shall expound. At the end of it all, I shall focus more specifically on how far ancient philosophers get in distinguishing between individuals and persons, before trying to shed a little further light on the problem by comparing, however briefly, some Christian and pagan evidence from late antiquity.

This will serve a number of useful purposes. First of all it will begin to pinpoint the differences, if any, between Christian and pagan theories about the value of man, at least in so far as those theories are the direct result of the work of thinkers and teachers. Secondly it will enable us to look at the still hardly-tilled ground of the positive (rather than the negative) reaction of Christians to pagan ethics—and that in a peculiarly important area of ethical concern. Finally, if different attitudes do emerge in the Christian writers, these will highlight the "pagan" theories by contrast. For it is always of almost equal value when comparing theories of the past with those of our more immediate acquaintance to consider what the ancients did *not* say—but which we might have expected them to say—as to note dutifully what they actually did say, and thus, even unconsciously, to strive to make them as like to ourselves as possible. For even though the value-systems of our post-Christian age may be growing more like those of antiquity in a number of important respects—this is what we might expect since more recently past centuries have existed on an amalgam of Christian and Greco-Roman moral theory, and the Christian is now being repudiated—yet it is still true that our *ideals*, as I said at the outset, seem substantially different from theirs. In recent times this point has been made by classical scholars versed in anthropology, such as E. R. Dodds, but it has never been seriously considered in relation to the value of man.

In a previous essay I considered a somewhat analogous problem at a more general level, the problem of "love" and of what Nietzsche called the "transvaluation of all ancient values" that is in Christianity.[5] But, as I tried to indicate there, the attempt simply to oppose the Christian and the "pagan" is misguided, partisan and seriously inaccurate. It will do for the ideologist or the religious fanatic, but not for the scholar or the philosopher. What really matters in a study of ideas in the past is to get the details right, for "blueprint" interpretations, though fascinating as fiction, are dangerous, sometimes even lethal, if taken too seriously as fact. The point of this study is not to show that ancient theses about the value of man were the same as our own—or as those of our best selves—or that they were different from our own, but rather how far they were similar to our own and how far they were different. It may also be useful to see whether certain kinds of *metaphysical* theses widely advocated in antiquity lead *necessarily* to particular value-assumptions about man, or rather whether they derive from any such assumptions, or whether both of these relationships are possible. Since there is at least something in Whitehead's claim that all of Western philosophy is a footnote to Plato, it is to Plato and to the Platonic Socrates that we ought first to direct our attention. But before that there are two preliminary matters to be considered, however briefly: the gods and the problem of usefulness.

CHAPTER ONE

THE GODS

The material presented in this chapter is in no sense intended as a summary or synopsis of the views of Greeks, or even of Greek thinkers, about their gods; it merely raises certain points about Greek religion which will help us to understand some of the ethical attitudes of the philosophers. Of necessity, discussion of these philosophers is at this stage only preliminary.

It is presumably part of the instinct of self-preservation to suppose that we are important. And at every stage of human society each man will recognize, even if unthinkingly, the importance of at least a few of those around him: his family, later his village, his class, and at a more advanced stage in Greece, his city or *polis*. And these acts of valuing can be viewed as extensions of the valuation of the self, of the most basic urge to survive and prosper. And whenever and however the gods come on to the scene, it will accordingly be natural to suppose that they too have their friends, have other divine (or human) beings whom for one reason or another they think important or more important than others. Thus in the *Iliad* and the *Odyssey* we find that the gods, apart from respecting one another as gods, have particular favourites among men. The values of the aristocratic society are projected on to the gods, and they in their turn are supposed to be the guardians of those values. They look after their friends and those who respect the code they guard; but only as well as they can, for who can fight against Fate?

We cannot forget the gods when we are dealing with the origins of philosophy in Greece, even with the origins of ethics which arose later than what the Greeks called *Physikē*, or the study of nature. For just as the philosophers, and Plato above all, claimed to be the successors of the poets in their traditional role as the teachers and educators of Hellas,[1] so the gods, whose histories and functions were "invented", as it was said by Herodotus (2.53.2), by Homer and Hesiod some 400 years before my time, were replaced to a very considerable extent by the "creatures" of philosophy in their roles as guarantors of society, whether actual or ideal. Hence when Xenophanes observed that Homer and Hesiod had attributed to the gods all that is disgraceful among mortals, stealing, adultery and deceit, and had thus set afoot that long history of bowdlerization which led through Plato to the Alexandrian grammarians and beyond,[2] we should be careful not to forget the baby (or at least the more positive and valuable theological items) which was thrown away with the bathwater. For the gods of Homeric, if not always Aeschylean, legend were not only immoral, brutal and unjust at whim; they were also, in a certain unclear but palpable sense, guardians of the traditional ways and the traditional values. Thus strangers, even occasionally (*Od.* 14.57-8) poor beggars,[3] were under the patronage of Zeus Xenios, and without that patronage we can be sure that an even greater number of them would have been robbed and murdered. When Zeus, and therefore, at least to some degree, Zeus Xenios was discredited,[4] the newly liberated believer might feel himself freed from all moral restraints, unless he chose to find himself new ones. Aristophanes and Euripides knew that well, as did Plato, who was perhaps aware that some compensation had to be found for the purely destructive side of his master Socrates' work.[5]

Socrates knew that the gods were beneficent. The gods, in particular Apollo, had sent him to do the Athenians a service. Perhaps the historical Socrates formulated no general theory about divine nature, but Plato's Socrates certainly advocated such a theory: God is obviously and necessarily only the author of good, never of what is evil.[6] That means also that the gods only value what is good, never what is evil, and that principle will apply to their treatment of human beings.

Plato's reformist attitude to the gods is at least in part conservative. Knowing that his more sophisticated age found too much to criticize in the traditional behaviour of the gods, but wishing to retain the gods themselves as the objects of respect, he found it necessary to reform their preferences and their scale of values. As we observed, in the "Homeric age" and in early Greece generally, the gods have their favourites, but their choice is not always governed by moral considerations of a sort such as would win the approval of Plato. Now for Plato since the gods are themselves moral, living exemplars of virtue, they must value human beings in so far as they live moral lives or attempt to do so. But in Plato's world, as we shall see in detail later on, the gods are not themselves the source of value; as the *Euthyphro* has it (10D-E), they honour the holy because it is holy, they do not make something holy by honouring it. Nevertheless the gods intervene, in some sense, in the world, for they have providentially arranged our lives so that the good will both immediately and ultimately be rewarded, and the bad will be punished. But it should be noticed that whereas in the older, pre-philosophical way of thought, human beings do what is "right" simply because that is what the gods want, in the Platonic version they must act rightly for the sake of rightness itself. This is indeed a more "moral" attitude, for in our terms at least merely *obeying* the gods because they have so directed may be pious or religious but can hardly be allowed to be moral.[7] But though the

Platonic gods may be more moral, their role as valuers is diminished. It may have been rather random and dependent on mere whim in earlier days, but now value does not depend on them at all. Clearly the world has changed.

What about the Demiurge in the *Timaeus*? Admittedly he is a special case, for he appears to be envisaged as in some sense the maker of the most important part of the human soul. But we hear nothing in the *Timaeus* of his attitudes towards what he has made, only about his reasons for making anything at all. And he is not the source of value in the Platonic world. In that role the gods have been replaced.

For Aristotle the traditional gods are often even less relevant. "God and nature does nothing in vain" seems to equate god with nature: god (i.e. nature) does nothing in vain. But nature has no mind, the traditional gods are banished from the scientific universe, and the unmoved movers and the Prime Mover are final causes only; they are not even efficient causes within the world, let alone guardians of value. They are sources of good, but not deliberately so, and what they cause is, from their point of view, "value-free". Even in the "theological" passage at the end of the *Eudemian Ethics*, God—and however the term is understood, he is certainly not a traditional god—is only the *object* of contemplation. Nor, as a rule, are Aristotle's philosophical divinities interested in human behaviour. "Superior" to moral virtue themselves, they have no concern with such virtue in others.[8]

As for Aristotle so for Epicurus, here perhaps, as elsewhere, under the influence of Aristotle. Epicurus' gods are not interested in the world at all; they are each and severally, like good Epicureans, only interested in themselves and their friends. There is, strictly speaking, no value at all in the Epicurean universe, so naturally the gods have no concern with it, unless one is to say that one's own pleasure is valuable. But Epicurus is interesting from another point of view. In some respects it may be said that the traditional gods have survived—certainly the traditional names are retained—but that they have been shorn of all traditional characteristics. True they are still anthropomorphic, modelled on the ideal of the philosopher, but it is a cultivated, not a traditional anthropomorphism. Some of them are indeed so characterless as to be indistinguishable one from another.[9] Epicurus has indeed solved one of the problems which worried Plato in the *Republic*: his gods no longer have favourites; they no longer bother themselves improperly and unworthily with human affairs. But the solution would have been anathema to Plato in that they now no longer concern themselves with human affairs at all, because human affairs are not only brief in time but without moral significance.

If Aristotle and the Epicureans have almost entirely banished the gods from ethics and from their accounts of value, the Stoics have in some respect done the opposite. For them God is everywhere, and since He is Reason and the Good Life, he is concerned through his Providence to reward virtue and punish vice. But though the Stoics have thus in a sense carried out the programme laid down by Plato for integrating the gods into a traditional schema, the end product is far from traditional in its emphases. When talking about ethics the Stoics do not emphasize the will or reason of God as determining what any of us is worth or what our behaviour is worth. It is not because God chooses us, or some of us, that we may be worth something, but because we are in a sense divine, because our ruling part is divine by nature.

Thus we may say that the traditional notion that God has friends and looks after his own has virtually disappeared among thinkers[10] once ethical philosophy gets a hold in the time of Socrates. What survives and replaces it is the doctrine of Providence, but compared to the personal relationship of the Homeric heroes and their divine protectors, that is a bloodless doctrine indeed. "Providence" is demythologized and rationalized even in Plato, more still in the Stoics. It is almost incomprehensible—nature working in a law-like fashion—in Aristotle, and non-existent in Epicurus.

It is only with a theory that the first principle of the universe is an efficient cause as well as a final or formal cause that there is any possibility that the traditional role of the gods might return in a less attenuated version. Clearly there is no likelihood of that in Cynicism or Scepticism. Only in Neoplatonism or in one of the other varieties of Platonism is such an eventuality available. For in Plotinus the One is both an efficient and a final cause of all that is, and he is endowed with the qualities, in some form, of Will and Desire (Eros). But we should remember that although Plotinus' One is the maker of all things and responsible for their continuation as beings, he leaves them, when created, outside of himself (*Enn.* 5.5.12.47-8). Nor does Plotinus specifically associate Providence with the One. Although both design and arrangement for the best exist at all levels in the Plotinian system, Providence, even in the somewhat attenuated Stoic version, only exists in the strict sense at the level of the World Soul. Similarly with Proclus: his "Providence" is associated with one group of gods in one limited part of the hierarchy of reality. But it might be argued that this is only the *word* "providence", and that the rational working out of the seeds of things exists at all levels of the cosmos. The word "providence" would then apply only to the destinies of *perishable* objects. Something similar exists at a higher level too, and in so far as the first principle is personal, something of the role of the gods in the earliest Greek belief has been allowed into the philosophical world-picture as a whole. But although it is hard to understand how God, as designer and maintainer of the world, does not value it, what we lack is the mention of any specific concern of the first principle *for* his products (or for any group of them).

Thus it seems that the personal relationships which Greek religion often emphasized obtain no pride of place with the major thinkers, even with those who put greater emphasis on the individual as a metaphysically significant substance. What often seems to be lacking among the philosophers we shall consider, that is, the major representatives of the principal schools from Socrates to Plotinus, is the sense of a personal, and above all a reciprocal relationship between man and the divine. In non-philosophical circles a sense of such relationships exists widely in antiquity; and a man like Apuleius who has certain philosophical pretensions is able to share in them. But although among the philosophers we often find a turning of man to the gods, in Epicurus who admires the gods as exemplars of Epicureanism, as in Plotinus who enjoys a personal union with the One, we certainly miss the sense of reciprocity, the relationship in which God concerns himself on a personal basis with man as well as man concerning himself with God. And without such a relationship the valuing of man in the eyes of God cannot easily occur. God for the philosophers is able to be the moral watchdog for man, but not easily the friend of man. In the course of this study we shall be considering various ways in which the valuing of man as such by God or gods is replaced, and we shall consider how effective the replacement is.

CHAPTER TWO

USEFULNESS

Before coming to more detailed consideration of specific ancient concepts of value, we must make a further series of preliminary remarks; this time about usefulness and its connection with goodness. For since what is useful is in some sense good, there will be a tendency in any culture and any language simply to equate the good and the useful. Hence the question must be raised in regard to that culture: is there anything which is thought good which is not useful? That question may be answered in the affirmative, in which case we may draw (and try to analyze) a clear distinction between goodness and utility. If the answer is in the negative, however, different problems require investigation. If all goods are somehow useful, what is the special "usefulness" of the good man? He may be useful since he is good *for* something, or good *at* something, or both good *for* and good *at*. Or could he be useful in some other special way?

We distinguish between objects and persons. Clearly objects may be good for something, but they are not good at anything. Those which are good for something have some sort of value, those which are good for nothing are worthless. With persons the situation is more complicated, for they may be regarded as good for something and "good" in no other sense; in which case they are treated more or less as objects, and as soon as they cease to be good for the purposes for which they are "intended", or for which they may be used—unless, of course, they can be put to some other purpose—they lose whatever value they may have had before. Under these circumstances the senile, the seriously deformed, the badly injured, etc., may lose all the value they ever had, unless they may perhaps be used as *examples* to other people of certain kinds of heroic behaviour and, as we may say, are useful for that at least.

We shall bear in mind the idea of being "good *for*" in the course of our enquiry: it is not an idea likely to produce a particularly high estimation of human beings. We shall certainly find it occurring regularly in antiquity, both among philosophers and in the society at large, but in a search for approximations to the notion of inalienable rights and basic irreducible value we shall probably advance further with the notion of "good at". For this notion suggests at least the possibility of man's being a free agent, not merely someone who is arranged or to whom and through whom things are done by others. Obviously what is "good for" something is going to be useful. But what is the relationship between what is "good at" something and the useful? Here we have a quite different question, though we should not make the mistake of assuming that someone who is "good at" something is necessarily a good man. "Al Capone was good at bank-robberies" does not imply that Al Capone was a good man, merely that he was a good bank-robber. And although good men may well turn out to be useful, good bank-robbers, assassins, con-men, etc. are not—except perhaps to "special interest" groups of like-minded persons. The point is worth making, because it seems that originally in Greek the words for "good", "excellence", "virtue" had no necessary moral connotations. You could be a good or excellent killer, and your dagger could have its virtue. So when we are considering people who are "good at" but who are also useful, we should not include all those who might be labelled "good at".

But what about the good man? Is he *simply* good, or is he necessarily good at something or some things too, and in virtue of this goodness is he called good? In a primitive society, for example, a man good at fighting and looking after his family and his people in general might for these reasons be called a good man. Nevertheless, even in such societies it is easy to imagine two "good" men, both good at doing those necessary jobs, but of whom one was kinder, more thoughtful, more generous than the other. He might, in virtue of these qualities, be called the better man. And it is not clear that in this context "better" means simply "more useful", say, to others. Certainly it may include that sort of connotation, but it is not limited to it. It looks as though it is difficult to reduce the general morally-approving word "good" to "useful" in such a social context.

Nevertheless, although it may be argued that "good" cannot be reduced first to "good at", and, via "good at", to "useful", it seems that in the sort of primitive society we mentioned, the good man will always *in fact* be useful, i.e. good at something, that is, that no one who is not useful can be called a good man. From that it would follow that no one who is not useful would have any value, unless he could be said to be "good for" something, that is, unless he could be valued not in the manner of purposive human beings, but in the manner of inanimate "goods" or of human units, that is, human beings viewed in this regard as though they were inanimate items.

From this it follows that in such a society as we are envisaging, to determine whether a man has value, and, if so, how much, we must begin by considering what he is good at or good for. If we find that he is good at, and even good for, nothing, we shall conclude that he has no value. At bottom such a model suggests that value depends on the ability to contribute in some way, either in a more human fashion if one is good at something useful, or at least in a less human fashion if one is good for something, i.e. can be put to some use in the society. Let us now look at what happens in a society which tends to think of value in this way in terms of the contributions of its members. Consider a few particular cases, beginning with slavery, an institution endemic and ubiquitous in ancient life. Slaves will normally be good at something, and, from the point of view of their owners, will be good for doing what they themselves are good at doing. They have a market value, and may or may not have a "personal" value to their owner over and above that. Many, of course, would have no personal value, and their market value would sharply decrease if they ceased to be able to do what they were previously good at. If, through injury or illness, they lose the ability to work altogether, they would also forfeit their entire market value, and in the cases where they have no "personal" value they would be left with no value at all in the eyes of their master or of society in general—unless, presumably, someone should be "generous" enough as to choose to do anything to help them. In ancient terms, such generosity would not be regarded as a moral obligation. We recall that in Plato's *Euthyphro* it is deliberately intended to be curious, and indeed paradoxical, that Euthyphro should be prosecuting his father over a serf whom the latter has killed. Normally, indeed, if a *slave* were killed—though there are modifications to this general principle—it was held that an offence had been committed against the slave-owner, not against the slave himself. To kill a man's slave was to rob the master of the slave's value.

Consider the case of an old, helpless man. He can no longer do anything for himself or for anyone else. Why keep him alive? At bottom why waste food on him? Children (and to a lesser degree other relations) will normally be supposed to have an obligation to do so; it is in part viewed as a compensation for nurture in infancy and childhood, in part as an act of piety towards the spirits of family and ancestors. But such ties apart, there is no obligation, no reason in ordinary morality why one should not let people die in ditches, or pass by on the other sides of roads. Of course killing by neglect and killing by direct interference are viewed differently. One is not allowed to take the life of an old and worn out citizen, even if he contributes nothing, though one may in effect leave him to die. Killing in such circumstances may be viewed similarly to killing a slave, that is, that the man "belongs" in some sense to his family; or perhaps a man has obtained as it were a pension of rights as the result of *past* services accomplished for the community. And beyond that there is the more "primitive" factor that any kind of killing might "pollute" the community in which it is committed. But all these explanations of the protection given to the old man have little to do with his value now that he is no longer useful.

Consider the case of women and girls. They are useful for child-bearing; but that can be a mixed blessing, for although male children in particular may be useful to work for the family, till the soil, etc., the number of them cannot be allowed to become too large, lest they become a serious economic liability. As for the other services which women and girls may perform, many of them, including obviously those of a domestic nature, could be equally well, and sometimes better, performed by slaves. And since women have virtually no public, as opposed to domestic role to play, except indeed as suppliers of "cannon-fodder", their value as contributors may thus also sink to a very low level.

When we consider the usefulness and the contribution of the good man, we shall not, of course, limit ourselves to "material" contributions, let alone to what an individual can be used for; there are also moral considerations which, especially in the case of "higher" class members of the society, may be regarded as much more important. For exemplars of virtue may be valued as much in terms of what they *contribute* to the society as in terms of intrinsic worth. Hence it might well be supposed, as it certainly is by many of the Greek philosophers, that moral superiority entails a *greater* degree of usefulness; and conversely that such usefulness may be an index of moral quality.

Consideration of the question of usefulness will also enable us to shed unexpected light on ancient utopias or ideal societies. The idea of the perfect society exercized a remarkable fascination on the philosophers of Greece for many centuries, and it is worth asking why this should have been so, or at least some of the reasons for it. Consider Plato's *Republic*, the most famous and influential example of the genre. One of the major features of this state, which indeed helps substantially to make it ideal in Plato's opinion, is that it affords an opportunity for each person to do what he can do best, provided, of course, that his skill is honourable rather than criminal or frivolous. Or rather perhaps we should say not only that the state provides opportunities of this kind, but that it is also founded on the principle that each person should "do his own thing" (*Rep.* 433A8), which will entail his contributing to the society to the maximum extent of his capabilities. Indeed, one of the principal attractive features of all ideal societies is that they seem to provide the opportunity to make use of capacities; but this may be interpreted differently: we may either think of the improvement of the individual and of his maximum development; or we may think of his maximum contribution to the society to which he belongs to the exclusion of concern with the man himself; or, of course, we may think of some combination of the two. Clearly when concern is only for one's contribution, we are dealing with a world in which value is entirely contributed by the society to the individual; and we shall examine theses of that kind in antiquity at a later stage. Plato's view and that of most other ancient utopians, however, is not of this sort: his primary concern is that the perfect society by definition provides the best environment for "soulmaking", or for improvement in the moral qualities of the individuals of whom the society is composed. Their moral qualities may be *measured*, partly at least, in terms of their contributions to that society, but their value is not determined by those contributions. For, as we shall see in Plato's case, the actions performed by the good man *flow from* his goodness; his goodness does not simply consist of the good acts which he performs.

The question of providence recurs at this point. For there is a sense in which a providential world, if one can be discerned, is a world where everyone contributes, willy-nilly, what he is supposed to contribute. Of course he may contribute to the sum total of good against his will. Like the Stoic dog behind the cart he may be dragged along,[1] but he contributes nevertheless. It is also true that his value is not necessarily related to his contribution; it may, for example, depend on the purity of his motives and his intentions. But the providential cosmos and the philosophical utopia are related in respect of the fact that on each occasion the individual is arranged so that he can (and does) contribute what is most in accord with reason or with some divine plan.

We shall consider at a later stage the case of the man who is more or less self-determining, at least in things that matter. Clearly his life need not be providentially arranged; indeed such a thesis of self-sufficiency might be wholly opposed to a providential view of the world. For the ideal of self-sufficiency may depend on a view that the individual is not *for* anything pre-defined or determined outside the bounds of the self; rather he is free to determine his own (moral) destiny. For such a man, of course, "contributions" and usefulness to society are entirely irrelevant. If he chooses to contribute, he may; but neither his moral worth nor his value are in any way connected to that decision.

I have thus far avoided detailed discussion of particular ancient theories, but these preliminary comments on utility should be borne in mind throughout the discussion that is to follow. We shall see that no important philosopher in antiquity claims that one's value depends on one's contribution to society ("from each according to his ability") without introducing further moderating factors; or rather other factors than utility are basic to ancient ideas of value, though considerations of utility are often intermingled with them, sometimes preventing us from seeing the wood for the trees.

CHAPTER THREE

PLATO: VALUE AND FORM

There is no reason to disbelieve Xenophon and Plato when they tell us, as they frequently do, that Socrates went about Athens asking people about moral qualities: what is courage?; what is piety?; what is goodness?. Aristotle thought that Socrates was looking for definitions, albeit real definitions, of these qualities. Perhaps eventually it came to that. But at first he was looking for a means of identifying and grasping them, seeking a distinguishing mark by means of which he could always recognize courage when he saw it.[1] For moral qualities are clearly important. They have value—indeed a traditional and well-known value—though Socrates did not express it like that.

Anyone can recognize a brave man, Socrates is told in the *Laches* (190E). He does certain things well: he stands in the battle-line and confronts the foe. Anyone should know what it is to be pious, Euthyphro suggests: I'm pious now in prosecuting my father for homicide because he killed a serf (5DE). In other words the traditional value-scheme tells us that by their fruits ye shall know them. A brave man acts bravely, a wise man acts wisely, a good man (*kaloskagathos*) acts well.

Sometimes books on Plato seem to suggest that Socrates rejects this traditional attitude in favour of a certain variety of "intellectualism". A good man, it might be suggested, knows what is right. But of course there is no necessity for the two views to be mutually exclusive. It is possible to do what is right as well as know what is right when one is a good man. Any *one* of these alternatives alone might be thought absurd. Clearly Socrates never believed or wanted anyone else to believe that a good man knows what is right and does *not* do it. Then he would be able to talk *about* goodness but not to practice it. That is like saying that a cyclist knows about cycling but need not be able to ride a bike. As we shall see, when in the *Timaeus* the Demiurge produces order out of chaos, Plato says that he does so because he is good (*Tim.* 29E). In other words "being good" entails "doing good".[2]

In the earlier, pre-Socratic days people may have assumed—this is what Socrates seems to complain of—that we speak and think as though there is no difference between being good and doing good, that in some sense "to be good" *means* "to do good", "to be brave" means "to act bravely". "Is he brave?" can then be answered solely in terms of "What does he do?". It is in the *Meno* that Plato points out that merely doing the right thing can be the result of "true opinion", not of knowledge (97BC); with that the traditional ethic of action is condemned as incomplete. But there is no suggestion here or anywhere else in Plato that an "intellectualist" ethic, in the sense of an ethic of merely *knowing* what is right, is designed to replace, rather than to reinforce an ethic of action. Yet this only brings us to the edge of our principal concern. We are to value the man who "is good" and "does good". But what of the man who is not good and who acts badly? What are we to make of him?

I presume that Plato wrote the *First Alcibiades*, but even if he did not, there is no doubt that it represents Socratic-seeming positions. The point of the dialogue is to identify the self with the soul; and to indicate that the philosopher's concern is with the betterment of his soul (*psychē*). That is in line with what we also meet in the *Apology*, where Socrates is found to have been exhorting the people of Athens to concern themselves not with money or fame but with the tending of their souls. Quite simply Socrates is urging them to be moral. To tend one's soul, or one's self in the language of the *Alcibiades*, is to be moral, to be a good man, to value what is really valuable. Notice of course that in the *Apology* Socrates does not merely urge the Athenians to look after their souls, but to concern themselves that their souls should be as good as possible, that is to characterize their souls in a particular way (29DE). The soul is valuable in so far as it possesses goodness, that is, a special kind of goodness. The goodness of the soul (moral goodness) is superior to any other "goods" which human beings can search for.

One point, of course, Socrates has in common with the searchers after other forms of goodness. Both he and they agree that in some sense the "goodness" which one needs is useful, that it benefits a man to have it. Clearly, one might suppose, the practitioners of ordinary goodness think the goods they seek beneficial. And from Socrates' point of view how could it not seem obvious that if you have a "better soul", if you are a "better man" (and a better man has a better soul), then you have profited in some significant way? What we do not find in the *Apology*, of course, is any statement by Socrates of *how* you become better, apart from the fact that you become better if you *look for* the good of the soul, or try to make the soul better. What we find is the urge to search; what we miss is the "content" of goodness.[3] What is this thing which makes the soul better and which it is so important to seek? Where is it to be found?

So we seem to find Socrates urging us to be better, but not telling us what it means to be better or how we are to become better. One solution to this difficulty must be ruled out. Although in the *Apology* Socrates is sure that the unexamined life is not worth living, there is no real evidence that he thought that the mere *search*, rather than the finding of "goodness" is what matters. Only one passage might give credence to such an interpretation. That is the section in which, speaking of the possibility of life after death, Socrates envisages himself asking questions of the Homeric heroes in the same way as he questions his contemporaries in Athens (41B). But even the prospect of seemingly endless enquiry after death does not mean that there is no end in view. Socrates is still interested in finding someone who is wise, who can explain the secret of wisdom.

The traditional word for what Socrates means by goodness of soul is virtue (aretē); hence it is not surprising that in the Socratic dialogues there is a good deal of emphasis on what virtue is. How can virtue be acquired? Is virtue natural or can it be taught? At an earlier stage of Greek society, as I have already briefly noted, a good man could be observed and recognized by his behaviour. He imbibed (or should have imbibed) his goodness—if he was from the right kind of family and class—from his family and his family's friends. Later, not replacing this notion, but rather superimposed upon it, came the view that virtue was not "inborn" in those of the right birth, but could be taught to anyone who could afford the time and money to study it with a professional teacher, or sophist. At least according to Plato, however, the sophists had no clear idea of what was involved in their teaching, or even, in a sense, of what they were teaching. In the *Gorgias* we find Gorgias purveying the art of fine speech; but when Socrates queries him about the *use* to which people might put such an art, he seems to find the question absurd. Everyone, he thinks, knows the difference between right and wrong. And when pressed, he says that if by some chance his pupils do not know the difference, do not know what right and wrong are, then he will teach them that too (*Gorgias* 459E-460A). He has given no serious thought to what is good, or, as we put it earlier, to the content of goodness.

In other words, there is a lot of evidence in the "Socratic" dialogues that, while Socrates and the Sophists are seeking for goodness, while the Sophists, though not Socrates, are trying to teach goodness, yet often the content of goodness is neglected, or, if considered, thought of in fairly traditional terms. In the *Protagoras* Protagoras' good man is able to run his property efficiently and to handle public business well: a quite traditional pair of responsibilities. And also, we should note, a pair different in their implications from any Socratic tending of the soul. They are "external" acts, rather than "internal" conditions. Which is not to say that Socrates' "interiorization" of morality would not, or was not intended to result in specific kinds of behaviour, though they might not be traditional kinds of behaviour. Socrates does not value his property or even his city so much as the state of his soul. He points to the neglect of his private concerns, and he only does what he is strictly required to do of ordinary public duties. He even neglects his family for the wider issues of a concern for the well-being of the *souls* of his fellow-citizens.

The Socratic shift of emphasis from the city or the family-estate to the self may be recognized as another way in which the problem of the content of goodness must have arisen. It is obvious, or it might have seemed obvious, what it meant to benefit the city: one conquered the city's enemies, and enlarged its territory or its treasury. And looking after one's property is similarly uncontroversial. One makes sure that the land produces, that the slaves work hard and carefully, etc. But doing good to one's self, or one's soul, is more difficult. What exactly should it consist in? In areas where traditional values can still be seen to be helpful to the soul, Socrates is able to fall back on them, sometimes bolstering them with more sophisticated argumentation. Thus in the *Crito* he can refuse to break the laws of the city; if he does it would be out of keeping and indeed unjust. He would in some sense become worse for such action. At the end of his life Socrates' number of choices was seriously curtailed, and in Plato's version he had no difficulty in deciding on the proper course of action. On other occasions the right decision, if not available from the resorted stock of traditional values, would have been much harder to obtain.

One of the problems about virtue confronting Socrates seems to have been envisioned by Plato, and probably by Socrates himself, in the following form. We know that there exist virtues, as well as goodness itself. How can we find out what sort of *things* these are? In the *Protagoras* Plato uses the word *pragma* (thing) of the particular virtue (in this case, courage) with which he is concerned (330C1, 330D4, 349B3, 349C1). Socrates came to think that he could find this quality, and other such qualities, in human beings and human actions (perhaps in the first instance primarily in human actions). Hence he gave up the study of nature, to which his earlier studies (perhaps with Archelaus) had been directed.[4] And he believed that unless he could identify virtue with certainty, he could not hope to acquire it; and that as a kind of teacher he could not teach it to others (as the Sophists were claiming to do) unless he knew what it is. The point seems to be made explicitly in the *Meno*, where a discussion which begins with the standard sophistic problem of whether virtue can be taught very quickly passes on to the question of how you can teach it if you do not know what it is. It seems likely that Socrates himself never came to any clear conclusions as to what it is. He was certain of its existence and of its importance, certain of the importance of looking for it, but uncertain what he was looking for and never clear that he had found it.

But what Socrates *was* clear about, as we have seen, was that the Good can be found among men. So his activities were limited to what we call ethics. And he seems to have believed that with a basic minimum of non-ethical assumptions, such as that of the existence of the gods, his difficulties about goodness and the virtues could be solved. That valuable thing, goodness, can be identified by a consideration of moral characteristics.

There are a number of passages in the Socratic dialogues where we get to this sort of position. In the *Charmides* "temperance" resolves itself into knowledge "concerned with good and evil" (174C), and courage looks as though it is "knowledge of all goods and evils" in the *Laches* (199C). One of the ways in which these dialogues end inconclusively is that the good(s) and evil(s) are left unspecified. But the most interesting comment on goodness in the "Socratic" group of dialogues is to be found in the *Lysis* (210CD), in a passage which has been analyzed at length by Vlastos.[5] Plato is dealing with the subject of "friendship", a theme which will constantly recur in our present study. The *Lysis* is his first approach to the topic, and the passage which concerns us argues that parents love their children (treat them as *philoi*) in so far as they are good and useful (210CD).[6] Goods (objects of love) are then arranged in a hierarchy. There is a first object of love on which all later "lovables" depend, a lovable which is lovable as an end and which provides the "lovableness" of all other goods which are themselves only means, that is, "good for somthing else" (219D). In the case of all these other goods, therefore, their goodness depends on their utility and on their providing a path to the true good, the "first lovable". Plato is reticent again, however, about the nature of this good. In fact again it seems devoid of content; or rather neither Socrates nor Plato is prepared (or is able) to identify whatever content it might have.

Vlastos has drawn attention, however, to the most significant point in this discussion; namely that Plato's implication is that friends, even sons and other "beloveds" (*philoi*) are only in some sense means to an end; they are in no sense goods in themselves.[7] Goodness is what matters, and it can be superadded to persons just as it can to all kinds of other "items" in the world. We remain puzzled as to what the nature of this superadded goodness might be.

In Socratic discussions moral excellence seems to have been originally attached to acts rather than to agents, and to agents in so far as they performed "good" acts.[8] This is certainly a somewhat more sophisticated version of the traditional moral notion that the "gentleman" knows how to behave, that he will know what to do in any particular circumstance. But it serves to highlight the point with which we are immediately concerned, in that a man's value seems to derive from what he does rather than simply from his being a man or even from his being a kind of man. How, then, are his acts evaluated? Almost certainly for the early Greeks, and indeed for most of the Greeks of the fifth century, they are evaluated (and hence he is evaluated) in terms of the traditions of a particular class or of a particular city; and somehow these traditions are thought to be guaranteed by the gods. (The gods also insure that they are such as to distinguish human from divine prerogatives). The assumption behind such a belief is that our local or familiar standards are objective, that our society is the right kind of society and its principles are the right principles. No-one really queries where these principles came from; they are given.

But with the coming of the Sophists all that was changed. Varieties of relativistic theory came into vogue. There were those who thought or claimed to think that morals could reasonably be different in Byzantium and in Athens. Others, like Protagoras, may have held that moral rules should be the same everywhere, yet it is up to man, presumably man as a species (though the Platonic Protagoras in the *Theaetetus* (152A ff.) goes to the more extreme view that each man is his own master), to decide the ultimate nature of the rules themselves. But despite this new sophistication, this new attitude towards the source of morality, there was, it seems, much less said about the *content* of morality. Novel proposals, indeed, there were, of which the most notorious were generated by the antithesis between nature and convention. But this seemingly outrageous doctrine exhibits just the weakness we have observed: it is remarkably low in specific content.

As far as we can perceive, the new doctrine of moral relativity, in its most generalized form, claimed that what often pass as ultimate moral principles are nothing more than local codes or conventions. Anyone who realizes that has no need to appear slavish by accepting them as worthy of obedience in the lands where they are current; if he is a real man, and lives according to nature, he will reject them all and enjoy an unfettered "natural" life. Such is the view attributed to Callicles, the probably but not certainly fictitious anti-hero of the *Gorgias*, and it certainly found its exponents in the ranks of Greek politicians. But what is the "good" of this "natural" life? As Callicles sees it, it is the acquisition of pleasure and the satisfaction of one's natural desires; and it is assumed that such satisfaction will usually be at someone else's expense. But in many respects Callicles' assumptions are crude. He makes no serious attempt to distinguish between pleasures, and he assumes that the strongest or most intense pleasures are the most worth-while. In other words it is the degree of wanting that matters. Whatever you want most is assumed to be a good for you to get. No account is taken of wanting being "mistaken"; there is no interest in the origin of wants. Note too how Callicles is shown up: when Socrates wants to know whether he should scratch if he itches and whether this is desirable for the naturally strong man, Callicles is embarrassed and tries to push Socrates back to "higher" things, thereby revealing his own illicit value-assumptions. His theory is simplistic in that he assumes he knows what nature is and what kind of behaviour is natural. Presumably intensity of feeling provides the criterion of the natural, though this is neither argued nor made explicit.

The interestingly cynical poem of the politician Critias, though not directly concerned with the antithesis between nature and convention, makes somewhat similar kinds of assumptions.[9] Critias argues that the gods are the invention of a clever tyrant who wished to keep his subjects in awe of him and thus unwilling to "sin" in secret. But the sort of sinning he has in mind seems to be concerned only with plots by members of the citizen-body against himself. The citizens are presumably to be rendered obedient to the laws that he has introduced (for his own profit). Certainly Critias' tyrant has no interest in their genuine moral improvement. He is only interested in people doing what they are told.

If I read him right, a somewhat similar thesis is offered by Thrasymachus in book I of the *Republic*. Certainly Thrasymachus is concerned to point out that in tyrannies there are "tyrannical" laws, in aristocracies "aristocratic" ones, etc. (338E); but beyond that he hardly goes. He thinks that the ruler will rule in his own interest, but has little to say about why ruling itself is advantageous. In a sense he is in agreement with Socrates; they both think that justice is (as a matter of fact) in the interest of the "stronger", but they neither of them bring out what it is for something to be in one's interest. Thrasymachus merely assumes that it is in one's interest to rule and that people will want to do so, while Socrates believes that authority is unwelcome to the good, but that they will exercize it for fear of tolerating the rule of the inadequate.

We may not unreasonably suppose that the fact that the historical Socrates did not or could not commit himself on the content of the good which is to be sought is one of the principal reasons for the apparently negative results of the early Platonic dialogues. Perhaps in this sense we should take Socrates' claim to "know nothing" seriously. He knows, or thinks he knows, something about how to set about searching for the good; what he does not know is what the supposedly objective good consists in. Perhaps it is in this region that we should look for the "move" from Socrates to Plato.

Or perhaps the question should not be posed in historical terms. It does not matter much whether the problem of the content of goodness, of the source of value, was set by Plato or by Socrates. My own view is that it is Platonic, but that is by the way. What is significant is that the *Republic* is the first Platonic dialogue in which the Form of the Good is discussed directly, and indeed almost the only one in which it is discussed at all. And the context of the discussion is metaphysical. The Good is introduced as the source of the being and knowability of the Forms. In other words it is through Forms that we come to know the ultimate source of value, and through a certain sort of metaphysical enquiry. We should note especially that even in the dialogues immediately preceding the *Republic*, the *Symposium*, that is, and the *Phaedo*, where we obviously do learn much about the content of goodness, the Form of the Good itself does not appear. The *Symposium* is perhaps the more informative as to why this is so. Here we find Socrates pursuing (with Diotima) the Calliclean problem of what we want. Only now the question is "What do we really want?" And for the first time we find a clear statement that we do not want bodily pleasures, or even pleasures of the soul, because they pale into insignificance in comparison with our real object of desire, the Form of the Beautiful. But significantly it is as a result of reaching for our wants, and for what gives us pleasure, that we come to this conclusion. In other words it is in direct response to the "Sophistic" concern with our "natural" satisfactions that we find, in the end, the Form of Beauty. Yet in the *Symposium* it is still only Beauty, admittedly more than aesthetic, but still lacking the universality of Goodness, with which we are concerned. By the time we have passed the *Phaedo* and recognized a whole string of Forms, certainly corresponding to all the moral qualities, we can come back to an ultimate source of value.

Socrates in the *Republic* declines to speak of the Good directly, for most of the time. He employs instead the three famous images: the Sun, the Divided Line and the Cave. For our present purposes it is the first of these which is the most significant, for the Sun is a necessary condition of life for all living things, just as the Good is in some way the necessary condition for the existence of the Forms. Let us consider exactly what the Form of the Good seems to contribute in the *Republic*. First what does the Form, any Form, contribute to particulars? Take the Form of Beauty. As the *Phaedo* put it, it is by Beauty that beautiful things become beautiful (100D). What does this mean? Presumably not that they *exist as such* "by Beauty", but that (being otherwise something else) they are beautiful by Beauty. If there were no Beauty in them, they would be something else. What if there were no Form in them? Does that mean they would not exist? Or does Plato envisage some basic "thing" which is formless and on which the Forms are impressed? In the *Phaedo* and the *Republic* there is no answer available to such a question. But it is very hard to imagine that

Plato would suppose that anything could even be "becoming" anything unless it were formed in some way. In other words everything *is something*. And if that applies to particulars, it applies *a fortiori* to Forms. The Form of Beauty *is something par excellence*; it *is* Beauty (and it is beautiful). It seems as though this could be generalized further: to be is to be something.[10] On this account there is no such thing, except presumably as an abstraction which can be identified by philosophers, as being itself. What then is meant in the famous passage of the *Republic* (509B8ff) in which Plato tells us that the Form of the Good provides the other Forms with their existence (*einai*) and their nature (*ousia*)? Not, if this interpretation is correct, that it simply gives them existence, but that it makes them *be something*. Seen in this way, the interpretation squares with what Plato says about cognition. The Form of the Good "enables" the Forms to be known. And to be known is to be known *as* something. Presumably Plato would think that unless the Forms were known *as* something, they could not be known at all. That is not, of course, to say that existence is unimportant to Plato; rather existence can only be found (and valued) in specific existents.

For Plato one of the chief differences between Forms and particulars is that particulars are imperfect while Forms are perfect; that is why Forms are knowable, for Plato thinks that there is a sense in which only what is perfect can be known. What then can we understand about the Good itself? That it cannot be known? No, we know that it can be known from the whole of this section of the *Republic*. It is certainly therefore perfect. Indeed, as Plato says, it excels the Forms in "being", that is in being something, and in power (509B8ff). What can excelling in being something mean? Obviously, as I have previously observed,[11] Plato does not mean that the Good does not exist. It must exist because it is something. What then does superior in being mean? The only meaning for which there is room is therefore that it exists as some higher or more valuable or more important thing. It is, in fact, the ultimately valuable thing in the world, and all else derives its value from it. It is also, in the genuinely Socratic tradition, the first desirable, the "first lovable" of the *Lysis*. Hence in order to determine what is valuable, we have to determine what is most like it. "Valuables" then can be ranked in order of approximation to it. Value is related not simply to being, but to being good.

What do we know about this source of value, this ultimately valuable being? First, that it is the cause of the "being something" which everything must be, lest it be nothing. Is it both a necessary and a sufficient cause of that "being something"? Plato does not raise such a question in the *Republic*, though his answer can plausibly be inferred. Consider an artifact. Plato need nowhere be saddled with the view that a chair comes to exist simply by partaking of the Form of Chair. There is always need of someone to give it that form. It seems likely that the *Timaeus* is to be taken more or less literally as an account of the temporal origins of the cosmos;[12] hence we can naturally and appropriately extend our argument about "efficient" causes to natural objects. Thus it would seem that despite the misleading phraseology "By Beauty the beautiful particulars become beautiful" (i.e. by F *x* becomes F), Plato never intended the Forms to be both necessary and sufficient conditions for the existence of particulars: the intermediary of soul is always required. The problem that remains, as so often in Plato, is that of the *nature* of soul. What is it and what is the nature of its relationship to Form? Above all what is its relationship to the Form of the Good?

Unfortunately these questions, so important for our study of value, are not at all easy to answer. Plato does not provide us with a definition of soul. All he can do is tell us certain things about soul. First of all, of course, we must avoid the Neoplatonic "interpretation": soul is not identical with Form. That is clear in the *Phaedo*, and the situation never changes. All that Plato says there about the relationship of Form and object is that soul is the most like to Form and that it is far nearer to Form than to body (79DE).

It is true that the way this is put is ambiguous. Socrates is made to argue that soul is "*homoiotatos*" ("very like") to Form; and the word *homoiotatos* would seem to hover in meaning between "very like" and "identical". Sometimes the two may be treated as synonyms, as when the Pythagoreans say that things *are* numbers, or are like numbers. Probably the explanation is that *homoios* should be taken literally as meaning "of the same kind", which might or might not involve identity. But when Hackforth spoke of the argument in the *Phaedo* as having a "disappointing limitation" in that Socrates only claims that soul is very like to Form, he is probably correct.[13] Were the situation otherwise we should find Plato advocating a position approximating to that of Aristotle that the soul is the form of the body.

Of course, the point of contact between soul and Form that is supposed to be established in the *Phaedo* is that the soul does not perish at the death of the body, that soul, in fact, is everlasting. It seems to have no beginning and certainly has no end at any point of time.[14] In this respect it resembles the Forms, which exist in a world which cannot be restricted by temporal limits. But although the soul lasts for ever it is unlike the Forms in other important respects. The soul, for Plato, as the *Phaedrus* and book 10 of the *Laws* make clear, is associated above all with motion and with the origin of motion. Soul is described in both the *Phaedrus* and the *Laws* as a self-moving mover. It moves itself at the same time as it imparts motion to other things. Now motion is some kind of change, most basically perhaps for Plato change of place. And change, alteration, for Plato must imply something like what Aristotle calls "potentiality"—which in turn implies inferiority, inadequateness, incompleteness in the changing subject. Now clearly Plato supposed that some movements are more perfect than others. Indeed the movement of the sun, moon and planets is the most perfect movement possible. But it is certainly different from, and in Plato's mind inferior to, the perfect unchangingness of the Forms themselves. Hence soul, even perfect soul, is lower in the hierarchy of value than Form. Put succinctly Plato postulates a sequence of existents of diminishing value. Form is the most valuable, and as things approximate to it, so their value may be said to be greater. When Plato is said to propose a theory of degrees of reality, we are not to think that he means that any existent has "more existence" than another, except in so far as one may exist for *longer* than another—a feature to which, however, he seems to have attached excessive weight; rather its existence is more important and more significant.

One of the corollaries to be drawn from this is that some things are of little or of no importance. Whatever exists is graded in so far as it approximates to the supreme objects of value, the Forms. In so far as an item is in no way characterized by goodness, whatever—if anything—it may be, it would seem to have no value at all. In Greek such an item would be *phaulos* (*phaulotatos*), and there would seem no reason why one *phaulos* should be more valuable than another. Now of course human beings too are capable of being *phaulos*, perhaps in some ways pre-eminently so. In this condition they would seem to have little to no value and should be eliminated. This would certainly follow if anything or anyone could be totally *phaulos*.

Such at least is the theoretical position. Let us consider a number of cases in which we may be able to see some practical implications, and thus test the theory.

(a) *Slaves*. In the Athens of Socrates and Plato slavery was the norm. Few indeed protested it as an institution, though some were aware of abuses of slaves within the institution and objected to them vigorously. None of the interlocutors of Socrates, nor Socrates himself, is shown objecting to slavery as such. In the *Republic* itself, it is true that slaves are not very visible in the Ideal State, but there is no reason to suppose that the institution has disappeared or is unnecessary.[15] Nor does Aristotle, in his series of detailed comments and criticisms on the Republic ever give the impression that Plato was fool enough to abolish slavery. What we find in the *Republic* is a ban on the enslavement of Greeks by Greeks,[16] but that is merely a part of Plato's panhellenism, a set of attitudes he more or less shared with many of his contemporaries, including Isocrates and Demosthenes. In the *Laws* the use of slaves is certain.

(b) *Non-Greeks*. Plato has considerable admiration for certain non-Greek peoples, such as the Egyptians.[17] He is aware of some of their contributions, or supposed contributions, to civilization. But there is no doubt in the *Republic* that the ideal state will be a Greek *polis*: probably racially Greek and certainly culturally Greek. There are admittedly passages in the *Republic*, including the famous one in which Socrates suggests that perhaps even now in some far away land the ideal society is a reality (499CD), where the possibility of a racially non-Greek *Kallipolis* seems to be at least implicit; but in his more "open" moments Plato apparently assumes that in fact the inhabitants of that happy land will be racially Greek as well. Indeed it is possible that he thought that only racial Greeks could be cultural Greeks. Against this interpretation, one might argue that the concern for the soul which in at least some parts of the *Republic* seems to be Plato's primary concern (e.g. at the end of book 9),[18] is preached to Everyman. But there are a number of plausible explanations of that: first that some men are more "human" than others, perhaps some do not even have human souls; second that he is writing for Greeks in any case and may be assumed to be addressing his remarks only to them. At any rate there is no doubt that there are a number of adult males who may be labelled "non-Greek" or "barbarian" who are congenitally inferior to "Greeks" in Plato's world.[19]

(c) *Women*. The position of women in Plato's ideal state can best be seen in relation to the Guardians, for they clearly represent his view of women at the limit of their capacities. The topic has been much discussed and I have no wish to go over it at length. The most salient points seem to be the following:

1. There are female Guardians possessing rights and responsibilities equal to those of the males.

2. There are likely to be, within any given equal number of men and women, a smaller number of women who are "Guardian material".[20]

3. Although Plato formally recognizes the absolute equality of men and women in the Guardian class, he sometimes speaks as though the Guardians are in fact male. This is particularly the case when he is discussing sexual matters, as in the famous "community of women and children". This *phrase* suggests that the women are shared between the men. Plato does not *speak* from a woman's point of view of a community of men, even though he does allow women equal promiscuity with men after they have passed the official child-bearing age.[21] In this language of "community" Plato seems to be operating with the traditional attitude

that women are used by men for procreating (as elsewhere they are important for pleasure, since although he speaks of more frequent sexual access to women as one of the rewards of the brave, he does not mention more frequent access to men (468C)).[22]

It is very difficult to put this "social" traditionalism together with Plato's theoretical advocacy of total equality. Certainly some women are equal to the best men, but that they are less likely to be seems to be the most important point. Plato cannot, even in his account of the Guardians, entirely shake off the attitude which makes him suggest elsewhere that if a man lives a bad life he will probably be reborn as a woman.[23]

(d) *Children*. There is comparatively little in Plato which gives us a clear idea of what he thought of the value or importance of minors. Except of course that exposure of physically inferior specimens is mandatory among the Guardians (460C1-5). Education is always uppermost in Plato's mind, but its main purpose seems to be to make sure that the children grow up into the right kind of adults. It seems a reasonable inference that children are valued in so far as they approximate to the ideal adult, and no further. Indeed as children, according to the *Laws*, they possess a fount of reason, but are crafty, fierce and given over to licence (808D). This general interpretation reinforces what we said earlier about the *Lysis*, where parents seem to value their children in so far as they are useful, that is good, that is lovable. Plato, of course, does not have the technical vocabulary to maintain that children are potentially human (*anthrōpoi*), but it is likely that his view—as the possession of a "fount" of reason suggests—and that of most or all of his contemporaries, was similar. Children are "half-human", half-man, half-slave, and should be treated accordingly.

(e) *The lower classes*. Here Plato's attitude is complicated and again difficult to see precisely. Clearly it is the function of the Guardians, as he says at the opening of the fourth book of the *Republic* (420B 6ff), to ensure the happiness not merely of themselves but of the whole state, that is, of all classes in the state and of all individuals within those classes. What "happiness" means for a member of the lowest class is not entirely clear. But let us pose a slightly different question: suppose a Guardian was in a situation where he could save the life of one Guardian or of a member of the lower classes. What decision would he take? His decision would certainly be based on a judgment as to which person is better, and would be more useful to the society were he to survive. In other words the life of a Guardian, who is "better", and therefore more useful, would certainly be given priority over at least one and probably more than one member of another class. Judged by such standards the lives of the lower orders are certainly worth less, however honest and law-abiding they may be, than the lives of the higher.

(f) *Criminals*. Like all Greeks of his time Plato would frequently impose floggings and executions, and perhaps also the infliction of torture on criminals, in his ideal society. The matter does not take up space in the *Republic*, but certain sections of the *Laws* are more explicit.[24] Clearly a man who believes in the immortality of the soul will have a different attitude to the death-penalty from one who does not, but the attitude towards unreformed and unreformable heretics in the *Laws* tells us a good deal: they are simply to be disposed of. Nothing can be done for their souls, which are presumably irredeemably corrupt; and such souls have no value.[25]

Looking through these various categories, we can see how the practical applications of a theory that human souls are of basically unequal value correspond to the theory itself. Women (in most cases), children, slaves, the lower orders generally, and *a fortiori* criminals are morally inferior to virtuous adult males. Hence they are less characterized by "the Form of the Good," and value is determined by the degree of such characterization. From Plato's point of view the same inferiority can also be seen in non-Greeks (whether defined racially or culturally).

Plato does not offer the proposal that we should seek "likeness to Forms" as such, though we frequently meet exhortations to acquire wisdom, to look after our souls and become more generally virtuous. When urged us to strive for excellence, we are told to look at the Forms as patterns in seeking "likeness to god".[26] Gods, therefore, and perfect souls must be assumed to be significantly similar. Both are characterized to the greatest degree possible in each case by the Forms. Certainly the gods are in some unspecified way superior, perhaps simply superior in power and range of activity, but they appear to be similar in kind. In the *Republic*, the Guardians are honoured as "divine men" at death or, if Apollo permits, as daimons (demigods).[27] Not, we notice, as gods but as godlike. And in the *Phaedrus* the souls of the virtuous dead seem to join the choir of some appropriate divinity to whom they may be assumed to be akin.[28]

Souls are not, and cannot be, Forms; gods are not, and cannot be, Forms. Souls can more or less approximate to gods in so far as they are more or less characterized by what makes the gods immortal, namely the Forms themselves.[29] Thus a good soul is a soul characterized in a particular way. What does this tell us about the souls that are so characterized? In the first place, it seems, that they are qualitatively identical, at least in all important respects. In so far as they differ, the differences are socially determined and hence are irrelevant to the value of a particular soul. In detail Plato is somewhat obscure about this in the *Phaedrus*. When he suggests in the myth that after death souls join the "choir" of a particular god, he seems to mean that there are various forms of excellence available, these forms being themselves different in kind. In practice it is hard to see what this is supposed to symbolize. Not, it would seem, that some are brave, say, but not wise, beautiful but unjust etc., for it seems to be Plato's view that the presence of any true and unshakeable virtue must entail the presence of other virtues. Of course, he recognizes the rarity of such desirable combinations in the imperfect world around us, as the *Politicus* makes clear when we hear how unusual it is to find temperance or moderation combined with courage (306 BC); but the suggestion that a Guardian might be just but not very brave seems ridiculous.

The notion of perfect but qualitatively indistinguishable beings is not alien to the Greek mind. Such divinities, the Graces, the Hours etc., existed in traditional religion, and Epicurus, or at least the Epicureans, wanted to perpetuate them:[30] there is one type of Epicurean god which consists of sets with identical members.[31] As Grube once put it, for Plato the perfect psyche "remains individual only in so far as it is imperfect".[32] The Guardians are all similar or of a very limited number of similar types. The uniqueness of any individual member has nothing to do with his value. Here we observe another respect in which Plato's notion of value differs sharply from what is current in our own society. For us there is certainly some sort of conceptual connection between the uniqueness of each individual and his value. His existence is uniquely his own and he is irreplaceable. He is not valuable because he belongs to a class of good men, but because he is a particular man, or perhaps, to come as close to Plato as possible, because he is a particular good man. Plato's view would appear to be that the value of each individual can be computed strictly in terms of the degree and number of good qualities he exhibits. We have the material, in fact, for a calculus of value. It has sometimes even been suggested that the Platonic individual is no more than the sum of his qualities. Porphyry seems to have understood Plato in that way at some ontological level, perhaps thinking of passages of the *Theaetetus*.[33] It seems highly doubtful whether Plato thought that the existence of individuals can be so explained; but at the axiological level, the level of value, the interpretation may be more nearly correct. Our conclusion must be, therefore, that Plato is not blind to the fact of existence, even perhaps to the logical priority of existence, but that he failed to connect existence, even human existence, necessarily to value. And he similarly refused to connect the "human" with the "valuable". Not only are humans, as we have seen, not all equally valuable; some have no value at all. Needless to say, therefore, no human has anything which could properly be called an intrinsic value.

Indeed if Plato had wanted to say that someone had intrinsic value or worth, he would have had no precise term to do the job. He could have used the word "good" (*agathos*), or "noble" (*kalos*), or "worthy" (*axios, spoudaios*), or "valuable" (timios), but all these terms, and perhaps particularly, the last, tend to be connected with one's position in society.[34] One is good at something; one is noble if one performs noble deeds; one might be worthy if one came from the right family or again if one did the right things. Plato does have a "technical" phrase which might suggest something "intrinsic": it is *auto kath' auto*. Typically it is used of Forms. It suggests that each Form is what it is "in itself" and "for itself", without any external reference. As Aristotle seems to suggest, the opposite of *kath' auto* ("in itself"), which is an attribute of Forms, is *pros ti* ("relative"), which refers to particulars.[35]

It would seem that value, in the sense with which we are concerned, is something which we have to acquire, or at least which we can try to acquire. However, the opportunities for such acquisition are unequal. Our likeness to the gods, our characterization by the Forms, depend on two factors, both of which are largely out of our own control: our original nature and our education. That our original natures differ in certain essential respects—at least from a Platonic viewpoint—is obvious: we are unequally intelligent, particularly unequally gifted in mathematical ability. The matter is self-evident; and it is one of the underlying factors leading to the "class-divisions" of Plato's state. Similarly with our education and our educational opportunities. Only very few men, like Socrates, can develop in an inadequate society, and even these must trim their sails, must take shelter against the storm. For most there is little or no opportunity for substantial improvement in morals any more than in more scholarly pursuits. Both our innate abilities and our educational opportunities are largely out of our own control, but they will point up Plato's attitude to human value. Our value is acquired as the result of processes largely set in motion by others. Rights are not distributed democratically, nor to each according to his needs; they are somehow determined by the ability to contribute and by the contribution itself.

What is the relationship in Plato's view between rights (depending on evaluation) and responsibilities? We normally operate on the principle that rights entail responsibilities, as though in some important sense rights are prior. But for Plato responsibilities are imposed, and we are educated to shoulder them. In accordance with our natural success in shouldering them, we may obtain certain rights. But even these rights are provisional; if we fail to fulfill our responsibilities, it would seem that not merely some, but probably *all* of our rights are forfeit. None would seem to be inalienable. For if we cease to be godlike, we lose our value: and obviously if we have no value we can hardly be reasonably thought to have rights.

That "rights" as well as values are comparatively unimportant for Plato is perhaps emphasized further by the inadequacy—which we have already mentioned—of the relevant terms in his vocabulary. The nearest, perhaps, to "value" is *timē*, which means "honour", but often has a rather prominently political and public flavour. To suffer loss of *timē* is to lose one's civic status, a fact which seems to emphasize that that is all one has. The man without civic status may become "stateless"; he has only the uncertain protection of the gods and of those who respect, out of deference to Zeus' will, the rights of strangers and the defenceless. If he is injured, the god is offended, and the offence seems to be religious rather than against the ordinary canons of criminal law.[36]

II

We now return to more strictly philosophical matters, to our earlier claim that Plato attempted to "flesh out" the nature of that goodness, of the good itself, which Socrates thought should be our over-riding concern. Our thesis that Plato was not prepared to put value on human existence as such, but on certain kinds of human existence, on certain qualities which themselves "derive" from the Good and the Forms, the ultimate valuables and sources of value, might seem to be affected if Existence itself were a Form. I have argued elsewhere, however, that it is not,[37] and our present consideration of value would seem to present *a priori* evidence in favour of that interpretation. When I speak of Forms in this connection, I refer to the transcendent entities of the middle dialogues, the separate sources of "reality" and "value".

Plato talks of the Forms as a whole, of the "intelligible world", as being (*to on*) or as reality (*ousia*). These terms thus often refer to "eternal" and unchanging realities in general, as distinct from the temporal; though both are objects of the philosopher's concern, for he is an observer of "all time and all being" (*Rep*. 486A8-9). Nowhere in the *Republic* (*or* for that matter in the *Phaedo, Symposium* or *Phaedrus*) does Plato speak of a particular Form of Being. It is only in the *Sophist* that what he calls an *eidos* (Form) of Being occurs. We need to know the meaning of that phrase.

If we follow G. E. L. Owen and others in believing that the *Timaeus* is earlier than the *Sophist*,[38] and that the *Timaeus*, where Plato undoubtedly accepts transcendent Forms, is the last dialogue in which he advocates them, it is clear that whatever the "Form of Being" may be in the *Sophist*, it is not a transcendent separate Form, and therefore not necessarily a source of value in the Platonic cosmos. So for Owen there need be no difficulty with the *Sophist*. Those of us who date the *Timaeus* late,[39] however, are faced with a problem in the *Sophist*, but it should be remarked that we can still accept an account of the *Sophist* acceptable to Owen without committing ourselves to his views on the dating of the *Timaeus* and his wider theses about the philosophical development of the "late Plato". In fact the belief that there is a discussion of *transcendent* Form in the *Sophist* depends on little more than the fact that Plato refers to his "greatest kinds" (being, non-being, rest, motion, etc.) as *eidē*, the word which one also has to translate as Forms. But the very description of "non-being" as an *eidos* should be enough to indicate that *eidē* in this dialogue are not Forms, but kinds or classes of things. What other word could Plato in fact have used?

It cannot be over-emphasized that the *Sophist* is a positive dialogue; it does not end on a note of perplexity. Progress is made and can be seen to be made quite apart from any question of value or of the transcendence of the Form. In other words there is nothing in the *Sophist* to suggest that we are dealing with transcendent (value-giving) Forms at all. The simplest explanation of the *eidos* of being in the *Sophist*, therefore, is that it has nothing to do with a Form of Being in the sense of Form with which the middle dialogues and the *Timaeus* in particular make us familiar. And if there is no Form of Being in the sense with which we are concerned in the *Sophist*, there is no sign of one in any other dialogue. We can assume, therefore, that it is not because of their assimilating themselves to, or being likenesses of a Form of Being, that any particulars acquire their value.

But, it might be objected, even if there is no transcendent Form of Being which might generate value, why should this not derive from the Forms themselves as "existents" (as *onta*)? At first sight this might seem to be plausible, but Plato does not emphasize their existence in connection with their excellence. Certainly they all exist; indeed the name of the Form X is *auto ho estin X*. But particulars exist in some sense too; they exist in time, that is, in Platonic language, they come into being and they pass out of being. This seems to bring us close to another part of Plato's structure of "goodness", a feature which Aristotle, who sometimes thought along rather similar lines, distorted in his criticism of Plato. In the *Nicomachean Ethics* (1096B3ff.) Aristotle observes that just as a white object which lasts a long time may be no whiter than one which lasts only a day, so the fact that the Form of the Good is eternal (*aidios*) makes no difference to the nature of its goodness. Plato, he suggests, equates mere long-lastingness with excellence; and at first sight this might seem to be correct, for the key difference between the two classes of existents which

Plato labels "beings" and "becomings" is that beings are eternal, they have no beginning or end.[40] It is in virtue of this eternity that they do not admit of change, of generation (from something imperfect) to destruction (to something imperfect).

But Aristotle distorts Plato if he suggests that mere long-lastingness is what Plato has in mind; the only long-lastingness with which Plato is concerned is *eternal* durability. Only in that sense did Plato associate the "goodness" of a thing, and hence its value, with duration. Now obviously the Form of the Good is the ultimate source of goodness in all else, including other Forms. And if the goodness of the Good is associated with its eternal durability, then when Plato speaks of the Good as in some sense the cause of the Forms, this must be one of the factors which he has in mind. For the Forms are what they are in so far as they are eternal and unchanging. It is this quality in them, rather than their bare existence, which *exhibits* their goodness, and which informs us best about the nature of the Good itself. That is not to say that the Forms are not *essentially* eternal, but that eternity comes to them from the Good. Even less intelligible would it be to say that as "eternals" they derive from a non-eternal. That is as absurd as to suppose that they are existents which derive from a non-existing Good. Certainly being and eternity are features of the Forms and of the Good, but it is eternity which *indicates* a specially "good" kind of being. Does this mean that in this respect too the Good is prior? Plato gives no indication of that. When he speaks of the priority of the Good to the Forms, he seems to think of being unlimited in scope, of having universal efficacy, as what is especially the mark of the Good. The Good is the source of *all* being and of *all* existence; its activity is ubiquitous, not limited to specific areas.

There is no clear evidence in the Platonic dialogues as to *how* the Forms relate to (or are dependent on) the Good. But they certainly share in goodness and in eternity. In what sense could Plato think that the Good is their cause, and what does this imply? Doubtless he would say "by goodness they are good"; and this goodness is in the metaphysical, not the moral, order. Without it they would not exist as goods, and indeed they would not exist at all. What kind of goodness could it be that has this effect? Plato seems to answer this in the *Philebus*. We reach the threshhold of the Good when we form notions of limit, measure and proportion. The idea is "Pythagorean". The Good is the source of limit; it limits all things, and nothing exists except in so far as it is limited and proportioned. We may conclude that what is limited exhibits form; and that where form is exhibited, there goodness will be found.

Let us for a moment turn from the realm of Forms to specific problems about individuals, and persons; and above all to the *Republic* to see how the principles we have identified are applied concretely. Then we shall be able to notice that in so far as an item is "limited", "specified", etc. it will be unchanging; and in so far as it is unchanging, it is eternal.

In the first place we should note the commandment to "do one's own".[41] There is a prescribed and optimum position and status for each member of the ideal society. If he steps outside his proper role, if he exceeds his area of competence, he enters upon vice and injustice: a clear example of limit. Now consider the parts of the soul. The good man is single-minded, set on the good; the tyrant is lost in an indeterminate plurality of conflicting lusts. He is multiform in so far as he is vicious. Naturally there is only one Form of the Good, one ideal constitution. All deviations from the norm—and variations are by definition deviations—are vicious.

The question of limit arises once more in a quite different context. Plato, in his later life, maintained that the Forms are all to be "derived" in some sense from two "higher" principles, which he called the One and the Indefinite Dyad (which latter is perhaps more informatively named as "plurality" by Speusippus).[42] Aristotle regularly complained that this theory conflicted with the original version of the Theory of Forms itself. We need not greatly concern ourselves with his objections, but unless Aristotle has totally misunderstood Plato's intentions, he provides some evidence that the Forms are to be regarded both as partaking of plurality—that is, perhaps, that there are many Forms—and also of unity—that is, that each Form is a perfect example of a limit. Plato himself seems to be thinking along these lines in the *Philebus* when he speaks of Forms as "henads" and "monads" (15B). But it is unity which in Plato's mind is associated once again with the Good. The Good, he seems to have said (to judge from Aristotle's account), is unity (or even is the One).[43] At any rate it is associated with unity or oneness, for Plato, whose approach to metaphysics is unashamedly epistemological, seems to have thought that only unity or unities could be the objects of certain knowledge. That fact may help us with some of our earlier problems about different individuals. Individuals must differ quantitatively to be individuals, for they are formed of different matter. But qualitatively, from Plato's point of view, they must be similar in so far as they are good. The better they are, the more they are characterized by the Form of Goodness, the more similar they will become to each other.

III

I shall consider Aristotle, Plato's most important pupil and critic, in a later chapter. But at this point in the discussion, it will be helpful to look briefly at two Platonists who remained in the Academy, Speusippus and Xenocrates. My treatment of them will be limited; I shall only consider whether the views of Speusippus and Xenocrates, as they are reported, help clarify some of the difficulties encountered in thinking about Plato.

Let us begin with Speusippus and his doctrine of the One. Like Owen's, but unlike Aristotle's, Plato, Speusippus abandoned the Theory of Forms, though he maintained that beings derive from the One and Plurality. His primary units are not Forms, but the objects of mathematics, a set of entities also recognized by Plato, but considered lower in the hierarchy than Forms, apparently because although each Form, say the Form Two, is one in number, mathematical twos are many, thus being further away from Unity itself. Speusippus abandoned the Forms, and held that goodness "arises" later than unity. What does this entail for a "Platonic" thesis in ethics? It might be supposed that Speusippus represents the *reductio ad absurdum* of the progression from Socrates to Plato. Socrates had concerned himself, as we have observed, with the search for moral norms. He was looking for "goodness" but seemed unable to identify its content, though he certainly thought that there was content to be found. Plato seems to have sought for Goodness primarily in unity or limit or some other such "mathematical" notions, but in associating or identifying the Good with the One, he always refused to abandon its ethical aspects. Plato's interests, as far as we can perceive them, were always to include ethics and politics, the good for man and the good for society; he did not lose sight of these studies even when seeking metaphysical aids in solving moral dilemmas. And his Forms, so far as we know, were always more than just the cause of particulars or the ontological basis for particulars; they were also the source of value. It seems as though Speusippus, who thinks that the One is not to be identified with goodness, is making a separation, of a kind unacceptable to Plato, between theory of value and ontology. For Speusippus agrees with the *Republic* in placing a first principle (for him, of course, the One, not the Good) "beyond Being".[44] And "beyond Being" is probably to be interpreted along somewhat the same lines as we have sketched for Plato himself.

If this approach to Speusippus is along the right lines, important results would seem to follow: first that there is a tendency to distinguish more than in Plato between existence and value. For now the two are not united in the Forms and the Good, but separated, for value must arise only with the (later) appearance of goodness. Thus one might expect to see in Speusippus an even harsher attitude towards the person than in Plato himself; and this seems to be borne out in a number of ways. First of all Speusippus is depicted by Aristotle as the enemy of pleasure, the philosopher *par excellence* who argued that pleasure is evil.[45] Secondly, according to the commentators on Aristotle, it is Speusippus' *alypia* (freedom from pain) of which Aristotle is thinking when he finds a philosopher advocating "*apatheia*", which probably here has the full "Cynic" sense of "absence of emotion", as the end of the philosophic life. Besides *alypia* (as opposed to pleasure *and* pain), we hear also of *aochlēsia* (Fr. 57 Lang).[46] It is hard to imagine the Platonic Socrates (of the *Symposium*), or even Plato himself, being "without any emotion". It is interesting to see here that the ultra-mathematically minded Speusippus finds common ground with the "proto-Cynic" Antisthenes, the man who would "rather be mad than feel pleasure".[47]

And in another respect too the Speusippean variations on Plato point towards Cynicism. Speusippus' "disjointing" of the universe cannot but have the effect, albeit unintended, of uncementing that composite of ethics and metaphysics which Plato had tried to construct in order to give content to Socratic goodness.[48] Value for Speusippus must reside in a sphere of rather lower importance. The real philosopher, preoccupied with metaphysics and mathematics and insensible to pleasure, will have, it would seem, far less value to put on the objects of moral concern, that is, on humans or on human souls.

When we turn from Speusippus to Xenocrates we move to a less original, but probably more immediately influential figure. Our present interest in him is again limited. He accepted Plato's Forms (though apparently wishing to dispense with mathematicals which he assimilated to the Forms) and presumably regarded Forms, as did Plato, as sources of value. His definition of soul as a number which moves itself was condemned by Aristotle as getting the worst of all worlds[49] (for soul is not a number and does not move itself), and is interesting only in so far as it tends to conflate a number of Platonic themes. But soul is certainly subordinate to Form and presumably, as for Plato, it is good in so far as it is characterized by the "ultimate" Form of the Good. Xenocrates was apparently much concerned with ethics, and if the story of his conversion of Polemo is to believed, he was possessed of a certain rhetorical power;[50] but from our present point of view we see in Xenocrates, in contrast with Speusippus, only a schematization of late Platonic positions. Where Speusippus seems to emphasize one facet of Plato's work, and Xenocrates tries (carelessly) to synthesize, both fail to reproduce its complexity.

IV

As already mentioned, we may accept the Aristotelian interpretation of the *Timaeus* (recently restated by Vlastos and Whittaker) that Plato intends to be taken more or less *au pied de la lettre* in his account of the Demiurge, that is, that he envisages an actual construction of the physical cosmos at the "beginning" of time by Mind or the Mind of God.[51] However, even if this overall interpretation of the dialogue is not acceptable, most of the following comments can still stand.

When the question is raised "Why does the Demiurge set about the ordering of chaos, the construction of an intelligible cosmos out of indeterminate matter?", the reply given is "Because he was (is) good". I take the imperfect to be gnomic: the Demiurge is, was, and will be good. But a more important question is the meaning of the reply. What does it mean to say that x does F because he is good? Two interpretations at least are readily available: that he recognizes the goodness of such action and therefore chooses to act accordingly; and that he simply acts in such a way because he is good, because that is what goodness is about. If Plato's Demiurge were a merely metaphysical principle, it would be much easier to take the passage in the second sense, but it seems that he is not; and even if he were, this interpretation is not necessary. We are certainly not dealing with a merely ontological *bonum diffusivum sui*. In fact, Plato himself rules out the second interpretation when he comments that since he is good, he *wished* to make everything as like to himself (as good) as possible (29E). Plato emphasizes the good will of the Demiurge and a disposition to act in a certain way. An easy misinterpretation should be avoided: we are concerned with a will to goodness, not with will as such; and in the Platonic scheme a will to goodness is inseparably linked, and indeed causally produced, by a "knowledge" of goodness. Knowledge is not simply propositional, but involves a turning of the soul[52] towards what is good. Hence it is a kind of attitude, a composite of cognitive and volitional elements; and the Demiurge is the example *par excellence* of the right combination of these elements. It is because he exhibits this combination that he is the "best soul", the most valuable. And in so far as others become like him, they acquire their value.

It is in this perspective that we should look even at the "political" side of Plato's thought to which we keep returning. When in the *Republic*, at the end of book 9, we learn that perhaps there will never be an ideal state on earth, that it may be only an exemplar laid up in heaven (592B2), we are told not to despair. What matters most is the *state* of our soul, that is, our attitudes and our choices; this is still the Socratic view of what "matters" as expressed in the *Apology*. Obviously there are many reasons for wishing to construct the Ideal Society, not the least of them being that it alone affords a certain opportunity for the development of numbers of "ideal" souls. But an ideal soul (like Socrates') may develop in any society; and although Plato plays with the idea that a soul is good in so far as it performs its role in a particular society (hopefully ideal) as well as possible, and may lose its value if it fails to contribute to that society any longer, it is important to note that it would lose its value not simply because it no longer contributes, but because it is no longer *of a kind* such as to contribute; it is no longer a "demiurge". Thus value is not bestowed on the individual by his society; in fact the reverse is the case. A society is valuable in so far as it affords the opportunity for excellence, for choosing the right; and the best society will contain the largest number of noble individuals. It is necessary to distinguish this position from that of Aristotle, which we shall consider later. For although Plato agrees with Aristotle that man is a social (political) animal, the interpretation of that phrase is different in the two philosophers. For Aristotle, as we shall see, the state provide an opportunity for excellence and those who cannot live in it are "beasts" or "gods", either above or below the normal level of "humanity". The "gods" have something of value for its own sake, namely their variety of intellect, but other human beings seem to depend almost totally on the existence of the state for their full development and cannot attain to excellence without it. True, in so far as they possess intellect they are "valuable", but there is far less emphasis that is to be found in Plato on that "Socratic" or "demiurgic" goodness of the individual soul which can be exhibited in any sort of society. The difference between Plato and Aristotle on this question depends on the fact that for Plato there is a source of goodness in the cosmos as a whole, entirely independent of man and society. That source is ultimately the Good, and dependently the world of Forms.

The Forms are "eternal"; the body, let us say by way of contrast, is not. What is unchanging and eternal is of greater value in that regard than what is subject to change and destruction. The human soul, so Plato claims in the *Phaedo*, is more like the Forms than is the body. As such it must be of greater moment. All souls, however, are equally immortal. As Plato argues in the last book of the *Republic* (610E), since vice cannot kill the soul, then nothing can. Now since it is the soul which is the immortal part of the person, will an examination of that part help to distinguish further among human beings, to place them more precisely in an order of value? Although in Plato's mature theory all souls are tripartite, that is, consist of a rational, a spirited and a concupiscent element, the capabilities of the elements, which are defined in terms of their goals, differ with different individuals. Thus an individual with a more powerfully rational soul is certainly capable of achieving a greater degree of goodness and of likeness to god. But that, of course, is a mere capacity. He is not to be valued in so far as he is capable of such excellence, but in so far as he achieves it. Thus a purely "psychological" examination of the potential of different individuals would not enable us to rank them in order of value. It would give us a list of theoretical values, but Plato never lets us forget that it is the potential Guardian, the man of potentially great virtues, who is also capable of choosing the greatest degree of vice, of being a "craftsman" of evil. It is important to note this distinction between actual and potential value, because Plato is not one of those—and there were many in antiquity—who ranked human beings according to the possession or non-possession of a particular faculty. For Plato it is the quality of goodness which finally fixes human value, as well as determining human choices; and that quality depends on the Forms. The different capacities of the soul are significant only in so far as they permit higher or lower kinds of excellence; or, as Plato renders it "mythologically" in the *Phaedrus*, the capacity which we possess determines whether, *if* we act and live well, we shall be able to join the choir of Zeus or whether we shall be restricted to that of Hera, Ares or Aphrodite.

V

Let us finally consider some curious anomalies in Plato's thought. It is certainly the view of Socrates both in the *Gorgias* and in the *Republic* that the good man would rather suffer evil than do it. Therefore in the ideal state we must assume that the structure of society is such as to minimize the harm done by the State to individuals regardless of their class. That should ensure even-handed justice and, one might have supposed, rule out degrading forms of punishment, particularly torture and above all mutilation. For, as Plato says, even in the case of slaves, degrading penalties nourish resentment, and the purpose of punishment in the Platonic state is to enable an individual to function better, if possible, in his society. But in fact there is only rather superficial discussion of punishment in Plato, and we cannot determine how consistent he was in this regard. We have already noticed in the *Laws*, however, frequent recourse to flogging, as well as branding for slaves and foreigners (854D); and a slave who murders a free man may be killed in whatever manner (however cruel or degrading) the relatives of the victim wish.

There is no doubt too that cultivation of the soul requires leisure, and that those without it, the *banausoi* of the *Republic*, those whose time is devoted to acquiring a livelihood, that is, a mere sufficiency of food to keep themselves and their dependents alive, have inadequate leisure. One might suppose, therefore, that Plato would make elaborate arrangements in his ideal state for the availability of leisure to all, and above all to allow the lowest classes, those whose work is necessarily (from his point of view) the most degrading, the maximum opportunities for such refreshment. But he does not appear to do this; no such elaborate arrangements exist. The state, it seems, does less than it could to prevent the *banausoi* from further injury to their souls.

Such carelessness is more than a little remarkable, for, theoretical considerations apart, Plato seems to have inherited from Socrates a considerable interest in craftsmen and their crafts. The work of the craftsman indeed almost parallels that of the philosopher-king, and the Demiurge (God) himself is, as his name indicates, a Craftsman. But Plato seems to be interested in the craftsman somewhat abstractly, that is, as an individual able to impose Form on matter. The process of imposition should, apparently, be effortless in an ideal world; at any rate it should not be time-consuming. Hence Plato's almost mathematical attitude towards the imposition of Form. The process of imposition in itself has no value, and gives no dignity. The ideal is effortless and immediate "creation". In so far as this is not attained, the activity is often degrading even when necessary, for it assumes involving the soul in detail. Slaves are best for that kind of thing; those, that is, who cannot be corrupted by it. If such can be found, so much the better. If not, the most slavish are the next best alternative and Plato is paradoxically unconcerned with the possibility of helping them improve their lot. At best they can be deceived into accepting it, as the myth of metals at the end of book 3 of the *Republic* suggests. In this matter, as in that of punishment, there is much inconsistency, and Plato's anti-humanitarian side tends to prevail when the logic of his normally impassioned call for justice fails him.

In a way, this should not surprise us. Throughout this discussion, we found Plato seeking a content for Goodness, a source of all value, in a metaphysical and supra-personal reality. In terms of value merely to exist as a man profits us nothing; we need to be good men, and others will not help us be good (and thus acquire value) as much as we would like. And if they will not help us in this regard, we turn to them only in so far as Justice impels us. We return to the Cave because *we* must *act* justly, not because we see human beings in need of help.

CHAPTER FOUR

ARISTOTLE: MIND AND PERSON

It is most unlikely that Aristotle ever subscribed to anything which might reasonably be called a theory of Forms of the Platonic type. Even if he did, he had abandoned it by the time we know much about him. The consequences of this for Aristotle's attitude to human beings and to other possible objects of value need to be worked out, especially since he held when young a very Platonic theory of the soul, much of which he never discarded.[1] For if in Plato value derives from the Forms and from characterization by them, above all from characterization by Goodness, then what happens when these sources of value disappear?[2] In a large number of areas which it would be inappropriate to enumerate, let alone discuss here, it can be argued that Aristotle tries to save Platonic positions, or assumes that such positions can be saved, even though the Forms have been abolished.

When considering Plato, we noticed that although the Forms are the objects of value, we are not invited to attain likeness to the Forms but likeness to God (*homoiōsis theōi*). Aristotle retains this doctrine in a famous text of the tenth book of the *Nicomachean Ethics* (1177B30ff). The whole tone of the passage is Platonic: we are to seek to immortalize ourselves as far as possible. The poets were wrong to preach that mortals should think mortal thoughts; we should think like the gods. But beneath the clearly Platonic surface lie substantial difficulties of interpretation. What gods does Aristotle believe in in any case? What sort of thoughts do they have? Perhaps we can get round these difficulties by supposing that by "immortalizing oneself", Aristotle is referring, somewhat vaguely, to conceptions of God different from his own. That is not very plausible in such a serious passage. Perhaps he is not alluding to God's thoughts, but to some other activity? That is not possible, since the whole passage is concerned with *theōria* (contemplation), an activity which Aristotle tells us man can share with the gods. So we are driven back to the problem that God's thoughts must be understood in the only way in which Aristotle allows them to be thought of, namely that we are dealing with God thinking of himself. And since god is to be identified with some kind of faculty of immediate apprehension (nous, noēsis), this must be also the highest activity for man. In the *Metaphysics* Aristotle specifically rules out the possibility that this immediate apprehension is of anything other than God himself (1074B); only since we know nothing of Aristotle's God except that he has such apprehension, we find ourselves unable to give any content to his thinking.

But we are not completely stymied at this point. The activity of "thinking" (if we may use that word for nous, noēsis) is certainly the most important phenomenon of Aristotle's world; indeed it is to be equated with life itself (*Met.* 1072B28). And the beings which are able to exercize it, and in so far as they are able to exercize it, are the most important within the Aristotelian world. In a revealing section of the *Metaphysics* Aristotle observes that it is more "honourable" (*timios*) for the Prime Mover to think itself than it would be for it to think of something else (1074B). And in the *De Anima* (430A18) we learn that acting is more "honourable" than being acted upon.[3] With the origins, murky as they may be, of this notion, we are not concerned, but an immediate contrast with Plato at a certain level should be remarked. The Forms do not *act* upon anything; they are the *conditions* for certain sorts of excellence; they are imposed on the cosmos by the Demiurge. In this sense the highest beings in a Platonic world are passive. But, as we have already observed, there is nothing corresponding to the Platonic Forms in the Aristotelian world. So he reverts, if you will, to the second level of the Platonic world for his supreme value, to the most active principle in the world, that is to Soul, or more precisely, to a certain function of soul, namely *nous*.

In Plato's *Laws*, in response to Protagoras' challenge that "Man is the measure of all things", Plato had laid down that "God is the measure of all things" (716C). The phrase contains a certain ambiguity; either God measures (determines) all things, or God is the standard by which all things are measured. The latter is in a sense Aristotle's position, for beings (particularly souls) are higher or lower on the scale of value in so far as they more or less approximate to the nature of the divine, that is to the divine mind. Obviously that means that above the level of man is not only the Prime Mover itself, but the other unmoved movers. That is clear enough, but when we come to the nature of man himself, the difficulties begin. The normal doctrine of the mature Aristotle is that man is informed matter, and that on the death of the individual the form (soul) disappears and the matter is recycled elsewhere in the cosmos. But there are two apparently divergent variations on this theme, one, that of the *nous thyrathen*, to be found in the "strictly" biological writings,[4] the other, involving the distinction between an Active and a Passive Intellect, in the *De Anima* (3.5.). Bot of these theories, the first of which seems to have certain affinities with Platonism, but is more probably of immediately "medical" origin, being associated with the notion of *pneuma*, seem to suggest that there is something in "us" but not of "us", where we are defined as being a soul-body complex.[5] The two theories appear to be incompatible, unless one supposes that the *nous* "from outside" is the Active Intellect; and that does not seem to be a suggestion one could deduce from reading the relevant texts.[6] At any rate in the *De Anima* it appears that were there no Active Intellect, certain types of mental operations, and those the "highest", would be impossible. But an examination of the nature of the Active Intellect does not advance our present investigation at all.

There must, it seems, be as many Active Intellects as there are human beings, and they must all be identical. If so, then differences in human character and personality do not arise from the nature of the Active Intellect, but from the nature of our individual soul-body complex. From our present point of view, however, it does not matter whether this interpretation of the Active Intellect is wrong, for the alternative version (that of Averroes) is that there is one single Active Intellect for the whole of mankind. A set of identical Active Intellects or one general Active Intellect makes no difference. What matters is the functioning of the soul as a whole. From this point of view the source of the Active Intellect is irrelevant. If, of course, the whole *nous* comes from outside, then the position is different, for presumably in those circumstances different persons' "minds" must be different *ab initio*. But we have no knowledge of this and will have to confine ourselves to the different functionings of the soul as Aristotle describes them.[7]

Aristotle's treatises on the soul and its various operations are to be classified with his biological writings. In the course of these writings Aristotle offers what amounts to a schematic view of living nature. All living things are to be seen on a continuum. The lowest of them possess necessarily the faculty of "nutrition and reproduction", and nothing higher. All higher beings possess this faculty plus that of "sensation". Men possess these two faculties plus the faculty of reason viewed in one of two aspects, the power of assenting to reason and the power to initiate rational actions (*N.E.* 1103A). As we shall see, however, some "men" do not exhibit both kinds of rationality.

We shall make further progress by considering the concept of nature. For Aristotle it seems that "the natural" is what is normally the case. Thus, he observes that what is "naturally just" is what is normally just.[8] The right hand is naturally (normally) stronger than the left. "Natural" behaviour seems to be determined not in relation to the activity of any individual (man or other), but to the behaviour of the species. But natural acts are not simply what "normally" occur in nature; they are teleological. The doctrine is of Platonic origin; thus in the *Laws* the "natural" use of sex is for procreation (839A, 841D). We may then assume that the use of the various features possessed by living beings is "natural". Thus men "naturally" (normally) reproduce (though some may be sterile), grow (though some may be stunted), perceive (though some may be, in our coarse parlance, "vegetables"), and think. But as we have already observed, the use of the "thinking" faculties is two-fold, and there are humans (admittedly such at *Politics* 1259B 27-38) who are only able to "perceive" sense in their masters and to obey, but not to originate rational activity. And some people are natural slaves; they "perceive" reason, perhaps somewhat like a domesticated animal. Certainly "perception" is the determining characteristic of animals, not of human beings. As Aristotle actually observes, slaves are used in the same way as tame animals (*Pol.* 1254B22), and, as Hesiod put it, the poor man who cannot afford an ox has a slave instead to do his manual work. It is noteworthy, however, that slaves can be "reasoned with"; they do not need to be merely commanded, like animals. So that they are still recognized as "men" (*anthrōpoi*) in the broad sense of the word, that is as belonging to the species Man, which has real content even in the individual case of the natural slave himself.

Before leaving natural slaves we should recall some further details. First of all the children of natural slaves are not necessarily natural slaves. This means that Aristotle is not, as it were, postulating a breed or race of "subhumans", but saying that because of a weakness of particular faculties some human beings are "less human" than others. We have already noted that these "natural slaves" can be reasoned with; they are also, to some degree, and perhaps rather strangely, capable of friendship. Qua slave they cannot be "friends" to their masters; qua man they can. But the interest of this is diminished when we realize that Aristotle identifies three different kinds of friendship, that for pleasure, that for utility and the higher form, for virtue. Obviously the slave cannot be a friend for the sake of virtue; the state of the personality of slave and master is too distinct: whatever friendship there is must be one of the lower forms.

Natural slaves are neither vicious nor bestial, though they do resemble animals, as we have seen, in certain important respects. There are certain other kinds of human beings, however, whom Aristotle seems to think of as "beasts" (*Pol.* 1253A29; *N.E.* 1145A31). Of these again there are three types: those who are converted into "beasts" by persistent vice or wrongdoing (*N.E.* 1148B17); those who are the victims of madness or some pathological condition; and those who, as it were, just grew that way (*N.E.* 1150A). These latter are like Cyclopes; they live by their own rules, which are essentially non-moral and non-rational. They are a different type of "subhuman". All the varieties of "bestiality" (massive folly, cowardice, licentiousness, harshness) seem to have irrationality as a common feature. The man of "bestial" folly lives entirely "by sensation" (*N.E.* 1149A10), in this respect having something in common with the natural slave. He shares with him a common "ambiguity" between the animal and the "really" human level.

Human beings are a kind of "animal"; they are animals fitted to live as citizens in a city-state.[9] They therefore share certain characteristics with the other animals, though not, of course, the characteristic of being able to live in a city-state. That means that those "hominids" *not* suited to living in this society as citizens are not human beings in the strong sense of the phrase, though, as we have seen, they are certainly human (*anthrōpoi*) in some sense. Those unable to live in cities are, as we have seen, "beasts" or "gods". Now we have already noted various classes of "men" who are unable to live in this way; and we have observed that they have not developed the "rational" faculty of men properly so called. There are other "underdeveloped" classes: women and children; and we shall consider these.

Before that, however, it will be valuable to turn briefly to the realm of embryology, to the problem of the development of men from the time of their conception. This is a subject to which Aristotle devoted a good deal of attention, and there are a number of texts which are relevant to our present concerns. At various places we read that an animal and a man do not come to be simultaneously, nor an animal and a horse.[10] The peculiarity (*idion*) of each thing comes when the process of genesis is complete. This seems to mean that an embryo, destined for manhood, becomes an animal, but not a specific kind of animal, before it becomes human, though it is potentially human. It is quite unclear, in fact, when it actually becomes human. At some stage of intrauterine growth it is fully differentiated as a human being physically, but it is by no means clear that Aristotle thinks that it is an actual human being at that stage. Certainly it is animal, and at the same time potentially human, but it appears not to be actually human. In some respects it may resemble the natural slaves and "beasts" who live by sensation alone. They are at the animal level. But much of the process of development from animal to individual human is not completed at all before birth. In the *Ethics* Aristotle suggests that *children* resemble animals in that they are underdeveloped morally (1100A2).[11] In an important respect they are not fully human. They cannot use their intelligence in the peculiarly human way which marks the perfectly mature and complete specimen. Mature specimens may be assumed to use their reason effectively to control their desires and ensure that the individual does not simply act instinctively. Thus from this point of view only adults are actually human. But even that won't do because some adults are not capable of controlling their instincts in the way Aristotle thinks that they should. We seem in fact to have reached an absurd situation. Practically no adult males will be human at all, only potentially so. Clearly this is not what Aristotle intends to say. We should probably make distinctions as follows: at some point before birth the animal may be said to be potentially human in one use of "potentially", that is "human" rather than some other species of animal. But the child is potentially human in a different sense; he is not simply "potentially human", but potentially virtuous human. It would seem to follow that just as the child would therefore be of greater value than the as yet undetermined embryo, so the man would be of greater value than the child. At any rate, as we have already noted, when dealing with another group of "defectives", Aristotle observes that a man rules his wife because of his greater value.[12]

We need go no further than this in identifying certain classes of defectives who are of lower value than the developed adult males of virtuous disposition. Apart from natural slaves, these include women and children. We might add, of course, that it would seem to follow that virtuous human beings are more valuable than vicious ones; and value would indeed be directly and entirely related to virtue. Hence there would seem, as with Plato, to be a group of people, hardened criminals, who would have no value at all and should, as in Plato, be eliminated. Finally, we should notice that in regard to women Aristotle's attitude seems to be rather more pessimistic than Plato's. Women are defective males, though there are exceptional cases of female excellence in "unnatural", that is unusual circumstances (*Pol.* 1259B3)".[13]

But even within the class of reasonably virtuous adult males we must be far more sparing with our accolades of value. Like Plato, Aristotle has little time for the *banausos*, the labourer. In Plato's Ideal State such people form the third class; in Aristotle's *Politics* they are to be excluded altogether from citizenship, for they do not have the time for the two necessary duties of citizens, namely participation in the machinery of government and in the courts;[14] hence they are not "productive of excellence" (1329A19-20). Aristotle does not even consider whether they are sufficiently well-endowed with practical wisdom to be helped to freedom from the time-consuming duties which prevent a man from developing the proper mentality of a citizen.

There is no doubt that whereas for Plato value is determined by the degree to which we approximate to God, and by so doing become characterized by the Forms, which are themselves the ultimate objects of value, in Aristotle it is by the achievement of our minds that we are measured. Again, as we pointed out earlier, this is a form of likeness to God; and again virtue (achieved virtue), with its necessary "intellectual" component is the precise measure of value. Aristotle in the *Nicomachean Ethics* pushes this as far as he can in a number of passages where he tries to equate "us" as far as possible with our contemplative "mind" (*nous*).[15] Notice however a difference from the position of the Socrates of Plato's *Alcibiades* that we should be equated with our soul. For the soul is concerned with a whole range of activities with which humans are concerned: sensation, thought, movement, etc. But *nous* is normally only a part or aspect of "soul"; and Aristotle's identification of "us" "more or less" with *nous* indicates that he believes that only those activities which are the "higher" activities of men are particularly important. Granted that, it would obviously follow that those (women, children, natural slaves, etc.) who cannot perform them are of proportionally lower worth. It is obvious that this identification—if that is what it is—of "ourselves" with "mind" is not entirely satisfying for Aristotle. There are *caveats* in the identification itself; we do not know why. And we can only assume that Aristotle remained somewhat uneasy with such an apparently reductionist view of what it is to be human, and of the unimportance of "non-intellectual" facets of the personality. It is the same kind of difficulty that many people—and startlingly in the ancient world Plotinus in particular[16]—have felt about Aristotle's concept of God. That is, perhaps God is to be sought along the lines Aristotle has suggested, but there must also be other lines along which the search can be pursued—with the necessary result that the concept of God must be more complex, possibly more personal, than Aristotle seems to have thought likely.

We can determine from the *Nicomachean Ethics* and the *Politics* the general lines of a hierarchy of human beings of declining value. At the top are the contemplators, who are in the city but not of it. The magistrates look after them in the same way as they "look after" the gods in their temples. Below them come the men of practical wisdom, and then follow those equipped with various other mental skills. It is not possible to work out from Aristotle's text exactly the sequence that follows, but we know that at the bottom will fall the natural slaves, those whose "best" life is to live entirely at the disposal of others. There are other indistinct features too: how does the value of a child, a potentially virtuous man, compare with that of an adult slave or a "banausos"? Luckily for Aristotle he was not obliged to spell out the practical details of the system. Had he attempted to do so, we could presumably have been confronted with an elaborate structure such as existed, for example, in the West Indies in colonial times, when one's value was rated in proportion to the fraction of whiteness in one's make-up, half-whites being higher than quarter-whites, etc.

But apart from practical difficulties of this sort, there is another strange feature of the Aristotelian "ethic of superiority". The standard is god; that is, human excellence is valued in so far as it approximates to something higher than the human level. Again there seems to be no account taken of the possible value in different kinds of human beings. Approximation to an impersonal, unfeeling, unchanging being is preferred to any diversification of human potentialities. That diversification, as in Plato, is due to matter; and the divine mind to which we are called on to approximate is non-material. We can certainly identify a "Platonism" without the Forms about all this; and it has survived to exist alongside Aristotle's doctrine of the soul as the form of the particular body. In many ways the two doctrines should not exist side by side. That they do is evidence of the importance Aristotle attached to the "ultra-Platonic" thesis about the relation of mind to self and to personality. It is, of course, a rather characteristic result of the Aristotelian method that such a situation should arise, for in pursuing his various problems Aristotle reaches a series of individual solutions, and he does not always get round to testing whether the solutions themselves are mutually compatible. Be that it may, Aristotle must have viewed his attitude to the relation of mind to self as of the highest importance and basically correct, for in this case the problems that it causes are patent. It is impossible to believe that he had no inkling of them.

Problems of method aside, however, let us revert to a topic which has already confronted us in discussing Socrates and Plato, and which was to be of great importance after Aristotle as well: the problem of the "content" rather than the "form" of goodness. It is clear both from discussion of the Prime Mover in the *Metaphysics*, and from Aristotle's remarks about practical and contemplative mind in the *Nicomachean Ethics* that the ultimately valuable in the Aristotelian universe is rationality as such. The universe is organized rationally, and mind at its best is able to recognize, and in Aristotelian terms, to be identified with, that rationality. Contemplative reason reflects on the nature of beings as such, while practical reason is able in matters of contingent fact, for example, to determine, that is to identify, the mean in relation to us. By "determine" we should note, is not meant create. Aristotelian mind does not create rationality and order. It exists as rationality; it recognizes rationality and tries to impose it.

Let us revert to Plato for a moment. In the *Meno* he distinguishes knowledge from true belief in a number of ways. Since "knowledge" in the special Platonic sense of the middle dialogues involves some kind of direct acquaintance by the subject with its object, whether that object be a particular, like the road to Larisa in the *Meno*, or the Form of the Good itself, the result of direct acquaintance is that "knowledge" can hardly be lost. If you've seen it, you've seen it. Or in a more modern parallel, it is strange for someone to say that he has forgotten the difference between right and wrong. Plato also supposed that knowledge of Form is of a very special kind in relation to the will; if one sees, for example, the Form of Beauty, as the *Symposium* tells us, one will try to "beget in the beautiful", to reproduce Beauty. If one is just in the Platonic sense, one will act justly, however hard that may seem to an outsider. "Why do you ask them to live a worse life when it is possible to live a better?", asks Glaucon in the *Republic* (519D8), speaking of the return of the Guardians to the Cave. Because they are just, is the answer, and since they are just, they will act justly, And finally the Demiurge wants to make all things as like himself as possible, i.e. as good as possible, *because* he is good. Thus we recognize that Platonic knowledge of Form so affects the whole character, not just the intellect, as to make action in a contrary spirit impossible. Were knowledge merely propositional, or some condition of the cognitive faculty in virtually any non-Platonic sense, such a thing would be impossible. Plato does not, however, spell out the psychological consequences of his own theory, indeed he could not have done so.

A corollary of Plato's account of knowledge, as book nine of the *Republic* makes clear, is that the so-called "reasoning" faculty is also volitional and appetitive. There is no distinction to be made between faculties of knowing and willing. The mind *wants* to know, craves to know, and is, as it were, emotionally affected by its knowledge. In this respect, of course, the human will, as the *Symposium* also shows, is different from the mind of the gods. The gods do not *want* to be wise (*Symp.* 203E), they *are* wise. But there is nothing in what Plato says in the *Symposium*—and indeed the reverse is implied—to suggest that the gods do not want to use their knowledge. They want to create, as is specifically said of the Demiurge. They do not feel the want that arises from "need" or "lack"; they do feel the want which arises from their character, their attitude of goodness. In this respect one might almost say that for Plato the *logistikon*, the *daimon*, the rational soul, is a personality in its own right. Certainly it is more than a cognitive instrument or unemotional principle of rationality as such.

Now it appears that in the tenth book of the *Nicomachean Ethics*, the thought of the Aristotelian contemplative is unplatonic in that it has no direct practical effects, that this knowing does *not* entail willing to act. In this respect the human intellect resembles the Prime Mover, for the thought of the Prime Mover is entirely limited to himself. But, it will be argued, there is a direct connection between the activity of the Prime Mover and the existence of motion in the cosmos. Yes, indeed, but the

Prime Mover is only to be regarded as the final cause. It is the effect of his existence to produce motion in the cosmos; he himself, however, is in no sense an efficient cause. Neither is the contemplative in the city-state. In fact he is not directly the cause of any kind of external effect at all. He is certainly bound up with himself; he exhibits nothing of the Platonic begetting and engendering in the beautiful. Such a distinction between Plato and Aristotle in the *Nicomachean Ethics* may be viewed as one of the effects of separating the "man of practical wisdom" from the "contemplative", the philosopher from the king—a separation towards which Plato was already moving by the time he wrote the *Laws* (710CD). It may be argued that it represents a devaluation of "practical wisdom".

Be that as it may, Aristotle's Prime Mover and "contemplative man" represent a more desiccated notion of the highest form of intellectual activity. The Eros of the Platonic Guardian has disappeared; the peculiar emotional force has been strained from intellectual life in its highest manifestations. No wonder then that Aristotle seems confused about the nature of Platonic philosophical "knowledge" in his attack on its "Socratic" version as failing to account for the phenomenon of weakness of will. Were Socratic knowledge the same kind of knowledge as his own contemplation, it would have no necessary connection, and perhaps no connection at all, with action. Indeed the disassociation of higher thought from action was to have longlasting effects—and to lead to strange attempts to affect a reconciliation. Yet from the author of the *Politics* with its brilliant central books on the manipulation of men and cities, the author of the biological works with their far from merely theoretical concerns, the disassociation is striking; one wonders whether Aristotle himself was fully aware of it. Perhaps, if Kenny's view of the development of Aristotle's ethics is right,[17] he attempted a correction in the *Eudemian Ethics*. But he could not have sorted out the problems satisfactorily without more awareness than he seems to show of the interrelations in Plato of ethics, axiology and metaphysics. In jettisoning what he jettisons, he seems to minimize the difficulty of retaining the remaining parts of a Platonic structure.

It might, I think, be claimed that Aristotle has gone along the path that Plato was tempted to pursue, but which his Athenian citizen interests, and the living memory of the attitudes of Socrates, prevented him from pursuing. Aristotle in the *Protrepticus*, with the younger man's enthusiasm, seems already to have advocated "pure research", the disassociation of the mind from society, to a degree which Plato could not have approved.[18] In the *Theaetetus* (174C ff) Plato outlines the claims of the wholly contemplative life; only, apparently, to reject them for human beings. Again in the *Philebus* the claims of *phronēsis* alone to represent the good for men are denied. A mixture of pleasure is necessary. Certainly Aristotle is not deaf to the challenge that pleasure might be the good;[19] but he seems prepared to advocate as an ideal for men, albeit a "pleasurable" ideal, a more purely "academic" life; or at least for a very few superior men, those capable of living at the "more than human" level.

What therefore remains is to consider Aristotelian *theōria* (and to a lesser extent phronēsis), as defined in the *Nicomachean Ethics*, more carefully. We have already noted a disassociation of contemplation from what may be crudely called the world of cause and effect. But its complete isolation from other forms of human behaviour raises still further difficulties. Despite a number of modern interpreters Aristotle probably thinks that the "contemplative" is in possession of at least a majority of the moral virtues.[20] For what will he do when he is not contemplating; and Aristotle realizes that he cannot contemplate all the time. He probably also possesses some of the other intellectual virtues. He will undoubtedly possess a certain power of immediate apprehension (*nous*) and presumably the ability to reason syllogistically (*epistēmē apodeiktikē*).

Yet strikingly Aristotle does not speak of the interrelation of the various intellectual activities. We do not know how he envisages that *nous* is affected by the activity of contemplation (*theōria*) itself. That there must be some interaction between the various intellectual activities, however, is not only likely on purely *a priori* grounds, but seems to be confirmed by Aristotle's view that it is "inhuman" to be alone. Of course contemplation is an activity carried on by the "soul" by itself; it does not need the presence of others for its continuing exercize; nevertheless it is remarkable that the clash between the impossibility of "loneliness" and the self-sufficiency of contemplation does not strike Aristotle as worthy of more comment.[21] He contents himself, as we have noticed, with pointing out that a life of contemplation is "above the human level" (*N.E.* 1177B27), and must therefore be of only limited duration.

For the insufficiency of contemplation to satisfy one's human needs—and I suspect that Aristotle is not merely thinking of the need to eat, drink and sleep—ought to provoke problems about the precise relationship between the contemplative mind and the man himself. Perhaps, however, that (or something like it) is what Aristotle was thinking of in those passages to which we have already alluded where he adds a *caveat*, a *malista* ("most strictly") to the proposal that *we* are to be identified with "mind". But from the point of view of value, even if this is the explanation, we have to conclude that, although Aristotle is honest enough to recognize that we are *not* "simply" to be identified with some form of mind, he seems almost to regret this and to treat the part over and above mind as of little value or importance. This alone—a tendency to think of the personality as composed of the mind plus the residue (of whatever size)—must be the explanation of why he does not discuss the effects of contemplation on the rest of the human personality.

In fact problems about contemplation are part of what seems to be a much more general difficulty in Aristotle's approach to psychology. Although Aristotle is frequently lauded for rejecting a "ship in the bottle" concept of the relationship of soul to body—his own theory of soul as the form of body avoids that—he fails adequately to discuss the interaction of the various other functions of the psyche—the nutritive and reproductive powers, the power of sensation; and he fails to deal adequately with the effects on these powers of the possession of mind itself. For it must be true that an Aristotelian faculty of sensation is affected by the presence or absence of mind. That is, my perception of a tree must be different from a dog's perception. Above all, in Aristotelian terms, the functioning of the common sense, the general perceptive faculty, will be different not only between men and animals but between different human beings. As we say, perceptions may be heightened by various other (mental or physical) experiences.

If we ask why Aristotle pays almost no attention to these interrelations within the psyche, we can only speculate. The most plausible suggestion would seem to be that again he is betrayed by an overplatonic model—indeed by a model which in some respects is more Platonic than anything in Plato himself. Although Aristotle concerns himself with faculties, capacities of the soul, he seems to operate much of the time as though these faculties were separate entities, rather than inseparable phenomena of an entire soul-body complex. Of course, in the case of *nous* (whether "from outside" or seen as an Active Intellect), we really do find a separate entity in a fully Platonic sense.

But difficulties of interrelation not only exist between the various faculties of the Aristotelian man; they also exist within what may be broadly called the "mental" (*dianoētikon*) itself. Presumably every human being possesses (or on the "Averroistic" view is affected by) an Active Intellect—though strictly speaking it seems difficult to understand how "natural slaves"—wholly devoid of the ability to formulate rational proposals, only capable of giving assent to such proposals when put forward by others—are able to use the Active Intellect even if they have one. Though perhaps even the recognition of reason in others requires such an intellect, it is hard to understand why it should only function in this limited way. Perhaps we have to say that in those cases it is the Passive Intellect (or even some bodily organ) which is defective.

But we must leave these wider difficulties and return to the contemplative. We cannot assume that he is *wholly* devoid of practical reason. Perhaps *some* contemplatives may be—though, as we have already observed, even these cannot be entirely lacking in the moral virtues, the virtues of habit. What then are to say of the contemplative who also possesses a certain practical wisdom? When Aristotle argues in the tenth book of the *Ethics* that contemplation is the superior form of activity and brings happiness in its train, his arguments illuminate his assumptions, even if they are not always persuasive. They run as follows:

(a) Intellect is the highest thing (*kratistē*) in us, and its objects are the highest.

(b) Contemplation is the most continuous activity.

(c) Activity in accordance with wisdom is "admittedly" the most pleasant kind of activity.

(d) It is reasonable to suppose that the possession of knowledge is more pleasant than the pursuit of it.

(e) Contemplation is the most self-sufficient activity; because while justice requires other people who may require to be treated justly, contemplation needs no such props. The wiser a contemplative is, the less he needs outside help.

(f) Contemplation needs nothing beyond itself.

(g) Contemplation is the activity of the "divine part".

(h) Contemplation is the activity of the dominant and better part of us. Who would choose to live not his own life, but that of some other?

Our earlier discussion enables us to comment on these arguments:

1. The argument about the objects of contemplation seems to beg the question, at least if the activity of contemplation is to approximate to the life of the gods. For among the gods it is mind itself (or rationality) which is the object of contemplation. In other words various assumptions about the nature of the objects of contemplation are needed to make the argument about objects of knowledge work. Beyond that there is simply the claim that the contemplative mind is the superior part, which may well be true, but is not self-evidently so. Nor, of course, does it help resolve the question of the relation between different mental functions: mind as practical reasoner and mind as contemplator.

2. When Aristotle specifically compares contemplation and practical reason (1178A20), he *distinguishes* contemplation as the virtue of our divine part from practical reason as the activity of the "composite"; thereby he again assumes that the activity of the composite is "lower" because the gods do not have it and because its objects are not eternal. But why thought of an eternal object should necessarily be "higher" than thought of a contingent one is not stated.

The most basic assumption, of course, underlying all the comments in this section of the *Ethics* is that within us there is something godlike, something more than human, which bestows value on the soul-body complex in so far as it is associated with it—a something which can approximate to a life higher than the merely moral life of that complex. We may have no objection to that thesis as such, but we must insist both that it is nowhere *argued* for in the text of Aristotle, and that it asserts the superiority of contemplation to practical reasoning, and the relationship between them, in a way which is incompatible not only with a genuinely Platonic account of knowledge, but also with a Platonic ethic. For in this regard it is the "other-worldly" Plato who sets higher store on dealing with contingent things, precisely because these things are what they are in virtue of a participation in Form. Whereas in Plato soul mediates between the world of Forms and the world of change, acting thereby both as an efficient cause and the conveyer of final causation to the world of particulars, in Aristotle the two worlds are separated in a more radical fashion—though, as we noticed, the more disillusioned Plato of the *Laws* seems to have paved the way. It is striking indeed that in the *Nicomachean*, though not in the *Eudemian Ethics* Aristotle has nothing at all to say about a man who could combine practical wisdom with contemplation, though perhaps the ideal king of his *Politics* would have been such a person.

The man of practical wisdom deals with contingent events and particular cases. His inferiority to the contemplator may be observed if we approach him in another way. What is the role of particulars, including human subjects, in the Aristotelian value-scheme? We know that for Aristotle it is species, classes of things, which are the concern of the philosopher as such, even though it is often particulars which are regarded as the basic furniture of the world. Here we seem to return to Aristotle's concept of the natural: "the natural" in living things is concerned with the maintenance of the species, not of the individual. Individuals may be understood (rather than merely "recognized") only *as* members of classes of individuals or of species. Of course, the species is not an abstraction; it is a collection of individuals, but the individual itself (and for itself) seems unimportant in the "natural" order. Perhaps Aristotle means that man's mind is his most valuable faculty in so far as it enables him to think not of individuals which are contingent, but of species which are enduring. This again points to the "superiority" of Aristotelian contemplation, which is presumably never of individuals as such.

It might even be argued that in general the species is what gives the individual soul-body complex, though not the individual mind, its value in Aristotle's axiology, though on the existential level it is only the individual which exists and lives. Man begets man, but Man does not exist. Peleus is the father of Achilles and your father is the father of you. Aristotle never faces the problem of the relationship between his axiological propositions and assumptions and his attack on Platonism in the interest of vindicating the existential priority of the individual. The problem, like others we have already mentioned, seems to have arisen because of the nature of Aristotle's chosen philosophical method. He may have been right in thinking that Plato tries to make his Forms, the sources of both "value" and "being such", do too much; but his pursuit of isolated philosophical problems has precluded his offering an alternative overall account of value: partly because of unresolved difficulties about the content of the highest kind of thought; partly because he has not adequately specified the relation of such thought to the workings of the practical intellect in the world of contingency. It is particularly interesting to notice that whereas Aristotle's emphasis on the individual as a compound of form and matter is overtly a critique of the Platonic tendency to devalue the "existence" of particulars, it breaks down as a theory of the nature of particulars precisely at the level of human beings where the question of value (in our terms) becomes acute. It is as though Aristotle supposes that when at the physical and biological level we have merely a compound of form and matter, the question of value hardly arises, or if it does arise, it only arises in some kind of analogical way (action being superior to passion, etc.); but when there are important questions of value (i.e. in beings possessed of *nous*), the hylomorphic explanation is inadequate.

A further negative comment should be made at this point. Aristotle never tries to "give value" to particulars, even particular human beings, by an appeal to providence. God is unconcerned with human beings; and the denial of Providence led some in antiquity to class Aristotle with the atheists. Hence human value, even the value of the mind itself, has nothing to do with the will or ordering of God. There is no connection in this area between value and the physical ordering of the cosmos.

Finally we may come to the question of "friendship" (*philia*), which provides a good example of the effects of Aristotle's ethic of superiority. In considering Plato, we observed that much of his thought about the ascent of the soul is related to his notions of friendship, and that human beings are valued, even held to be worthy of "friendship" or "love", in so far as they exhibit good qualities. Aristotle often thinks in a similar way; certainly he disallows the possibility of true friendship if individuals are "mentally" too far apart. God cannot be the friend of man, he holds. This must be true even on an apparently "popular" view of God; on the Aristotelian metaphysical view it would follow necessarily from God's nature, not merely from the nature of the highest kind of friendship.

Friendship is indeed important for Aristotle, and at its highest level it involves valuing one's friend as a second self. But that means that the better a man becomes, the more "god-like" he becomes, the fewer friends he will normally have. It looks as though, if a single perfect man were possible, he would value no-one at all as highly as himself. Other people would be valued at less, and in proportion as they approximate to himself. They could not be valued for the sake of virtue, for his own virtue is complete; still less could they be valued for the sake of utility or pleasure.

Aristotle's attitude to "friendship" has a number of important similarities to Plato's attitude to "love"; and indeed the same word (*philia* or its cognates) is used by both Plato and Aristotle to deal with an emotion, an attitude, which we could only designate strongly enough by the word "love". But just as in Plato the "love" for the individual's soul is transmuted into love not of individuals but of the Forms themselves, so in Aristotle "friendship" is more appropriate not to the highest kind of man, but to the second, the man of practical wisdom. The problem with friendship for Aristotle, as indeed with all the practical virtues, is that it is not self-sufficient. It requires the existence of another for its exercise, it is an external good;[21] and although that presents no difficulties for man when he lives at a purely human level, as a "social animal", it is inadequate when he exceeds that level to live like the gods, or to achieve immortality as far as he is able. For Aristotle, therefore, as for Plato, we may conclude that the love of immortality (now seen as rationality) transcends and supersedes the love of persons. God is not a person, he is a principle, even if one may justly conclude that he is the principle of rationality.

With Aristotle we must conclude, as we began, with Plato and the areas of his influence. We have observed in Aristotle's "ethic of superiority" a number of unresolved problems about the relationship between "mind" and what we may crudely call "the whole person" or "the composite". We have found Aristotle at times almost (but not quite) limiting the "we", the self, to some kind of mind. We have made no attempt to link this to more general problems of Aristotelian metaphysics; nor would it be appropriate to do so now. But it would not be satisfactory to discuss Aristotle's attitude to our "real self" without noting that there are undoubted similarities between what he says about whether "we" are *nous* and his doctrine that the essence of any particular (the "what it is") is somehow the substance of that particular. As mind is to our whole self, so, in certain respects, "essence" is to substance. Or perhaps the former relationship is an example of the latter. But Aristotle does not discuss these relationships, and it is not possible to explore them further here.

We conclude that for Aristotle human value depends on the nature of the human mind; and, as we first observed, this might be thought of as an example of Platonism without the Forms. But our study of contemplation has marked out certain peculiarly Aristotelian tendencies: because of the separation of contemplation and action the best man, at least in the *Nicomachean Ethics*, is curiously unconcerned with his fellows. Goodness, that is, has tended to shed its ethical features; and that is appropriate in a scenario where mind has replaced the Good as the fount of value. And the psychological counterpart of this is that the highest thought has lost its power to motivate social action. Nevertheless, at the level of practical wisdom and below, where man is still viewed as active in a social context, we also find the equation of mind with value maintained. As we pass from the man of practical wisdom to the natural slave, we find the value of man proportionally declining.

Finally we should notice that Aristotle's scale of value is not substantially affected by the fact that in book 3 of the *Politics* (1286A) he allows that there are many occasions when the collective wisdom of a group may prove superior to that of any individual member. Leave aside the fact that Aristotle seems more or less unaware in this section of the special pressures towards irresponsibility and spinelessness inherent in the behaviour of groups (who, he thinks, are less corruptible). Merely observe that there is nothing in Aristotle's account to suggest that he would want to modify his view of human value in the light of the possible collective wisdom of groups. Any similar group of people will be equally effective. The credit of the group contributes nothing to the personal value of its members, who, from this point of view, are human units.

CHAPTER FIVE

FREEDOM

In considering Socrates and Plato, we observed a number of the roots of the particular concept of freedom with which we are going to be concerned in this chapter. Contemporary discussions of freedom tend to start with the now well-known distinction between "freedom from" and "freedom to". In Greek times most, though not all, discussion of freedom was in terms of freedom from, of "unrestraint". Even "positive" freedom, i.e. the right of participation in the government or the judiciary, was often viewed in this light.[1] The very words *exousia*, *autexousia*, often the philosophical equivalents of *eleutheria*, which is a term drawn from the political domain,[2] indicate a "permission to", or a "lack of restriction from". Of course, an important part of "doing what you like" is saying what you like; and freedom of speech is the watchword of democracy and the "finest thing there is" for the Cynic Diogenes.[3]

It was the Sophistic movement which primarily brought the notion of freedom *from* to philosophical attention, though of course the development of political democracy in Greek society, and in particular in Athens, depended on a recognition of the importance of freedom from arbitrary restrictions, and in particular from arbitrary acts of the ruling group or the "tyrant". Hence the importance of fixed law, as both Plato and Aristotle recognized. But with the sophists we come to a fully developed antithesis between "convention" and "nature", which carried with it the claim, urged forcibly by Callicles in the *Gorgias*, that obedience to the laws of a city or the customs of a society is a kind of slavery; the free man, therefore, is the natural man, the man who can break through the various chains which lesser human beings have imposed on him. In less violent versions of this thesis than that espoused by Callicles, such as, for example, that offered by Glaucon in the second book of the *Republic* (359Aff), we find the view that states, societies, laws and conventions grow up as a kind of covenant, being in this sense a man-made rather than a "natural" product, designed by the weak—and most men have to recognize their weakness—to protect themselves against the strong. It would follow from this version of the antithesis between nature and convention, as for the Calliclean version, that a naturally strong man might choose not to abide by the conventions, and profit by such action, being free from the restraints that they impose.

There is no doubt that it was not only intellectuals like Euripides who were fascinated by the development of the concept of nature in this sense.⁴ Critias' poem indicates a similar interest in that crafty oligarch; and we can assert without hesitation that Callicles, who is depicted as a political manipulator and demagogue, is designed to represent a type of "new politician" who is able to exploit the novel understanding of freedom to his own personal advantage. It need not only be aristocrats, as Callicles himself shows, who might think along these lines. Indeed the type of politics one espouses may not matter at all. The ideology, the political programme, can be tailored to suit one's own advantage with the maximum dishonesty one can muster. Aristotle's catalogue in the *Politics* of the ways in which power can be maintained probably indicates a long history (starting from the fifth century) of "academic" interest in such manipulation; and it seems that at some time between the *Republic* and the *Laws*, or between the *Politicus* and the *Laws*, or perhaps even while writing the *Laws*, Plato had become much more conscious of the dangers and attractions of power as such, and the inability of any man to resist its attractions.⁵

Such attractions need not be justified by a "sophisticated" thesis that power is naturally sought, that might is naturally right. But ideas of that sort were widely current and could not but affect the ordinary politician, indeed the ordinary member of the public. And the attractiveness of power as such might well be associated with a belief that restraint of any kind is the product of society, that it has nothing "natural" about it, indeed that it is artificial. A simple lust for power might look attractively like a new kind of freedom, as Polus in the *Gorgias* seems to suppose, and as is documented in the case of the "democratic" and "tyrannical" men of the *Republic* (560-1ff). Here Plato's characters, though not, of course, Plato himself, think of freedom exclusively as a lack of restriction, an ability to do what one likes, or, quite simply, as licence.

This sort of freedom has much to do with an ideal which we have already discussed, that of self-sufficiency (*autarkeia*); and at this point it seems to come into contact with apparently more reputable, less anarchic, political or philosophical ideals. For the self-sufficient man, whether in Plato's or in Aristotle's version, is free of the hypocrisies of bourgeois Greek society. He does not accept moral values and rules simply because of what Plato calls "true opinion", a mere adhering to convention. (Those who do that, as the *Phaedo* (82B5ff) succinctly puts it, will be reincarnated as social insects like bees or ants). The self-sufficient man, according to the philosophers, accepts conventions when he chooses to and because he judges it right to do so. He is able to judge them freely and dispassionately. The point may be illustrated by considering certain incidents in the career of Socrates.

In the *Apology* Socrates strives to show that he has exhibited to a high degree all the qualities of a patriotic Athenian. But beside mentioning his distinguished military service and his rare (though striking) forays into the political and judicial arena, he also claims that his unusual and unconventional behaviour, his quest to save the souls of his fellow-Athenians for virtue, is politically and socially right. In other words he tries to prove that his somewhat eccentric life, his admitted neglect of his family and his own affairs, is fully in accord with the conventions of society, and indeed determined by the basic principles from which such conventions have rightly developed.

Consider another instance: Socrates' behaviour, as described in the *Crito*, when he is offered the chance of flight to Thebes. He argues that he has always accepted the laws of Athens and has no reason not to do so now. He has chosen to remain in Athens and live under Athenian law when he might earlier and easily have gone elsewhere. His choice is a kind of contract which at this late stage it would be improper for him to violate. Thus Socrates claims not just that he accepts the laws of his city, but that he has *chosen* to accept them. Where he has been "conventional", it is a choice of convention. Where he has been unconventional, that was his choice too.

For in the history of ancient thought Socrates is not only the predecessor of Plato, the inspirer of the philosophy of the Forms and of the Academy; he is also a star instance of the free man, the man who is afraid neither to behave conventionally, nor to behave unconventionally. How does he reach this position? Because, as we have shown, he has discovered the form, if not the content, of a truth which transcends conventions, though he is able to use these too when the occasion is right.

In this important sense, Socrates is the heir of the sophistic antithesis between nature and convention. Competing with Callicles he is able to appeal to a *higher* nature, while at the same time remaining the master of convention rather than its slave.

He is free even from the conventions which he chooses to adopt; and it is his search for truth and for virtue which grants him this freedom. Plato is genuinely in the Socratic tradition when he thinks of the Forms as existing "by nature", and Xenocrates is in the genuinely Platonic tradition when he quotes as a definition of Forms acceptable to Plato himself the phrase "paradeigmatic cause of the things that exist in nature".[6]

But Socrates, as we observed, was the ideal of other traditions than the Platonic, the teacher or at least the inspirer of other philosophies than the theory of Forms. Within a very few years of his death there were those who claimed that Plato's portrait (especially, but not only, in the *Apology*) was radically misleading. Socrates was not a dogmatic philosopher: as the probably anachronistic story in Diogenes Laertius puts it, "What a pack of lies this young man (i.e. Plato) puts into my mouth?" says Socrates on hearing Plato read the *Lysis*.[7] Even in the Platonic writings themselves we can glimpse a quite "unplatonic" kind of person who nevertheless regarded Socrates as a hero in his way of life, and who copied him, one might almost say parodied him, in the details of it: Apollodorus in the *Symposium*. Above all, however, we should think of Antisthenes in this connection, the alleged founder and certain predecessor of Cynicism. Like his Cynic successors Antisthenes seems to have sought happiness above all in freedom from the conventions and in freedom from the passions.[8] Probably it was among such people that the concept of *apatheia* first arose, though, as we observed, this was also promoted by the quite different thinking of Speusippus.[9]

Let us look at the Cynic tradition more closely, concerning ourselves less with the historical circumstances of the personalities involved and their "doxographical" connections, than with the "philosophical" links that join them, with particular reference to the notion of freedom. Diogenes himself, seeking to avoid enslavement to the passions, is reported to have advocated "Reason or the Rope (i.e. suicide)",[10] and Antisthenes said that he would rather be mad than feel pleasure.[11] Diogenes, the Cynic *par excellence*, tried to live with as few of the enslaving "necessities" of life as possible, and was said to have wandered about Athens with a lantern saying he was looking for an honest man. When the Stoic Zeno had abandoned his earlier Cynic associates, for reasons which we may shortly consider, he was accosted by Diogenes with the taunt "What are you doing among us free men?"[12] In all this "Reason or the Rope" brings us closest to the heart of the issue, for it asserts that Reason alone distinguished the life worth living; such unfettered reason is passionless, and seemingly inhuman. One might suppose that a life of reason alone would have brought the Cynic nearer to Aristotle, whose ideal in the *Nicomachean Ethics* is that of the free and unrestricted life of the contemplative intellect. To understand why it did not involves not only more discussion of the problem of pleasure, but a more fundamental analysis of the importance of the content (as against the form) of the moral life.

Plato's portrait of Socrates, we suggested, appears authentic in that he is depicted as "living" a mode of ethical enquiry while offering no specific moral theory. But Socrates did not give up the search for virtue, and, as Plato maintained, it may be genuinely Socratic to believe that the "content" or nature of goodness could and would be discovered. There is no good evidence to support the later and frequent claim of the Sceptics that Socrates himself was sceptical about the possibility of knowledge.[13]

But the example of Socrates the searcher overshadowed in many minds the question of the subject of his search: in the eyes of Apollodorus, of Antisthenes and of the Cynic tradition in general, Socrates is already the truly virtuous man, the Heracles of the "modern" world, the man who is already free from that enslavement to convention which oppressed the majority of his contemporaries. Indeed not only is the question of the content of goodness neglected; it is positively asserted that the way of life itself is the good for man; and of course the way of life now differs from the Socratic, even while sheltering under his name. For although Socrates may be cited as an exemplar of the kind of free man with whom the Cynic tradition was concerned, he did not *claim* that this freedom was of great importance to him. In Cynic terms Socrates acted freely; in Socratic terms his freedom was a means to an unaccomplished end. But we must concentrate at this point not on Socrates, but on what the Cynics made of him.

Before leaving the historical Socrates altogether, however, we should consider the matter of his public image, of his political reputation, and more specifically his attitude towards Athenian democracy. As we have already observed, freedom, and in particular freedom of speech (*parrhēsia*), were among the more important democratic watchwords. Socrates himself was widely recognized, as we have seen, as being "free" from human conventions in the accepted Greek sense; and he was certainly also characterized by his freedom of speech. Socrates was the last man to mince his words or to avoid dangerous topics, whether dealing with the highest or with the lowest members of society. But his attitude to democracy, even as portrayed by Plato in the most "Socratic" dialogues, the *Apology* and the *Crito*, was not hostile. In these works there is none of the rancour, born in part from the killing of Socrates himself, which marks the more "Platonic" texts of the *Meno* and the *Gorgias*—not to speak of the *Republic*.[14] Admittedly in the case of the *Apology* at least it might be objected that Plato is doing his best to conceal any anti-democratic leanings that the accused associate of Alcibiades and Critias, notorious enemies of the "people," may have shown; but we need not doubt that Socrates' view of "virtue" as "democratically" available to *all* is historically correct.

There is no particular emphasis on distinction of intellect in Socratic morality. What matters is a particular mental orientation, use of the talents that one has to tend one's soul, and intellectual honesty. Socrates finds nothing strange in looking for virtue among the craftsmen and trademen of Athens as well as among the learned and well-born; and he demanded no special intellectual training and endowment beyond a certain basic intellectual integrity which could be achieved by rich and poor, oligarch and democrat. In fact, he himself seems to have given up the study of the natural world because, so he claimed, his mind was inadequate to make good use of the data of the physicists;[15] and he certainly thought that no extra-ethical study is required for the practice of virtue. Socrates made no effort to "save" ethics by the introduction of metaphysical theses in the manner to be attempted by Plato, and in this too the Cynics followed him closely. For them intellectual work could very easily turn into mere hedonism—the pursuit of intellectual pleasures—a goal which, as we have noted, Aristotle himself was at one point tempted by Eudoxus to accept.

Let us consider the implications of Socrates' more "democratic" approach to ethics in detail. If "freedom" is available to all, and no particular intellectual gifts are required—Antisthenes and Diogenes too seem to have thought that the rationality which is the only alternative to suicide is within the grasp of the whole human race—then the source of human value must be very different from that espoused by Plato, and even more from that of Aristotle. What matters is how free one is. The opposite to "free" is "slave", and there is every reason to suppose that the Cynic tradition, and indeed the general tradition which we shall dub that of "freedom alone", put no more value on this kind of slave than natural slaves were accorded by Aristotle. Thus again we have an ethic of superiority. We may expect to find in this tradition that, although all men *can* be equal ("democratically"), those who do not choose freedom when it is available are to be treated as worthless and contemptible. There are exceptions to this principle, as we shall see, but in general it should be observed that the Cynics lashed rather than loved the human race.

The second feature of Socrates to which we should draw attention is related to this "contempt". For although it would be false to maintain that Socrates was contemptuous of the human race, or even of many members of it, as was Diogenes, the view that his "failure" was a "failure in love" must be taken seriously.[16] Not all would regard it as a failure, but Plato seems to be in the genuinely Socratic spirit when he thinks in the *Symposium* of the love of individuals as something to outgrow. It is probably true that the formal account of this "outgrowth" in the *Symposium* is unsocratic, but Socrates' concern for the souls of his fellow-citizens is strangely impersonal, at times almost callous. He makes them look ridiculous, mocks them for their failures, and is hated for it. Clearly it cannot be argued that he did not realize the effects of his behaviour;[17] clearly he could have achieved many of the same or similar intellectual effects less brutally, and perhaps even more persuasively. He seems not to have cared about such things. It seems to be no accident that his vision is associated with Apollo, the god of rationality, but a strangely impersonal, if not terrifying and even sinister being. Socrates (and Apollo) is in this respect Aristotelian, above the human level, unconcerned with human feelings, undisturbed by pity, to us seeming rather hard. There is no necessary conflict between such attitudes and care of souls in the Socratic sense, but taken to further lengths by the Cynics, Socratic teaching could degenerate into brutal and contemptuous harangue.

There appears to be no compelling philosophical reason within the tradition of "freedom" why harshness should mark the approach of the free man to his fellows; but an attitude of "independence", of being one of the few "free" among a herd of slaves would, one might suppose, encourage it. Hence it might be supposed that where a kinder, more "humane" attitude to others arises in this tradition, it is emotionally, if not intellectually, out of keeping. In fact, from the time of Crates (early 3rd century B.C.) down to the time of Demonax (2nd century A.D.),[18] a gentler voice is heard alongside the harsher "calls to repentance" of the Cynic preachers. Sometimes—and this stream had its influence beyond the numbers of the Cynics themselves—those to be treated more harshly are distinguished from those to be treated more gently. Harshness is to be reserved for philosophers or would-be philosophers whose pretensions must be ruthlessly denounced. In this tradition is the anecdote of the meeting of Zeno and Crates, the point of which is to expose a bogus sort of claim to independence. Crates asks Zeno for some oil. Zeno refuses with the words "Which of us is the more shameless?"[19] But Crates himself is one of the more striking examples of the gentler version of Cynic freedom. Humanity is to be gently upbraided, persuaded with kindness rather than taunted and condemned.

When we considered Aristotle, we observed that, although it may not be possible to spell out all the different grades of human beings, there must certainly be such differences, and indeed, that the scale of human excellence and therefore human value must be a continuum. But with freedom, with being "free", we are in a different world, which one might rashly call the world of instant salvation. Although it is possible to imagine grades of freedom, it is also very easy to argue that one is either free or one is not. "What are you doing among free men?" The point may not be very logical; but it is emotionally plausible. There are the wise and the fools, the slaves and the free: in other terms the saved and the damned. At this point there will arise the question of whether the wise have any responsibility for the fools. And if they have, why should they have?

Consider a problem I have discussed elsewhere, the relation between the Cynics and the Stoics.[20] There is no doubt that Zeno, and at a later date Chrysippus, were impressed by the Cynics: Zeno indeed is listed in the doxographical tradition as a follower of Crates, and it is said that his *Republic* was written "on the dog's tail".[21] Nevertheless Zeno probably broke with the Cynics over very specific issues: and it appears that one of these was the content of goodness and of nature.[22] For Zeno accepted and continued to accept the Cynic call to "follow nature"—the latter day equivalent of the Sophistic rejection of convention—but he was not satisfied that in practice "nature" can be found simply by casting off the traditional restraints of morals and society. Some more formal study of nature is necessary.

Such study may be regrettable and certainly is not to be undertaken "for its own sake"; but it is essential. Hence in Stoicism the danger of a return of the "intellect" as the marker of value. And certainly the abandonment of the "Socratic" and "Cynic" way of "ethics alone" might tend to imply that "freedom" alone is inadequate to mark the wise man. It seems, however, that the Stoics never really admitted that, for they maintained at most periods of their history numerous links with Cynicism, and some of the later Stoic preachers and directors of conscience, such as Epictetus, even called themselves Cynics, the terms "Cynic" and "Stoic" becoming almost interchangeable.[23] Yet for all that Stoicism differs substantially from Cynicism in offering a content for the good and for virtue: that is, a wise man is not simply a man who acts freely from pure motives; he is also the one who knows and does the right thing. There are types of behaviour which are objectively right, such behaviour being guaranteed to promote the divine order and rationality in the cosmos and to be in harmony with it. This divine order and rationality is itself to be discovered by a proper use of the mind in the study of nature.

In general, we may say that within Stoicism the search for freedom and the ideal of the free man generate difficulties whenever the question of the importance of knowledge arises. Such difficulties arose first with Zeno himself, and with his own abandonment of Cynicism, and the reformed Cynicism of the Stoa did not bring the dispute to an end. Indeed one of the earliest of his own followers, Aristo, wished to revert to the Cynic way of "ethics alone" and condemned all concern with physics and logic.[24] Interestingly enough, another of the earliest Stoics, Herillus of Carthage, took exactly the opposite route.[25] For him the good is knowledge, and in rejecting this alternative Zeno tried to find a middle ground between Cynicism and a position which gave an uncynic importance to the intellect. The move from Socrates to Plato was tempting but was not to repeat itself in the new Stoic context.

It is important to recognize, therefore, that among the Cynic advocates of freedom, and to a lesser degree among their Stoic successors and rivals, it is not really the mind which is free. We are not concerned with a freedom of the intellect to roam at will, but with what we might call a freedom of the individual, of the I, to act freely. In Stoicism this "I" is viewed psychosomatically, as a disposition of the "ruling part". Originally, at least, there is no technical term for the whole self, or for what the Stoics seem to have regarded as something like the moral personality, but at some point in later Stoicism, and presumably in Cynicism too, the word *prohairesis* began to be used to convey the appropriate sense.

In the *Nicomachean Ethics* of Aristotle *prohairesis* has its basic sense of "choice" (1111B4ff). Virtue is a disposition concerned with making certain kinds of choices. By the time we read the writings of Epictetus,[26] the word has taken on the full sense of "moral self", "moral personality". At least in Seneca and almost certainly earlier it seems to have a Latin equivalent in *voluntas*; and this may help us with the new technical sense of *prohairesis* itself. *Mens et voluntas*, the whole phrase, seems to have been thought necessary by Cicero to convey the meaning of the Greek word *nous*.[27] For Cicero seems to refer both to the mind which forms the idea on which the intention is based and to the intention itself; that is, the word *nous* is both cognitive and volitional, bearing a double connotation which is clearer in *dia-noia* and its cognate verb *dianooumai*, and which helps to explain why on purely linguistic grounds it was easy for Plato not to separate "knowing" from "willing" or "intending to perform". Now for purely linguistic reasons, reasons, that is, which were quite unrelated to philosophical intentions, Latin was compelled to separate the cognitive and the volitional. *Voluntas* thereby came to be associated primarily with intention, and with moral choice, thus resembling *prohairesis* in its original Aristotelian usage. And yet, as we have said, the Greek equivalent of *voluntas* in Imperial Stoicism seems to be *prohairesis*, but *prohairesis* now extended in its meaning from "will" or "choice" or "intention" to comprehend the moral self as such.

Whatever the history, it is the *prohairesis*, the moral self that matters for Epictetus, not the intellect. Like all the Stoics, but with a particular vehemence of his own, Epictetus condemns learning for its own sake, even the reading of the logical texts of Chrysippus. Who has read them?, he asks. What does it matter?[28]

Curiously enough the term *prohairesis* does not seem to stand for the "soul" alone. The "soul" is often distinguished from the "self" or rather the "moral self", as though there could be various other selves (or at least aspects of the self) which *prohairesis* does not cover. In particular *prohairesis* seems to indicate the *conscious* self, as contrasted with the hidden desires of the soul which may be suppressed. Thus the *prohairesis* may be not simply the self, but what matters in the self. In this connection there is a parallel to the Aristotelian notion of intellect, for the usage would seem to imply that there is a part of the self, i.e. the *prohairesis*, which matters, and a part which does not. But in other respects the term is quite different, for it preserves the black and white qualities to which we have already alluded. Whereas with the Latin word *voluntas* we may speak of a good or bad *voluntas*, we think of a *prohairesis* not as the act of choosing but as the disposition or character from which good or bad choices actually arise. What is, more, according to Epictetus, this *prohairesis* itself is free: we are always able to live rightly. Epictetus certainly maintains the traditional Stoic distinction between the wise and the foolish, but the foolish are still free enough to be able to improve themselves if they choose to. In this sense morality is indeed a matter of will. But Epictetus does not go the whole way with the Cynics: something of the Stoic content of virtue is maintained. Why should this be so?

It seems that among many of the Stoics, though not among the Cynics, the doctrine of freedom is not the sole source of value. There are two reasons for this, both of which require consideration. First there is the theory that each of us is a "spark" of the divine (*apospasma*). It is unclear where this thesis originated, but there seems to be no particular reason to deny that it comes from the earliest period of the school. It is a "democratic" doctrine, and in this respect consorts well with the theory of freedom, in that all of us share in the divine "gift"; but philosophically it raises considerable difficulties in that we may wonder why the divine spark is so easily concealed in the great crowds of "fools" who surround the wise man. Here, of course, the doctrine of freedom helps, for although we can all be wise, we do not all "choose" to be so. Nevertheless the doctrine of a divine spark introduces a second source of value.

Indeed one must suppose that even the fools, the "unfree", have a certain value if they have the divine spark in them. Little more need be said about this now except that it may help with a question which always arises when we consider the relationship between Cynicism and Stoicism; namely, why does the wise man think it advisable or desirable to do anything for his fellows. We have already observed that for the Cynics, where we are concerned with the "pure" doctrine of freedom, where the free are of value and the rest seem worthless, there is little reason why anyone should do anything for anyone; and some at least of the Cynics, perhaps including Diogenes himself, operated on that sort of principle. But the "divine spark" enables us to avoid such a "solution"; let it await further discussion at a later stage.

Let us now return to an important feature of the "freedom" approach to value which marks it off sharply from both the "formal" and from the "mental" approaches, and from the corresponding theses of Plato and Aristotle and their followers. In the view of the partisans of "freedom" there is common possibility of freedom and therefore of value for the whole human race. But while the area of value is enlarged in this domain, it is presumably diminished in others. For Plato everything animate and inanimate ought to have value in so far as it is characterized by Form, though Plato does not in fact draw this conclusion. Indeed it should follow that value is coterminous with existence and that man may not occupy a position of pre-eminence in this regard different in *kind* from other beings. Certainly it is Plato's view that there are beings more valuable than man to be found in the heavens. Man is not the measure, as it is put in the *Laws*; God is the measure (716C). Similarly in Aristotle beings are apparently valued in so far as they approximate to some form of Mind, a position which is certainly less generous than Plato's to the inanimate, but again embraces much more than the human, both above and below the human. Now with the "freedom", the black and white, approach all humans are "eligible" for value, but nothing else is, unless there be something above the human level—and the Cynics at least do not seem to have "pushed" the existence of the gods with any great vigour. Hence the world may seem not only more democratic but also more anthropocentric—another feature of Cynicism which the Stoics were at pains to correct. The study of nature provides a wider context and a wider content for man's activities. For, as we have seen elsewhere, the Cynics appealed to "nature", but offer little clear opinion on the "content" of nature, and seem to have thought it of no interest to investigate it.

The Cynics rejected the conventions of particular *poleis*, the centres of civilized Greek society. They took the title "citizens of the world"—which originally had a negative connotation; it meant that they rejected the citizenship of any particular and individual city.[29] In its earliest appearances the term suggests no loyalty to anything beyond the "community of the wise"; only in its Stoicizing and Imperial Roman version does it seem to have referred to something more like cosmopolitanism in the modern sense.[30] In its "late" and developed form it is linked with a belief in providence, which seems not only out of keeping with "pure" Cynicism, but alien to the whole theory which we have been discussing that "freedom" is a primary source of value. "Freedom" above all links value to human decision, to an attitude adopted. The gods are irrelevant to that decision. It is true, as we observed in another context, that the Cynics do not deny the gods; rather they are uninterested in them. It is not the gods, but what amounts to an act of will which fixes our worth.

A final point about "democracy". Both Plato and Aristotle hold that some people have no value at all, or lose what little they may have had. We noted the gulf between this attitude and that of the concept of "basic human rights". Do the Cynics offer anything new in this regard? In the last analysis we must conclude that they do not. The "unfree" are slaves, and worthless. Who cares what happens to them? Admittedly the gentler "voices" we mentioned do not make this explicit, and inconsistently may not have accepted it. But the Diogeneses rejoice in its relentless consistency. You can be free and virtuous; if you choose not to be, to hell with you.

CHAPTER SIX

DIVINE SPARKS

In the course of some earlier remarks on Epictetus, we had occasion to mention a further source of value, in the theory that man or a part of man is some sort of "segment" or "portion" of the divine. We observed that, although this theory normally identifies the "divine spark" with a particular aspect of the human being—the mind is usually the prime candidate for such an identification—it also suggests that all human beings are in a similar or identical relation to the divine; and in this respect it differs basically and "democratically" from, for example, Aristotle's version which insists that it is the *quality* or *capacity* of a mind which determines what, if anything, we are worth.

It is unfortunate that we began the discussion of "divine sparks" with Epictetus. It was necessary to do so, however, because we observed that this theory cut across and correspondingly modified the Cynic-Stoic attitude to freedom, and we could not avoid introducing it at that point. But the thesis in various forms is older than the Stoics and Cynics, older than Socrates in his role as the inspirer of Cynicism. I do not intend to pursue its origins into the murky regions lying behind Greek philosophical enquiry; I shall content myself only with a few comments on Heraclitus, before returning again to Socrates and Plato. My justification for this procedure is that almost nothing of pre-Socratic thought was "historically" understood in the later period of Greek philosophy with which we are presently concerned.

Ēthos anthrōpōi daimon. I understand this phrase as indicating that a divine being is our inner self or character.[1] Hence when Heraclitus says that he sought for himself, he means that he was looking for the real self who is more than human, in fact a *daimon*. It is the *daimon* in us that matters; the rest is a mere corpse. Such ideas are also to be found in the *Purifications* of Empedocles,[2] where the true self, the *daimon*, wanders in its fallen state through various incarnations until it eventually attains blessed release from the cycle of births and deaths. The difference between these ideas and Aristotle's notion of making ourselves immortal is apparent: in Aristotle, although we are invited to disregard the poets and think more than mortal thoughts, our best *human* life is at the "social" level, the level of practical wisdom.[3] If we transcend this life, this mode of existence, it is for brief periods only. We do not aspire to such a state as a permanent condition. Whatever survival "we" may have after death, it is an emotionless, passionless, memory-free existence for the Active Intellect at best.

It was through the Pythagoreans that the notion of a daimōn within us became particularly influential in Greek philosophy—and through Pythagorean influence on Plato. What is taught is a dramatic history of mankind. After a primordial fall, it is necessary for all human souls to be purified by passing through a series of bodies; it is hoped that in the end freedom from an otherwise endless progression will be attained. But the differences between varying teachers as to how purification can be achieved concern more than merely ritual techniques. There are more fundamental disagreements about the nature of the fallen *daimōn* itself. In so far as the proposed purifications are purely ritual acts (abstinence from animal foods, for example), we might say that they imply a "democratic" theory of the nature of the *daimōn* within us. All human beings, qua human, are identical in this regard.[4]

However, although the matter cannot be argued in detail here, it is widely believed, and probably rightly, that in some forms of Pythagoreanism a certain "academic" proficiency, the study of mathematics, was regarded as purificatory. That theory could lead us to a more "Aristotelian" position, to the thesis that a limited number of "humans" have the mental gifts to achieve freedom. We do not know whether, or how far, the earlier Pythagoreans moved in this direction. They may have thought that the limited mathematical skills required were within the capacity of everyone; they may even have kept up such a claim long after its verisimilitude had vanished. And with the "mathematical" theory of purification we would seem to be confronted with the awkward situation that unless each man has the requisite intellectual ability, some *daimones* are fated never to be released; hence they appear to be radically inferior. Of course in some circumstances degrees of inferiority and superiority could have been acceptable; Plato appears to accept them in the myth of the *Phaedrus* when he describes the "choirs" of hierarchically distinct divinities (247A). But in this version although all souls (*daimones?*) are not equal in all respects, they have a basic equality in so far as they can all be saved, all be freed from the cycle of births and deaths. Purification by mathematics should not allow as much as that.

Plato, as we know, frequently alludes to the *daimōn*. The Guardians at death may be honoured as *daimones*;[5] Socrates is a Silenus-like *daimōn* in the *Symposium*, as is the Eros of which he is almost an incarnation.[6] In the *Timaeus nous* is a *daimōn* within us;[7] and in the *Republic* we each choose our own *daimōn*[8]—a slightly different though related notion with which I shall not be concerned here. But Plato seems uncertain or unclear on an important point, as were the Pythagoreans: that of the exact relationship between the *daimōn* (which is our soul or some part of our soul) and the gods.

Daimones and gods must differ significantly for two reasons: the human soul falls, but the souls of the gods do not; even in their purified state human souls are still, strictly speaking, not gods but *daimones*, belonging to the "choirs" of various gods. There is no explanatory comment on either of these matters to be found in the Platonic dialogues. Plato merely makes such assumptions. He seem to suppose that it is by participation in the Forms that Gods and souls become perfect, and that it is simply in the nature of things that gods can be the more fully characterized by goodness. What this means is not discussed. It is clear from the *Phaedrus* that the souls of both gods and men are similarly tripartite, and that at their best they are all fully characterized by unifying goodness;[9] but it is also clear that they are so characterized in proportion as they are capable of "receiving" this goodness. But the nature of such a capacity remains obscure: human and divine perfection is described in terms of the presence (or degree of presence) of the Form, and that is all; except that our earlier discussion should lead us to assume that Plato would regard the matter of the exact nature of the *daimōn* as unimportant compared with that of its observable degree of closeness to the Form of the Good. For it is on such closeness that its worth depends.

Most of the problems about the Platonic *daimōn* arise because, like Aristotle's Speusippus, though less radically so, Plato is a "disjointer";[10] that is, there is no overall single cause of things in his system. In the *Timaeus* we find that to explain the existence of the material world around us we need to postulate three principles: Mind or God (the Demiurge), the Forms and matter. There is no hierarchical relationship between these three factors; no one is the efficient cause of the others. As for the human soul, and even more for mind (*nous*), there is an immense problem of interpretation, for although soul is somehow dependent for its being on the divine mind, it is certainly to be thought of as eternal, that is, without end. In this respect souls constitute further examples of the demiurgic principle, for they are *naturally* immortal. Such *natural* immortality was recognized throughout antiquity as a peculiar hallmark of "Platonic Hellenism".[11] But its consequences for axiology are substantial, because it seems that in terms of value the ultimate relations between the various "basic" elements in the Platonic universe are arbitrary. It is only when Plato speaks as though the Form of the Good is in the strongest sense the cause of all, that relative values can be more strictly determined. The myth of the construction of the soul in the *Timaeus* seems designed to help alleviate difficulties in this area, for it seems to reduce the number of further entities to be accounted for (apart from "space" and the Demiurge himself). According to the myth, the souls are dependent on the Demiurge, and their value is thus entirely derivative; but, as we have suggested, this sits uncomfortably with the doctrine of the natural immortality of the soul or of some part or aspect of the soul.

For a *daimōn*-theory to be fully coherent, to form part of an adequate account of the nature and value of man, it must probably be integrated with a "non-disjointing" account of the world. But Plato's account of the origin of value, as we have seen, does not ultimately depend on an analysis of the nature of the souls or of the *daimōn*; and he did not attempt to forge precise metaphysical links between the *daimōn* and the Good. The Stoics, on the other hand, with their quite different metaphysical structure and their pantheistic God, were at considerable pains to do so. We recall that it was with a late Stoic, Epictetus, that we were compelled to begin this part of our discussion of human value. And we have seen enough of Epictetus to know that his brand of Stoicism would not easily confound the *daimōn*, or the divine spark, with reason alone. Rather the divine spark is in some sense the moral personality.

In Stoicism, from the beginning, the Forms are gone. The Stoics had their explanations of the existence of universal terms: they are mere concepts[12] which Platonists make the mistake of reifying. For the Stoics, as normally for Aristotle, what is real is the individual. But the explanation of this individual, the approach to the individual, is quite unaristotelian. Let us content ourselves with human individuals at this stage. They must not be viewed as some kind of compound of Form and matter; they are a psychosomatic whole. Ultimately there is to be no distinction between mental and corporeal events. Judgments are closely related to emotions, which are indeed explained psychosomatically by Chrysippus as themselves judgments, valid or mistaken.[13] The individual is indivisible; he is not to be approached in terms of class membership. We do not start with "All x's are F (All men are mortal), but with "If there is an x, it is F".[14] Clearly therefore any value-scheme of a Platonic type is ruled out. Forms cannot bestow or be the cause of value. Individuals in such and such a condition are the ultimately valuable furniture of the world. The world itself is a similar individual.

In the Stoic cosmos all the particular individuals, including all the psychosomatic entities, or persons, are interrelated and jointly related to the world as a whole, which is called God, being immortal and unchanging in its nature. We are exhorted to live in harmony with ourselves, with our own nature and with Nature as a whole.[15] The linking factor is our "ruling principle" (*hēgemonikon*) which is in some sense identical with the ruling principle of the cosmos. It would seem from this that all human beings should be of equal value and equally able to achieve excellence. And indeed according to the Stoics such equality is possible. That is one of the implications of their much misinterpreted maxim that the only good is virtue, the only evil is vice, and that all else is "indifferent". Virtue is a disposition or attitude which can be equally present in all men. Neither their social status, their wealth, nor their fortune makes any difference to this basic capacity. In this entirely "moral" sense all men are equal, all are divine; all in some sense are good. We do not hear specifically in early Stoicism of "likeness to God".[16] We hear of the perfect happiness of the good man, the indefectibility of virtue,[17] the unimportance of social position or even of social justice in so far as it need not affect the happiness and the importance of the individual.[18]

It might be supposed that Stoic metaphysics would always tend to place value on the individual as such, but the "divine spark" theory, the notion of man as part of the cosmos, works both for and against such a position. The Stoics wish to emphasize, against Plato (and presumably Aristotle), that no two members of a class are identical. Even if they cannot be distinguished, like two snakes who pop out of a hole, and even if the wise man has to suspend judgment about the nature of the difference between them, this difference is always present. It cannot be removed; nor is it to be viewed platonically as the result of successive and various approximations to an ideal type which can only be imperfectly instantiated in particulars. But Stoic metaphysical theory does not lead in ethics to great emphasis on the value of the individual person, nor, of course, to any kind of moral relativism. This can only be understood if we realize that individual differences, though necessarily present, and metaphysically significant, are morally and axiologically unimportant. For the Stoics not only hold (against Plato and Aristotle) that differences of intellectual capacity have no necessary bearing on questions of value or of rights; they also hold that all personal differences, except of course differences of moral character, are ethically and axiologically trivial. What matters are not individual characteristics as such, but only degrees of virtue and vice. The virtuous man (and we can all be virtuous) is more important than the vicious. We should consider two questions with regard to this: 1) Is it a reasonable thesis?; and 2) how does it square with the theory that man is a part of the cosmos?

The first question can be posed in its sharpest form in the context of a banal and hypothetical situation. Suppose I am in a boat with two other people, one, a particularly good and kindly man who has devoted much of his life to the cure of the sick, the other an ex-convict who has done time for robbery with violence, and who I have every reason to believe will soon be back in prison for another piece of gratuitous savagery. Neither of my two companions can swim; the boat capsizes and I can only rescue one of them. Most people would think that the good doctor would be the more worth saving. In other words they have made a judgment about the worth of the two men in terms of moral qualities or, as the Stoics would prefer to phrase it, in terms of virtue and vice. The example shows clearly that the Stoic position is both reasonable and apparently commonsensical. It also shows that many people would think that this position is not incompatible with a theory of the intrinsic value of human beings and their possession of basic rights. Virtue would then appear to add something to a basic minimum of value which every human being possesses. The Stoic position should probably have been formulated as something of this sort, for they hold virtue and vice to be characteristics of the individual person, who is himself in some sense identical in his reason with the Reason of the cosmos. But, as we shall see, they do not appear to have recognized this.

Philosophically, virtue can easily be understood as a quality of the ruling principle, but vice is harder to deal with. If the soul or the "ruling part" is a piece of the cosmos, a reason which is part of Reason, how can it ever be vicious, for vice is certainly to be identified as a kind of irrationality? To answer this fully, one would have to outline the complete Stoic theory of the origin and nature of evil,[19] but that is not necessary for our present purposes. A few points from the theory will suffice. First of all it seems that the nature of reason is affected by its objects and the purposes to which it is put. Thus a vicious man is, as we might say, using his reason to rationalize, or to excuse, rather than to think. If not that, he is planning to carry out what his passions prompt. Reason is "following" the passions rather than leading or directing them. But, it might be objected, that would be satisfactory enough were it not precisely for the theory with which we are at present concerned, that is, that the "ruling part" is a fragment or portion of the Reason of the cosmos. If the Reason of the cosmos is good, how can its parts have the alternatives of being good or bad?

Fortunately, the ancient evidence lets us see how the Stoics would answer this objection. They would appeal to the illustration of pictures or of stage-plays. In a picture some parts of the whole may seem, when viewed by themselves, to be ugly or deformed, but when taken in conjunction with the whole work they fit in perfectly and the result is admirable. Similarly on the stage: it would be a poor play if all the characters were good; but bad individuals make no difference to the different kind of goodness of the play as a whole. Needless to say, these images are not satisfying. For they seem to suggest either that the vice of the individual soul is something akin to an optical illusion, or that vice does not matter in the individual so long as the whole is providentially arranged. But the Stoics do not regard vice as an illusion; and they do think that questions of virtue and vice are important.

The only way the Stoics might have been able to lessen these difficulties is, I think, closed to them because of their emphasis on individual morality. It would be a variation on the Greatest Happiness Principle, by which it might be argued that a certain amount of vice or imperfection is necessary for the maximization of virtue. Something of the sort is already present in Aristotle,[20] when he argues that the various practical virtues need scope for their exercize: thus the man of practical wisdom is not self-sufficient. And we seem to be on similar ground over the argument which apparently arose about whether a doctor should wish for people to be sick in order that he may effectively pursue the practice of medicine and be successful in healing.[21] Would such a wish be compatible with, or even necessary to, the notion of the good doctor? Now it might be supposed that the Stoics would have allowed or even encouraged the existence of certain "apparent" evils, such as pain or poverty, for example, in the interest of promoting the greater good of the whole, the greater well-being of society and indeed of the cosmos. Or the institution of torture might be defended, as were gladiatorial shows by Pliny, on the grounds that it sometimes afforded instances of bravery which would be a great inspiration to those who observed them or learned of them. But although the tolerance of certain kinds of vice might be conducive to the exhibition of various forms of virtue, and although we might argue (on the picture analogy) that this would increase the sum superiority of virtue over vice in the cosmos, the Stoics were not prepared to accept any such "trade-off". The reason for this is plain enough: it is because the cosmos is a whole being and the individual reasons are in some sense its parts. Hence if one of them is vicious, it is as though the organism is *sick* in one of its parts rather than that it is (or appears) ugly or even deformed.

II

It is in the doctrine that "we" are at any time to be identified as a ruling principle in a certain condition that we may find the key to how the Stoics combined their notion of the individual *logos* or mind as part of the divine with their ethical theory of virtue and vice. Qua ruling principle in the individual there is no necessity for mind to be in good condition. It must, however, remain an irreducible centre of ethical consciousness. The Stoics, in taking such a position, have separated the realms of existence and of value less sharply than they may have intended. For if one were to take *au pied de la lettre* the doctrine that virtue is the only good, and therefore the only thing to be prized as good, then one might have to say that the corrupt "ruling principle", though still a part of the divine, has no value at all—which the Stoics would not, I think, want to say. Perhaps they would defend not drawing this conclusion by arguing that no "ruling principle", however vicious, is able altogether to cease functioning in some way as a "seed" of providence, a source from which (in part) the divine plan of the universe flows.

As we have already suggested, the difficulties which confront the Stoics cannot be properly faced unless we identify the *metaphysical* status of evil in Stoicism. Essentially this problem comes down to the metaphysical status of *moral* evil, for other "natural" evils, plagues, famines, disease, etc., are not evils at all to the good man. So what has to be explained is the nature of the moral evil in the bad man. How is such moral evil generated? The only possible answer to this is that it is present in the mind of the individual himself, in his "ruling part". Events in the Stoic world are in some sense determined, but our attitude towards them is not.[22] We can go willingly behind the cart, like a dog, or we can be dragged along. It seems that our moral *attitudes* are somehow outside the causal network in which the Stoics lived, and that the "partial" nature of the individual ruling principle is responsible for them when they are malign.

Presumably the Stoics held that if one "listens" to Nature, and attends to the consistency of one's behaviour, one can somehow identify more and more with the whole of which we are only parts. Their doctrine of *oikeiōsis*, of "reconciliation", runs along parallel lines.[23] When we are born, we find ourselves "akin to ourselves", in other words we have an instinct for self-preservation. As we grow, the realm of our concern expands, at least in the fully developed Stoic view, until it becomes as broad as the cosmos itself, embracing the notions of both social and cosmic justice. At such a time we recognize fully the relation of our reason to Reason as a whole. In so far as we do not, in so far as we are misguided, blind or ignorant, hence follows our moral evil. Thus moral evil is in some sense a negation of the possibilities of the self, a malfunctioning of the self, or, as the Stoics were frequently prepared to put it, a sickness of the self.

If we view moral evil in this way, we can understand how it might be argued on purely Stoic grounds that the divine spark does not lose its value even when guilty or "sick". For it would not seem to be necessarily true that a man becomes more or less valuable in proportion to whether he is sick or healthy. He may of course be more or less able to perform a particular function well. He may be a more or less good writer or hockey-player or soldier. But the Stoics should not be concerned with that, for that would be to argue that value depends on the ability to perform certain functions in a society either well or ill, whereas the Stoics are concerned not with function but with general *moral* character.

In fact a certain division of opinion on the issue of "sickness" and "health" may be identified in Stoic writers. There is a note of ferocity towards the mass of "fools" which may be clearly detected among the early Stoics, and which may be associated with the Cynic roots of the school. For the Cynics, with their theory that value is related to "freedom", regarded the unfree as slaves, to be treated with the lack of respect due to slaves as such.

It might be supposed that the comparison of virtue and vice to health and sickness would only be appropriate in a context like that of Stoicism, where man is viewed as a psychosomatic unity. But the idea far predates Stoicism, going back at least as far as Alcmaeon.

For our purposes, however, Plato, as early as the *Protagoras* (313E2), is again the point at which we may begin. And in the *Republic* we find the language of sickness and health appearing alongside the theory of the tripartite soul. Sickness arises when the relationship between the parts is incorrect or distorted (571-6). Plato in fact is particularly inclined to view the life of the tyrannical man as a kind of mental sickness, for he is the victim of conflicting desires which cannot be reconciled and almost tear him apart. And the Platonic account of mental sickness, despite, or possibly even because of, the fact that it is hard to reconcile with the theory of the tripartite soul, seems to have been particularly influential on the Stoics.

Although the theory that the vicious soul is sick was certainly advocated by Zeno and Chrysippus, it seem to have come into even greater prominence in at least one important respect in a later period of the school; that is, after Posidonius had "heretically" introduced the Platonic doctrine of the tripartition of the soul into Stoicism.[24] It is true that full Posidonian unorthodoxy did not persist, but an abiding strand of Platonism can be found in the Stoicism of Seneca, of Marcus Aurelius and even of Epictetus. Within this tradition we notice a tendency to revert (less sharply than with Posidonius) to a Platonic dichotomy between soul and body; but within it too comes the ideal of the Stoic as a kind of "spiritual director", someone responsible for the care of sick souls.

The philosophical school, for Epictetus and for Seneca, is a clinic where maladies of the soul may be cured. We see here the gentler attitude, more appropriate, one might judge, to a view that the soul really is sick—though one may admit that revulsion too is a common reaction to many symptoms of the more nauseating types of illness. Epictetus recalls both Socrates and the Cynics as masters in his therapy, but he has little of the genuine Cynic ferocity and is in many respects (not least intellectually) less demanding than Socrates. If one adopts this kind of attitude, of course, it means that one recognizes the irreducible worth even of those deep in vice; and that accords with the "divine spark" theory. It is Marcus Aurelius who develops this theme to its furthest point in his vision that each of us is some kind of "limb" of the cosmos (7.13). Of course, that might not give any of us any "absolute" value after all—limbs may have to be amputated!—but it suggests a serious attempt to draw out the genuinely "democratic" aspects of the divine spark theory. With Marcus and Epictetus the feeling of equality at the level of "moral character" seems certain, though in Marcus it is always tempered by his unstoic and even unplatonic tendency to view the world as an illusion. Marcus is inclined to give all men an equally "unimportant" rating on the grounds that they will soon all pass away: "Remember the courts of Augustus, Trajan, Hadrian; see how they busied themselves; now all are dead".[25] Epictetus, for his part, seems inclined to accord value, but not rights.

Here indeed we touch on another genuine problem: a modern problem at least, though with clear reference to ancient practice. There are two sharply different ways in which we can view people as of equal value. They may be equal individuals, to take the extreme position, each endowed with an immortal soul and an eternal destiny and each equally beloved of God. They are all equal and all valuable; all are unique. The other view is the opposite of this: they are all equally worthless. Among a mass of slaves none need have any value at all, though they may all be treated equally. "Divine spark" theories of the type which we have been considering should enable us to avoid the latter version of "democracy"—the version which we may not entirely flippantly call that of a "People's Democracy"—and normally they will do so. But in Marcus, in so far as a somewhat Platonic view of the "divine" nature of the "ruling part" (or *nous*) is associated with the notion of the unreality of all transitory things—indeed of all things other than the most basic principles of the physical world—then the "mass-democratic" view, the vision that human beings are mere units, or at best comparable to social insects, may reappear.[26] One should say, at once, that this view, in so far as it exists in Marcus, is wholly in conflict with the principles and practice of orthodox Stoicism, with its emphasis on the moral importance of all human acts and its metaphysical doctrine of the primacy in reality of the unique and in some sense irreducible individual.

In another respect, however, we should notice that certain types of "divine spark" theories are more likely than other theories of value to *submerge* the individual in the "good" of the whole. For whereas in Plato and Aristotle the State is a kind of abstraction—what ultimately matters is the good of the individual and his fullest development, the State being nothing apart from the individuals who compose it—in Stoicism, as in any pantheistic theory, it is tempting always to argue in cosmic terms:[27] that the good of the whole, not merely of the majority of human beings, but of the cosmos as a whole, in fact the good of God, must always be given priority over the good of the individual or even of a collectivity of individuals.

But Marcus' attitude to individuals, that their petty doings seem so trivial, is quite unconnected with this. It is akin to the Cynic side of Stoicism, for there the emphasis is Socratic in so far as it is placed on the freedom of the individual sage or on the community of sages. Such a view of the community was probably also to be found in Zeno's *Republic* written "on the dog's tail",[28] but the more the Stoics came to emphasize one's membership in the cosmos, one's part in the Whole which is divine, the more tension appeared between this and the more "Cynic" creed of individualism. Emphasis on the "sympathy" of the different parts of the cosmos was a Stoic doctrine, as far as we know, from the beginning—though scholars have often claimed to associate it particularly with Posidonius[29]—but some Stoics probably emphasized it more than others.

If we call the emphasis on the individual and his morality the "ethical" aspect of Stoicism, and the emphasis on "sympathy" and the universe as a whole the "cosmic" side, we can see that where the "cosmic" side predominates, there are at least *a priori* grounds for de-valuing the individual. Perhaps it is in terms of an antithesis like this that the problem should be posed even for Posidonius. Perhaps the reality lying behind the impression that has frequently been made on scholars that the "cosmic"—the doctrine of "sympathy"—is to be specifically associated with Posidonius should be rephrased in terms of this cosmic-ethical tension. Certainly the "cosmic" interests may explain the erudition of Posidonius, his somewhat unstoic penchant for learning and his own success as a polymath. But in the history of ideas the views of individual thinkers can rarely be reduced to pure examples of a particular type of thought—books which show them to be so are often much valued, impressive and simplistic; normally any thinker, even one in whom a particular type of thought is dominant, will not exhibit it in a "pure" form; modifying factors from his heritage will always demand consideration. And so it would seem to be with Posidonius. For beside the cosmic "sympathy" and the far-flung concerns of the polymath is the Platonic theory of the tripartition of the soul to which we have already alluded, and the reinstatement of the soul as immortal. This last is asserted not only against his immediate predecessor Panaetius, who had claimed that the soul perished with the body, but against the earlier Stoic view that all souls, or at least the souls of the wise, have only a limited duration after the death of the body, continuing, in the latter case, until the conflagration at the end of their particular cycle of the cosmos.[30]

With Seneca, Musonius Rufus and Epictetus, the problem of the "cosmic" and the "ethical" scarcely arises, for with their emphasis on spiritual direction the cosmic almost drops out of sight and the well-being of the self at the moral level is the almost exclusive concern. With Marcus, however, the cosmic city plays a very important role and combines in this regard with the tendency to think of the individual's doings as petty to the point of unreality that we have already considered. The "Dear City of Zeus" is Marcus' ideal,[31] rising above the trivial and infuriating concerns of this world. Marcus is not a Stoic teacher, nor a spiritual director. His imperial position too cannot but impel him to think at a "grandiose" level. He is helping to organize the cosmos, though the details are trivial and the temptations to abuse of power are many. But the scale of the cosmos is so vast that even imperial concerns, indeed any concerns of our little world seem to get lost. Here the "cosmic" has not simply dominated the "ethical"—in a sense it does not do that in Marcus; it has destroyed the social dimension of human life and rendered the whole of our planet insignificant.

However one may look at first principles, that is, whether one considers them to be atoms and void, with Epicurus, or the pantheistic Reason of Stoicism,[32] any part of the structure seems lost in the vastness and impersonality of the whole. For Marcus' world is certainly impersonal:[33] the fate of Christians is unimportant, personal problems like love are only the opportunity for moral renunciation (Thank God I did not touch Benedicta and Theodotus...).[34] The divine spark, if you will, has become so small that it has almost died out. All are passing units; it is vanity to think of ourselves in higher terms. Interestingly enough Marcus is notable in combining this attitude with an absence of positive cruelty or savagery. Quite the reverse, he tried to live rationally and to govern well in accord with his Stoic principles. But in such a world it is easy to see why the human units should not be endowed with much value (everyone is worth what they set their heart on).[35] They are there not to be respected but to be organized.

The tension that we have observed within Stoicism, even within those Stoics whose version of the system places the most emphasis on the "divine spark" theory of the soul, can perhaps be illuminated by a Christian parallel. The problem seems to have been that in so far as the Stoics emphasized the Whole, or God, there was a tendency to de-emphasize the self, to the point of an almost total disregard. On the other hand it could be argued that Stoics like Seneca, Epictetus and Musonius Rufus, who act primarily as spiritual directors, almost lose sight of the cosmos altogether—ethics alone comes to be the philosophical outlook; a mere glance at Seneca's *Naturales Quaestiones* is sufficient to show that though the author is interested in his subject matter, he does not accord it tremendous importance. Interest in the cosmos as a whole has become diluted. A school tradition and the need for mental relaxation makes Seneca talk about the physical world; and Epictetus hardly bothers to do that. But the "divine spark" is treated with a care and a kindness almost out-of-keeping with traditional Stoicism, let alone with the indifferentism of Marcus. Similarly in the Christian tradition it can be argued that where interest centres very strongly on God the creator and on the vastness of his cosmos, the human soul seems to be diminished. If this can happen within Christianity where the doctrine of the Incarnation is available to "protect" the human soul from disappearing into the greatness of God—and it can be seen happening, for example, in Calvin's view of the utter powerlessness of the human soul or in Barth's emphasis on the vastness of the gulf between human and divine—then one can justly recognize it as a tendency of human thought. At the opposite extreme, in a Christian equivalent of the ancient thesis "ethics alone", we sometimes find that God is diminished to the status of a "benevolent uncle". Here human dignity is purportedly maintained and divine glory diminished or neglected.

How should we summarize our findings about "divine spark" theories? That they can be of at least two distinct types. In antiquity the divine spark is sometimes identified with the reason, sometimes rather with moral personality, sometimes with an amalgam of the two, with reason viewed as in some sense identical with the moral personality. The greater the emphasis on reason, the more likely it is that the theory will assimilate itself to a different account of value, namely that value depends entirely on degrees of intellectual capacity and achievement of some kind or another. In this form it is less "democratic", for "moral personality" (which often becomes identified merely as control of the passions) is equally common to humanity, whereas intelligence, meditative power, or whatever else *nous* may be is not. Perhaps both versions of the theory of the divine spark may be said to allow a minimum value to all human beings, but the "moral personality" version is more fitted to raise the basic level of value, and hence of rights, which we are all to be allowed. And we may conclude that wherever we find the theory of a divine spark, the dominant ancient thesis that there are a number of human beings possessed of no value at all has met a potential, though rarely an actual, challenge.

CHAPTER SEVEN

SOCIETY AND THE STATE

In a study of this kind it is impossible to avoid overlap. The question of man's value being bestowed on him by society has come up already, particularly in our consideration of Plato and Aristotle. But though the estimation of society is recognized by both Plato and Aristotle as important for a consideration of the value of man, it is not the most fundamental factor. For Plato, that is the Form of the Good and the relation of that Form to the individual soul; for Aristotle it is the nature of the mind. Nevertheless, since both Plato and Aristotle, perhaps particularly the latter, are concerned with man's development in a social context, we shall have to consider them both again when we investigate whether or not value is the gift to the individual man of the society to which he belongs. In discussing this issue, particularly in the case of Plato, we are treading much frequented ground. I shall make no attempt to enter into every controversy that has arisen, let alone acknowledge all those who have contributed to our understanding of the problems involved. I hope, however, that at least the main lines of my approach will be generally acceptable.

Those who have wished to turn Plato into a stateworshipper, that is a thinker or propagandist who holds that the state itself is a living organism, or like a living organism, have tended to rely heavily on such passages as the one in book four of the *Republic* (420B) where Socrates, discussing what are to be the conditions of life for the Guardians, asserts firmly that it is not the good of one class that is his concern, but the good of the city as a whole. It should not be necessary at this stage to argue that the "good of the whole city" means for Plato the good of all the members of the city, or the good of the greatest number of the members of the city. It does not mean the good of any one class, not even the ruling class, at the expense of the others.[1] That is the whole point of Plato's insistence that the kind of person who would make a good Guardian would not wish to rule, but would only do so after an honest appraisal of the fact that the alternative to his ruling himself would be that he would be ruled by someone inferior. It does not positively benefit the ruling class to rule; it would positively harm them (and others) to live in a state where they were not the rulers.

But although Plato does not regard the state as a living entity or a metaphysical being with some claim to a "higher existence" than that of the individuals of whom it is composed—nowhere does Plato claim that "reasons of state" justify behaviour which would be morally abhorrent if performed for private or personal reasons[2]—he might seem to advocate the thesis that a man's value in the state is to be measured in terms of what he can contribute to it. If he is suffering from an incurable disease, he is not worth keeping alive; if he is born deformed he should be exposed.[3] Now we should notice, however, that Plato is *not* talking about the absolute value of the individual, but his value *in the society*. He may have, or his soul may have, a value outside the society, though it must be admitted that his good outside the society seems very easy to forget if it appears that he has no value inside it.

Now there is no doubt that Plato is speaking in terms of contributions to society when he says that we are not legislating for one class, but for all. Were it not that their contributions are of supreme importance, we might wonder why the Guardians should be expected to make them. But the significance of the work of the Guardians is not simply that they help the collectivity; it lies in the fact, as Plato himself says of the return to the Cave, that we can expect just deeds of just men (520A). In relation to his society, therefore, one may say that the Guardian has the highest value because he is the best, the most godlike, and, as we have seen, the nearest to the Form of the Good.

The point is no small one, for in our search for the perfect man and the perfect society, it may be that we shall find the perfect society beyond our reach. But since a man's value is ultimately not to be determined by his contribution to society, but by his goodness and his likeness to God, we can see why Plato is not to be dismissed as merely pessimistic at the end of book nine (592B2), when he says that even if the Ideal State is only a "paradigm in the sky", we can still perfect our souls. That is not a *pis aller*. Indeed to read the middle dialogues of Plato in any way other than as a guide to the perfection of the soul is to lose sight of the whole message of "Socrates".

But although we must reject the view that for Plato value is simply bestowed by the state or exists in terms of what we contribute to the state, we cannot pass on without considering in what sense and to what degree the state is necessary for the well-being and full development of the individual, and the nature of the claims, if any, which this would give it.

Clearly Plato does not think that a wise man can only exist in a perfect state; Socrates (and earlier Pythagoras) was a living example to the contrary.[4] Plato probably supposed, however, that the existence of some form of *polis*-society is necessary for such maturity to develop to the fullest extent. Good men can live in bad states, but some form of organized society and certain minimum patterns of tradition and education cannot be dispensed with. And in most societies it is only the exceptionally well-endowed individual who will be able to rise above the inadequacies of his upbringing and of the world in which he is compelled to live. His life too is liable to be cut short, for excellence is hated and misunderstood (496D); he will have to shelter behind the wall and weather out the storm. Nevertheless, the fact of his existence indicates that the potential of being a philosopher-king is partly inborn, requiring nature as well as art. And nature "will out" in some ways despite an extremely hostile environment. Value cannot thus be wholly dependent on society; in part it must be providentially bestowed by nature.

But, one might say, since some form of society is necessary for all human existence, may it not be argued that if one's excellence at the "political" level can only arise in a "human society", then to an admittedly restricted but still significant degree society *bestows* it? Not so, for all we have admitted is that each member of society (those who in one's own generation and its predecessors have developed an environment in which human excellence may flourish) has within society the opportunity and responsibility to try to promote the well-being of his fellows. We have said nothing about the chances of his being successful, but spoken merely about the arena in which he works; and Plato, who argues through the mouth of Socrates in the *Gorgias* (479E) that it is better to suffer injustice than to inflict it, is the last man to confuse human excellence or human value with the "physical" fortune or misfortune of the individual in his attempts to live virtuously in societies of varying degrees of inadequacy. Society, then, is to be viewed at best as an opportunity for an individual to develop the potentialities he has. In an ideal society he is helped to contribute by a kindly environment, and if he fails to contribute in such a setting Plato thinks he is worthless; in a normally "inadequate" society he gets very little help, except from certain individuals (parents, friends, good men in general) who are probably in a minority.

No one is born virtuous or vicious; virtue and vice are acquired. And it is among men, good or bad, that they are acquired. Does that imply that without society no one could have *any* value, that is, granted for the moment that value depends exclusively on virtue, that this virtue must be viewed positively as a contribution of some sort to society? Or is the nature of virtue such that the future Guardian is worth more than others even when he is still undeveloped? The answer, from Plato's point of view, is that if virtue can be recognized at all, its possessor is worth more. Otherwise there would be no grounds for preferring those who look (physically and mentally) able to contribute more to those who are physically and mentally defective,[5] and therefore unable to contribute anything of "significance". What about past contributions? What happens if someone ceases to be useful? Certainly, as we have seen, he will not be "needlessly" kept alive if he cannot contribute; after all he has an immortal soul. Yet, there is no reason to think that Plato would wish to eliminate him if he could contribute anything at all. And contributions may be moral as well as physical. In other words his virtue in itself would be classed as a "useful" asset. He would only cease to be "useful" if he became vicious. But the matter of his becoming chronically ill, or a "vegetable", needs further thought. He will not be kept alive; but will he be killed off? There is no evidence that he will, even if he contributes nothing; and it seems at least plausible to suppose that Plato would regard it as ungrateful to reward past services with execution. And the situation is probably similar among the lower classes to what it is for the Guardians.

There is no doubt that for Plato the state is a natural growth, for man is naturally social and his needs are best met when we have the sort of division of labour which the state alone can supply. But constantly in Plato, from his Socratic apprenticeship till the end of his life, the state is a means, not an end. In the *Republic*, at the time of the most optimistic belief that the skills of the philosopher and the statesman can be combined in a single person, as well as in the *Politicus*, where Plato emphasizes the public suspicion that no ruler will remain uncorrupted by power, and the *Laws* where the two ideas are separated and Plato fears to entrust absolute power to anyone,[6] it is the soul that is in the centre of the philosopher's quest. Why then is Plato so politically-minded when Socrates seems to have eschewed politics? The traditional answer alone can be seen to be the right one. Plato came to believe that *unless* there was some sort of "philosophical" control over the state, good men (like Socrates) would not be allowed to flourish; and the majority of mankind would thus be deprived of almost all their opportunities for the good life. Just as in the first book of the *Republic* we learn that the "real" ruler rules when he has to (to avoid worse), so throughout Plato's political writings the State appears as an unfortunate necessity of the fallen human condition. Happy indeed it would be for the philosopher (king) if he could leave politics aside; among the gods he would be able to do so. But the practice of politics is a demand of justice,[7] and so he must involve himself in it. In these circumstances, despite Plato's suggestions in the *Republic* above all that one's survival and value in an ideal society would depend on one's contribution to that society, we have to re-emphasize against too many interpreters, that the value that society puts on a man, and society itself, are ultimately unimportant in comparison with the tendence of one's soul. For all his concern with politics, Plato is the antithesis of the picturebook political tyrant who has often been presented as the author of the *Republic*. Plato would like politics to come to an end, not to deprive anyone of his rights, but to allow him to grow; but he is realist enough to know that there will never be a time when it is possible for the state to wither away.

II

When we turn from Plato to Aristotle, on the relation of society to the individual as in so many other areas, we find both startling similarities and important differences. Their own positions in society were dissimilar. Plato was able, if he chose, to enter politics directly, and to act personally in the affairs of his home city; Aristotle, the son of the court physician of the king of Macedon, lived much of his adult life in a city where he had no political rights, and where he could not even own property. Furthermore, although he spent more than twenty years in the Academy, the Platonic "school for tyrants", his earlier interests seem to have been predominantly in logic, rhetoric and scientific matters. Neither ethics nor politics played the role in his development that they had done for Plato.

But Aristotle shared Plato's admiration for the city-state, and like Plato believed it to be the only potentially satisfactory form of political organization. Of the other basic forms of society he knew, tribal life or autocratic monarchy, none seemed comparable, none offered the development of the personality that the city-state could provide. Man—and here Aristotle means adult males—is naturally suited to live as a citizen in a city-state. We have already discussed the inferior value of women, slaves, non-citizens, etc., and need not revert to these matters here. Let us consider the adult males: they are the active members in the process of the formation of the city-state; they form such societies for the sake of staying alive, but it is the city alone which offers the opportunity for the "good life". Only for those few mortals capable of living above the "human" level is such a society unnecessary; and Aristotle, who lived outside such a society himself in Athens, perhaps thought of himself as a member of this godly group.

We pointed out earlier that value, for Aristotle, depends on the quality of a man's mind. And for all but the few "contemplatives" the exercise of this mind depends on the society. A good example of how this works in practice is provided by the virtue of justice. It cannot be exercised unless there are people for it to be exercised on;[8] otherwise it remains an unfulfilled potentiality, and we are not praised or blamed for what we are potentially but for what we are actually. Furthermore we recall that all the moral virtues are acquired by exercise;[9] just as it is by running, by the practice of running, that we become runners, so it is by the practice of virtue that we become good. Hence if we live by ourselves, there are very few virtues which we could ever acquire and use.

Quite literally the state gives us the opportunity of separating the men from the boys. While we are children, we resemble animals more than mature humans in one important respect: we lack the ability to control our instincts by reason, because the reason is undeveloped and unexercized; and hence we are unable to make moral choices. Only in the environment of the state are we able to make the full range of such choices and to learn to make them. It is not clear from the account Aristotle gives in the *Politics* whether he thinks that living outside society would entail a total lack of moral development; probably that is not his view. Perhaps even in the family which "precedes" the state as a natural unit a certain development is possible, but the overwhelming impression that Aristotle leaves with us is that for full development or even the possibility of full development the existence of a city-state is essential.

It is important to distinguish Aristotle's position from Plato's in a number of important respects. While both Plato and Aristotle think that many men (if not almost all men) need a society in which to grow, their positions certainly differ sharply as regards the desirability of political life. Plato, as we saw, distinguishes an "ontological" from a "social" level of human value. At the ontological level society may help man to grow, but his basic value has nothing to do with his contribution to the society itself. For Aristotle one of the functions of society is to provide a place where the virtues can be exercized; for Aristotle, therefore, it would be incorrect to say, as we said for Plato, that he views politics as a necessary evil, a call on the just man which he will obey because it is just to do so. For Aristotle the ordinary adult male, whom I have described elsewhere as a "man" in the narrow sense of the word, needs society not only to develop, but to practice what he has developed, to be a man in the strict sense.[10] Now, as we have seen, being a man in this sense is to be associated with a certain kind of intellectual activity, or activity of the mind; and without this intellectual activity our value declines. Hence for Aristotle all men, apart from the contemplatives, are necessarily lessened in value if they do not live in the sort of society which enables them to function "morally". The problem here seems to arise from the theory of potentiality and actuality, and from Aristotle's view that moral virtues do not exist unless they are exercized.

Now it may be objected that the contrast we have drawn between Plato and Aristotle is between the Plato of the *Republic* and Aristotle, that had we considered the *Politicus* and the *Laws* the contrast would have seemed far less sharp. For partly in the *Politicus* and wholly in the *Laws* Plato has separated the functions of "philosopher" and "king", having, it seems, despaired of combining the two roles in the same person. Does that mean that his attitude towards the "king" would be the same as that of Aristotle towards the man of practical wisdom? There is no reason to think so, for although it is true that in many respects Aristotle in the *Politics* follows the "late" Plato rather than the Plato of the *Republic*, there is nothing in the *Politicus* or the *Laws* to suggest that Plato's attitude towards the relationship between "care of the soul" and political life has changed.[11] The statesman will rule, in association with the philosopher, when necessity arises, just as he does in the *Republic*. His virtue is not merely potential if he does not use it, nor does he need people on whom to practice his politico-ethical skills.

Where then precisely does the difference between Plato and Aristotle lie? The real answer to this is that it is in their concept of human excellence. For Plato the goal of a human being is to attain likeness to God, through development of the general quality of goodness which is more than an intellectual quality. (In the case of the souls of the gods in the *Phaedrus*, it is a quality which is held in common, for example, by all parts of the tripartite soul.) Certainly Plato accepts the view that man has a "function" (*ergon*), as argued by Aristotle in the *Nicomachean Ethics*; probably the concept was common ground in the Academy.[12] But Aristotle wanted to identify the human function as closely as possible with use of the mind; and certain kinds of mental activity are performed in society if they are to be performed at all. Hence Aristotle's notion of the origin of *actual* as opposed to potential value in human beings is much more closely tied than Plato's to the existence of society itself.

There is the further factor of Providence, which we have not considered so far, but which affects the present issue in a number of important respects. For Plato the world is providentially arranged; Socrates seems to have thought of himself as having been providentially sent to stir up his fellow-citizens of Athens;[13] the laws of nature, in which Plato is as firm a believer as Aristotle, are also the product of a providential ordering. God (gods) is concerned with the world directly, and above all with the human world;[14] any other view of him would be unworthy. Hence the "ontological" view of the world of which we spoke earlier is in some sense to be understood as a "god's eye view", as the *Laws* would have it, thus controverting Protagoras' "Man is the measure".[15] But Aristotle's universe is quite different. God is not concerned with the world; he is "non-moral" and unmoved by human virtue and vice; the laws of nature do not point to a planning intellect, but are a pattern which can be recognized by the intellect. Frequently in antiquity, as we observed, the Aristotelians were regarded as atheists—and as a rather "low" type of atheists at that—because of their denial of providence. But as far as our present concerns go, what matters is that whatever "providential" factor there may be in Aristotle's cosmos, society itself is man-made. Certainly the state is a natural growth, but like other natural growths it has no divine artificer or organizer. It is produced by the instinct in men to keep themselves alive, to protect themselves, and later, when they become conscious of its value, to enable themselves to live the good life and to develop their full capabilities. But the fact that this society is entirely a human product and is quite devoid of divine surveillance, means that the "good" in it is either intrinsic to the society itself or derives from those who produce it. In such a situation, as we have seen, the temptation (or the possibility, if you will) of deifying the society so necessary for the excellence of its members is increased. Aristotle does not succumb to this temptation. Society still remains a means to an end, as it is for Plato, but the end, "the good for man", is much more fundamentally tied than in Plato to the society itself. It has lost the impetus to transcend society which the theory of Forms and the works of Providence provide.

In a Platonic state "likeness to God", characterization by goodness, are possibilities to some extent available to all; they are not tied to the ideal society, or indeed *necessarily* to any society, though society certainly makes them easier to obtain; for Aristotle, only the contemplatives seem to have attained this possibility. For them a quasi-Platonic ideal remains, dependent on the individual soul and its "apotheosis" as far as possible. Aristotle seems in the end to have split human beings—even those mature adult males who are capable of human excellence in a strong sense—virtually into two classes; when he refers to those who live "above" society as gods, the point is made clear. They are almost different in kind from the "society-animals"; they are the remnants of a Platonic ideal.

III

If Aristotle has developed the social aspect of Plato's ideal, the Cynics were bent on abandoning it altogether. We have already observed their treatment of the Socratic concept of freedom. With this went an exaggeration of the "apolitical" features of Socrates—up to the point of maintaining that society is nothing but a aggregation of individuals. Such a position is the exact antithesis of Aristotle's. By implication it denies that society is any kind of natural growth, and *a fortiori* the Stoic position that we are "limbs" or "living parts" of a wider unit, whether social or cosmic. If society is a mere aggregation of units, it follows that there is no benefit whatsoever to be obtained by being a member of the collectivity—whatever form it might take. Indeed there are not, strictly speaking, forms of agglomeration. Different political structures are all, as one might put it in a contemporary idiom, in some kind of bad faith. Their existence asserts, wrongly, that there are goods which can be bestowed on an individual by his society, and others which are bestowed on the society itself by the individuals who compose it. Diogenes, the most notorious Cynic, was determined to put the worthless coinage of all current societies out of circulation,[16] to defy or distrust the various conventions of the cities. In so doing he was affirming them valueless, having nothing to offer. This is a strictly anarchic position. We should notice that the Cynic does not say, in some Thrasymachean fashion, that societies operate for some particular person's advantage, be he ruler or subject. In terms of value they are strictly neutral; they have nothing to offer and nothing need be offered to them. The story of Diogenes and Alexander is *ben trovato*. When Alexander asked Diogenes what he could give him—and Alexander is representative of Power and of organized political structures—Diogenes mocks him with the retort "Get out of my light".[17] The king has nothing worth accepting. His role is merely one of blocking off a "natural" good, something which can be enjoyed by anyone who is not interfered with. One has to admit that the Cynic position, if unacceptable, is relentlessly logical. With the primacy of freedom to be asserted as the only good, and that primacy being within the grasp of everyone, it is necessary to affirm, and to keep on affirming, that society contributes nothing.

As so often, it is interesting to compare the Cynics with the Stoics at this point. There are striking similarities and dissimilarities between the "schools", just as we should expect since the Stoa was founded by an ex-Cynic. That Zeno's *Republic* was written while its author was still a professed Cynic is unlikely, but that it was greatly influenced by Cynicism is certain. It is noteworthy, therefore, that Zeno seems to have gone to considerable lengths to demolish all the "public" features of the traditional Greek *polis*:[18] there are to be no baths, temples or other public buildings, and no coinage. There are to be no magistrates, for in an assemblage of units it is worth showing that the hierarchies of society have no importance. Other marks of distinction, such as differences of clothing, also disappear; all dress alike, both men and women. Such uniformity represents what is natural and is a rejection of distracting and misleading convention. Scholars who have supposed this city is any other than a community of the wise have mistaken its whole nature. Like a true Cynic, Zeno believes that society contributes nothing to the moral well-being of the sage.[19]

But whereas the Cynic thinks that society is irrelevant to the sage in that he does not need it, and that he contributes nothing to it but an invitation to others to leave it, the Stoic, thanks to his metaphysics and his construction of the physical cosmos, is obliged to "construct" the world in an almost Platonic manner. It makes no difference to his moral virtue if he fails; but, as we have seen, unlike the Cynic, he finds nature outside of his own mind and will as well as inside it. And society is not simply a part of that external cosmos; it is precisely the part in which the moral virtues may be exercized. Hence it can be said that the Stoic gives but does not get from society, unless it be some near approximation to the society of the wise, for his role is not to be developed by society but to develop society into a somewhat less imperfect form.

At one level, we shall note, the Stoic's attitude is in its own way as far from that of Aristotle as is the Cynic's. For while in the Aristotelian world society is constructed naturally by men, in the Stoic cosmos it is merely a further manifestation of the destiny of God. Hence the notion of society bestowing value on the individuals of whom it is composed would seem particularly strange in a Stoic context; for the Stoic man, the individual, is real, and society is what he constructs by recognizing what is natural and rational. There is no doctrine of actual and potential virtue to worry the Stoics. Their sage has all the virtues, but he obviously cannot exercize them all at the same time. Nevertheless he is still entirely wise, entirely happy, equal to Zeus apart from his (im)mortality.[20]

Yet in contrast to the Cynics, Aristotle and the Stoics have Nature as some sort of point of contact—particularly in respect of the fact that they equally recognize natural laws, and natural laws which are objective. These natural laws demonstrate that the state, that society itself, is natural, and therefore that it is in accordance with reason to busy oneself with it. However much they may differ in other respects, Aristotle and the Stoics agree that political and social activity need not conflict with freedom, even though they also seem equally to seek a somewhat homogeneous collection of individuals in their ideal societies. Here too they agree with Plato, and we find lurking behind the different theories of the nature of the state the Platonic idea that there is one, or at least a very few, perfect *types* of individual, to which all approximate. In so far as this ideal is merely that all should seek goodness, it is doubtless innocuous enough; but we cannot neglect the fact that goodness consistently seems to lead towards the generation of identical or substantially identical individuals, or human units.

It is clear that the Cynic version of the theory that society is an agglomeration of individuals is sharply opposed to the views of Socrates, Plato and Aristotle, and that in a number of important respects the Stoics refused to accept it. The Cynic view might seem to be as far from worship of the state or from any theory in which human excellence depends on the state as it could be; but the Cynics were not alone in holding such a view. Indeed in some ways Epicurus advocated an even more extreme version of it. For the Cynics were Socratic enough as to admit, and indeed positively to affirm, the importance of virtue, including the virtues which might tie us to others, such as justice. Such virtues are undoubtedly "real" in some quite unspecified moral sense in the Cynic world. They are "natural", though this concept of "naturalness" is as devoid of content as is the related Cynic concept of "goodness". But Epicurus denied all the virtues in their entirety. They contribute nothing to human happiness as such, and unless they are pleasurable, they have no connection with the good for man. "I spit on virtue unless it brings pleasure" is the Epicurean watchword.[21] If it pays, the Epicurean will turn "criminal", though it will not normally pay: either his "bourgeois" conscience or fear of the law will disturb his peace too much.[22] In contrast to the Stoics, and to the intense irritation of right-thinking Romans like Cicero (as the *De Amicitia* bears out), the Epicurean would also act criminally if necessary for his friend. While the Stoic Blossius, when asked if he would burn the Capitol for Tiberius Gracchus, could reply, "Yes, but he would never ask me such a thing",[23] the Epicurean would have no moral scruples about asking it, only the scruples of convenience. Compared with the Cynics also, the Epicureans were able, or claimed to be able, to offer theoretical justification for their position. The functioning of society, they held, has no connection with the laws of nature; the Stoics and Platonists are seriously mistaken in that regard. The so-called natural bonds of society are merely man-made conventions, which may be useful if they give pleasure, but which should otherwise be ignored. Not only is there no providence in the Epicurean world, but there are no natural bonds other than those of personal pleasure between human beings.[24] That means, of course, that from a "God's eye view", no human being has any value whatsoever; in his own eyes, yes indeed, he has immense value, and for the sake of his own value he may choose to designate other people, especially his friends, as valuable too.

The Epicurean conception of friendship is at this point exceptionally important. We have already observed that the calls of friendship will, if appropriate, run counter to the demands of conventional law and justice. The Epicureans rejected society *in toto*; it can be *used* for their own purposes from time to time. Monarchies are perhaps particularly valuable in so far as they offer less likelihood of disturbing changes to which the good Epicurean must constantly readapt himself. You know where you are with an autocracy of this type; and there are not too many people to be placated.

But obviously neither monarchy nor any form of organized society will have anything to do with the value of the individual either to himself or to anyone else. The Epicurean community is an island in a basically hostile world.[25] For the Epicurean, therefore, friendship plays the role which membership in a larger political and social community plays for other people. Within the Epicurean "cell" the development of happiness (pleasure) is more easily attained; some at least of the unpleasantnesses of fortune can be warded off. The other members of the community can be trusted—which is more than can be said of anyone outside—because their very membership is the sign that they recognize the advantages of belonging. In such a context one can see why renegades from the Epicurean group were bitterly and relentlessly abused. Their mere existence would appear to be a threat to those who remain. They are a symbol of the uncertainty of human dispositions and the ease with which false opinions may get a hold.

Perhaps all we have said here, however, is that the Epicureans view their smaller society in the way other philosophers viewed the larger; in other words that the Epicurean community is a kind of *polis* by itself, a city within the artificial city of the unenlightened. In order to emphasize the contrast between the Epicureans, on the one hand, and the Stoics, Platonists and Aristotelians on the other, therefore, we must insist that even friendships *within* the Epicurean community cannot be classed as "natural". They are produced by a kind of contract between the various partners.[26] "Natural", as we have already observed, has to do with what is normally the case in nature; and no human relationships can, for the Epicurean, be thought of in terms of what is normally the case in nature. They are in fact epiphenomena of atoms and the void.

Perhaps the greatest difference between an Epicurean community of friends and the more usual philosophical conception of society or the state, is that for the Epicureans membership in the community is entirely the result of personal choice. Here again, as in the notion that society is a mere agglomeration, we see a point of contact between Epicurean and Cynic. The associations of the wise are free associations for both, and all other associations are entirely worthless. Epicurus went out of his way to emphasize that we need contract no relationships which we do not want. The wise man normally will not marry.[27] Normally he will not have children; children if born to the Epicurean woman (or couple) are normally to be exposed.[28] Thus it seems that the point of Epicurus' rejection of familial relations is that they are imposed on us—if we allow them to be; they are normally not freely chosen. Obviously some familial relations are unavoidable, though Epicurus wants to make it clear that the obligations they are normally supposed to bring with them *are* avoidable.

However, if one wishes, one may, by choice, assimilate family relations to relations of friendship, thus entering by choice into a contract which, for the sake of pleasure, brings obligations in its train. For example the Epicurean will normally expose his children, but if he brings them up, he has entered by choice into some kind of quasi-contractual relationship with them or, perhaps, with their other parent. It would therefore be the height of illogicality to bring someone up and maltreat him in the course of doing so. Such behaviour would be totally inconsistent; it would entail choosing one thing and then choosing its negation. The wise man's behaviour is not inconsistent. Inconsistency must imply either a recognizably mistaken original choice or outright folly.

Such being the Epicurean view of the family, one can see the rationale for their view of what Plato wished to think of as an extended family, namely the state. Society is in general a source of danger and contributes nothing to our worth or in itself to our happiness. If we can make use of it, so much the luckier we. If not, we have to put up with it as best we can, above all by becoming entangled with it as little as possible. Society does not provide us with a desirable environment, let alone a necessary one for our growth. We have to make our own environment largely by our own choices, making use of the circumstances into which we are born, however unfavourable they may be. There can be no such thing as an ideal society.[29] Societies, of their nature, tend to be hostile to the well being of an individual, that is, to his acquisition of pleasure.

To conclude this section of our study, it is worth going back to Marcus Aurelius again. We noted a number of passages in the *Meditations* where Marcus seems unconcerned whether the Stoics or the Epicureans give the ultimately correct answer to the problems of the nature of the cosmos.[30] Whichever way it is, he suggests, our normal human behaviour seems trivial. Human beings are like ants, startled mice, puppets on a string or dogs worrying over a bone.[31] In his emphasis that what matters in this isolated and alienating situation is the moral personality, Marcus is totally un-Epicurean. But in his sense of the triviality of the human units the wise man is shepherding, he has certain affinities to Epicurus. Marcus affirms (in some kind of "cognitive" faith) that a man has obligations to his fellows; but emotionally he is at one with Epicurus, who thinks he has none. Or rather with what Epicurus more logically perhaps should have been like, for Epicurus, unlike Marcus, is a man of violent personal loves and hatreds.

IV

Our general conclusions about the role of society in bestowing value on the human individual must be restrained. There has been a tendency to overestimate the importance of the State in the view of ancient philosophers. In fact while certain ancients assert that all morality is bunk, no ancient philosopher of significance at any time holds the view that there are "political reasons" to justify behaviour which should be condemned if performed privately. There is in the *philosophy* of antiquity no higher morality of the state, for both in historical terms and in the theory even of men like Plato, the state is viewed as no more important than the individuals, larger or smaller in number, who direct it or at least participate in its activities by their own consent. In this respect the philosophers, it must be admitted, are entirely affected by the nature of the political societies around them. Compared with ourselves, the ancients lived in a world where, even if the State had wished to permeate society and to direct it in detail, it was largely unable to do so. Lacking means of communication, in particular, ancient rulers could often only make their authority felt when they, or their legal representatives, were actually present. There was very little of what we might call the "machinery of government", or institutions designed to act executively on behalf of authority.[32] Power was viewed, for good or ill, individually, in terms of power-holders, and in the case of the less highminded of them at least, of their perquisites. Of course there was a city-loyalty, normally focussed on a patron god or goddess, but that too, as strikingly in Periclean Athens, was almost a personal loyalty. In Roman times we should note that it proved expedient to encourage the cult of Rome by associating it with that of Augustus, or with the individual ruling emperor.[33] Whatever the disadvantages of such a system, it had the advantage of tending to prevent patriotism degenerating into some kind of idolatry of the state.

Plato, of all the thinkers in antiquity, was perhaps the most interested in government and in the proper exercise of power, and his solution to the problems of civil strife which were virtually endemic in Greek society was to try to persuade his citizens to regard their city as a vastly extended family. Among the Guardians at least, the primary purpose of the so-called "community of women and children" as well as of the common ownership of property, was to encourage unity, the unity of a single large family. Aristotle applauded the aim, but thought that Plato's means of achieving it were likely to be quite ineffective: "Better a real cousin than a Platonic son".[34] The reason why we tend to exaggerate the importance of the state in ancient thinkers, and in the case of Plato in particular, is that they were so conscious of the lack of what we should think of as a state, so aware that Greek society carried almost no loyalties which were not personal loyalties that they seem obsessed by the problem of the unity and the homogeneity of society.

This being so, it will seem less surprising that even in Aristotle, for whom society contributes the most to the value of human beings, its role seems to be modest compared with theories of more modern times. Perhaps, it may be objected, we have made a mistake by talking simultaneously about the *state* and about *society*. But whatever validity such a distinction may have in recent times, it has almost no meaning in antiquity. There is no separate word for "social", as distinct from "political" in Greek. "Man is a political animal" *means* that man is a social animal: and vice versa. Certainly one could be "social" in antiquity within the context of the family and friends, as for example, Epicurus might have wished; but beyond the family and friends there are only "political" or commercial relationships—and commercial relationships are normally regarded by the philosophers as a necessary evil at best and as a degrading evil at worst.

At best, then, the role of state and society is to afford an opportunity for excellence—and in the most developed form of that thesis, that of Aristotle, this is only true of the second best class of humanity. In this area, as in many others, as a result of our contemporary attitude to the state, we have greatly overestimated its role in ancient thought. Plato in particular, who has been constantly accused of subordinating the individual to the state, must be viewed in a wholly different light. It is not so much that he did not subordinate the state to the individual, or the individual to the state, as that to pose the question in terms of subordinating is to mis-state it entirely. When Plato urges execution for the habitual criminal, he argues that death is *both* in the criminal's interest, and in the interest of society (*Laws* 862D). If then our question is misstated, a wrong answer is thus guaranteed. Starting from the correct premise that "ethics" leads to "politics", in Greek thought, we have then drawn the false conclusion that the individual either is or is not subordinated to the state. "When did you stop beating your wife?". It is probably safer from our point of view to say that "politics" is that brand of ethics which deals with the individual's relationships beyond the family. By phrasing oneself in that way, we avoid a misleadingly modern idea of the State while emphasizing the genuinely ancient view that political life is a matter of direct personal relationships between rulers and ruled, and that these relations are controlled by the same ethical principles as govern one's private affairs.

CHAPTER EIGHT

PLOTINUS

Plotinus thinks of himself as a Platonist, but his philosophy differs from that of Plato in a great many ways,[1] of which the following are among the more important:

1. Plotinus' One, unlike Plato's Good, is the cause of all that is. Mind and matter both derive from it.

2. The goal of the human soul is union with the One, not a vision of the Form of Goodness or of Beauty.

As far as questions of value are concerned, the second of these points is particularly important, for it enables Plotinus to combine in an unusual way a version of what we have called the "divine spark" theory with the traditional Platonic view that one's value depends on the degree with which one is qualified by the Form of the Good. It also gives man, despite Plotinus' tendency to deny the fact when treating of Gnosticism, a very particular position in the cosmos. For man alone is apparently capable of attaining this special kind of union with the One; he—or at least his soul—is, in the famous phrase of Dean Inge, the wanderer of the metaphysical world.[2]

The key to Plotinus' doctrine of human nature is to be found in particular in two treatises: 1.1 and 6.8. Both these tracts were composed fairly late in Plotinus' life and may certainly be regarded as products of his maturity. 6.8. may have been provoked by the reading of a treatise on the nature of God, possibly Christian or para-Christian, now lost to us. We shall return to this question shortly.

In 1.1 it could be argued that no specifically new theories about the human soul appear, but that the resulting synthesis is new in a number of very important respects. Here (and also elsewhere) Plotinus distinguishes between the empirical self (the "I", or "we", as he calls it),[3] that is, the mode of consciousness we have at any particular time, and the soul, which is the totality of our psychic powers whether we are conscious of them or not. These psychic powers may be described, in value terms of Aristotelian origin, as either "above" or "below" the level of consciousness and the empirical self. Highest of them, of course, is the so-called undescended part of the soul, which is always in contact with the Divine Mind and the world of Forms, that is, always characterized perfectly by the divine "archetypes" of things. Because of the existence of this aspect of the soul, we are able to learn, that is, to call into consciousness, facts and values of which we are not always *aware*, but which are the characteristics of that higher part of the soul. For in Plotinus' words, each of us is an intelligible world;[4] not, that is, a potentially intelligible world in some Aristotelian sense, but an actual intelligible world; not, however, in respect of our conscious self, but of our "upper" soul, our real or true self. We shall have to consider the relationship between our "true self" and our "empirical self" later.[5]

Below the level of consciousness there are other psychic activities, and subconscious desires, which may come to the surface as we "identify" with them from time to time. Plotinus does not specify much about the nature of these desires "locked up in the desiring faculty", except for a few isolated but important items of information: that they are irrational and thus tending to non-existence, and that within the lower part of the soul they resemble the upper soul in that they share in immortality.[6] At the ontological level the problem that this seems to pose is of the nature of the existence of the "we", or of consciousness itself. It seems to be, though it is not, some kind of epiphenomenon of the soul when engaged in certain kinds of activity. Thus "we" would be merely a name given to the various functionings of the soul in so far as there is consciousness of them. But that does not seem to help very much, for the question obviously remains as to *what* is conscious. A more hopeful approach seems to be that the "we" is to be identified with our "outer" self and the soul (or rather the upper soul) with our "true self" or "inner self"—the inner man,[7] as Plotinus sometimes says, making good use of Stoic (and Platonic) terminology. Now if this is the explanation, then the inner self is some kind of soul in the *Platonic* sense of the word, while the outer self, the "we" is inferior, but capable of rising above this inferiority. Somehow, therefore, when we identify with the upper soul, we do not change that upper soul of itself, but we realize our whole being in a kind of harmonious relationship. Thus the distinction between the inner and the outer self disappears.

This interpretation may be challenged on the ground that the "outer man" or "outer self" is usually identified in the text of Plotinus with the life of sensation and of the passions. How then can it be that it could be called the "we"? Because, it may be supposed, all that involves our *individual* life, our personal experiences, is mediated through the "outer self", which thus plays a role not dissimilar to that attributed by Aristotle to the Passive Intellect, the "soul", and the body over against the Active Intellect.

The Aristotelian Active Intellect cannot remember; that is why after death, when the Active Intellect alone survives, there is no memory. However, the Plotinian "upper soul", unlike the Aristotelian Active Intellect, is not devoid of thought-content. On the contrary its object of thought is the entire intelligible world. It does not need memory, therefore, for at the level of Form it has a constant and present awareness.

Whenever the "we" is identified with the upper soul, it is characterized by the Forms, and we know the Forms in some kind of immediate apprehension. At other times we lose this awareness and have "forgotten our origins".[8] One can recognize in this Plotinian doctrine of the "we" something of the account of the unification of the parts of the tripartite soul by goodness that Plato describes in the *Phaedrus*.[9] There is no "we" apart from the "upper soul" and the passions, etc. There are only different types of relationship between the inner and the outer man, between the upper soul and its lower manifestations. Such a theory, where the highest state for a man is the integration of his levels of activity, and the "completion" of the "we" by this kind of integration, would suggest that man in his highest "version" is more than any of his "parts", including the higher soul before it is brought to consciousness. It would also imply that each individual man is in some sense unique, not merely a man with the characteristics of men, but a man whose specially integrated personality is somehow "greater" than would be the case were he merely an *example* of the form of Man.

I believe it may now be assumed, for various reasons which we need not specify in detail here, that Plotinus was one of those Platonists who subscribed to a heretical version of Platonism according to which there are not only forms of species but also forms of individuals, at least in the case of individual men.[10] If our account of the nature of the "integrated" human being is on the right lines, it becomes clear that here too there would be a further reason for maintaining such a thesis, though Plotinus does not allude to it in this context. Perhaps, in fact, he did not argue for it on these sorts of grounds, but for other reasons of his own (and because the Stoics had awakened him, and presumably other Platonists, to the problems of uniquely qualified individuals). Be that as it may, a belief in forms of individuals is consonant with the attitude towards the integration of the personality which I have just described.

If this approach is correct, however, a perhaps even more fundamental divergence from traditional Platonism than the theory of forms of individuals seems to emerge. For we took it as a dictum for Plato that "individuality" is something to outgrow, something which is merely the mark of that imperfect realization of the Forms which all particulars exhibit. For Plotinus, therefore, individuality will be the necessary mark of the perfected self, at least of the self raised to the level of a conscious integration of the inner and the outer man.

"Many times have I woken up to myself out of the body", says Plotinus (4.8.1). The passage may not refer to union with the One, as Porphyry seems to have thought, and as I have interpreted it before,[11] but to the raising of the "we" to the level of the upper soul and the vision of the Forms. We note that it is "I" who am raised. The passage is one of the few "personal" sections of the *Enneads*, indicating that "personality" does not disappear at this level.

But it is not only at this level that the "I" remains. At the level of the union of the self with the One, we hear of the union of the "alone with the Alone", of the two becoming one, etc. These texts, as I have argued elsewhere, are to be interpreted theistically; they concern the relationship of the self with the One.[12] But even if they are to be read monistically, as dealing with a reassimilation of the self in which all individuality is lost, we should still have to say that at the level next to that of union with the One, there is something of "personality" that remains. It is not the form of Man that attains union with the One; it is I who attain to such union, just as it is I who awake out of the body to the eternal life of the forms (and beyond).[13] Such ideas make it clear that if Plotinus did *not* posit forms of individuals, if, that is, he thought that the individual differs only in so far as he is inadequate, then he is wildly inconsistent. For the "I" that eventually attains union with the One is not an imperfect being, but a perfected being, living a life at the level of the intelligible world. Thus, if there are not forms of individuals in the Plotinian world, they would have to be invented; they ought to be there.

All this should leave us in no doubt that the question of the value of man in the Plotinian world must be considered quite separately from the view of Plato. Two other points should immediately reinforce this conclusion. The first arises from the "monistic" structure of the Plotinian world as a whole, a world, as we observed, in which everything that exists owes its existence and its nature to the mode of its derivation from the One. The human being is immortal; above all his soul is immortal. But his immortality *depends* on the nature of the One; were the One non-existent, there would be no human soul, no human being. Yet since the One exists, the human being is by nature metaphysically perfectable, able, when he wishes, to return to his Source without any kind of further divine intervention which would compromise the unchangeability of God. The human being is generated as he is as a result of the One's nature. He is the only being that is able both to "fall" from perfection and to rise to it by his own actions. Above the level of the individual soul beings do not fall; there is no fall of the World Soul: for Plotinus such a fall would amount to dualism;[14] the World-Soul would come to look like the Sophia (or one of her offspring) of the Gnostic myths.

Yet nothing below the level of man is capable of rising, of being the "wanderer of the metaphysical world". All below can only "strive for contemplation" obliquely, in an "unseeing" or "unconscious" fashion.[15] But the human being, with his unique powers of both ascent and descent, is in a position to exercize his will in a special way which, as Plotinus explains in *Ennead* 6.8, perhaps the most remarkable of all his treatises, resembles most closely the "attitude" of the One itself. Man can learn to do what the One simply wills to do. We shall consider this in more detail later, but one point may be made at once: Plotinus could not have proposed a view of this kind were it not for the fact that he has merged the Platonic Good and the gods. Plotinus' One, as distinct from Plato's Good, as we have seen, is a living being from which both Forms and divine souls spring. Indeed Forms and divine souls (or at least divine Minds) are two aspects, both real, of the same phenomenon, the Intelligible World. This world, therefore, has to be "experienced and shared" rather than "seen" in the Platonic sense; and, through this experience, the life of the One itself can be shared by the human soul.

The second point in favour of viewing Plotinus in his own right, not merely as a Platonist, is a corollary of the first. For Plato, although the Form of the Good provides the "existence" as well as the "knowability" of the Forms, and hence of the particulars which come to resemble the Forms, yet all derived existence depends also on a second "causative" element: the "great and small" in the case of the Forms; "space" or "the receptacle" in the case of particulars. In other words, although Plato holds that the Good is the cause of existence, at another level its powers as cause are circumscribed; whereas Plotinus constantly emphasizes that the One alone is the cause of existence. For Plotinus, far more explicitly than for Plato, goodness *is* existence, evil *is* non-existence. The latter version of the equation, explicitly spelled out and worked out in at least two treatises of Plotinus (1.8 and 2.4), is only implied at best in Plato. Plotinus is to be regarded, therefore, despite many of his interpreters, as much more conscious of the significance of existence, and of the relation of the existence of particulars to the One's existence.

Nor is it from Aristotle that this emphasis has entered the Plotinian world. Like Plato, Aristotle assumes the existence of things, indeed more so than Plato in so far as he argues for the eternity of the world and of its species in a way which the *Timaeus* seems to rule out.[16] For Aristotle, and for those most influenced by him, what needs to be explained is the rest, and above all the movement, of natural objects, of particulars; their existence is taken for granted. For Plotinus it is their existence which first of all demands explanation. Hence there are no Aristotelian arguments in the *Enneads* about the origin of motion; the One is not introduced in such terms. The One appears when we try to explain why things exist and why they are as they are. The latter is an Aristotelian question, as the opening of the *Metaphysics* makes clear. But Plotinus would place the emphasis differently; for him, the problem is why they *are* as they are.

The novelty of Plotinus' view in the context of the major currents of thought in antiquity cannot be over-emphasized. But, it may be objected, surely it is merely another version of the old puzzle of the One and the Many? Surely Parmenides is an obvious precursor? In one sense that is true, but the problem is posed by Plotinus in a quite different way. In the world of Parmenides, what is real is the One, Being;[17] all else is appearance or the deceitful ways of opinion. We are dealing with true and false ways of looking at the same phenomenon. But in Plotinus there is no problem of the illusion of material things, or of a false description of the world. We have a quite different problem of derivation and of causation. Certainly, in some respects, the Stoics were Plotinus' predecessors in this regard, but with the Stoics we are still dealing with a restatement, a description of the contents of the world in different ways: either the one God or Matter—they are two ways of looking at the same thing. Certainly God (Reason) organizes and in a way generates the cosmos, but he is also to be identified with the cosmos. We have no problem of the origin of the existence of things, still only the problem of their organization, of their being something.

Perhaps we now seem to have veered far from our original problems of value, but, as we shall see, that is not the case. Plotinus has combined something of the "divine spark" theory of the soul with an unstoic principle that this divine spark is *not* the organizer, but is the product of a "transcendental" organizer to which it can return in a mystical union. In a way it is back to the pre-Socratics, for Plotinus is less worried by the Parmenidean dictum "nothing can come from nothing" than are most of his predecessors. It is true that the world arises "from the One" in the Plotinian system; but things which exist are not parts of the One or transformations of the One.[18] They are new beings; the One has left them to be "by themselves". This is the significance of Plotinus' teaching a monistic version of the Pythagorean theory of "first principles".[19] The Dyad (matter or a material principle) does not exist alongside the One; it is generated from the One and returns to it to be formed. Among the Milesians and early Pythagoreans this notion of new beings arising from a First was unknown; and Plato, Aristotle and the Stoics were still sufficiently under the spell of Parmenides for them to assume that not only could nothing be formed out of nothing, but that nothing wholly new could be formed from anything without that thing being itself diminished. There is a kind of metaphysical principle of conservation of energy. But although Plotinus would doubtless have accepted that in relation to being in time, he abandoned it in relation to eternal being and eternal generation. It is part of the One's "infinite power" to be able to leap over the Parmenidean hurdle.[20]

We are confronted, then, in the Plotinian world with a fully developed thesis that at any time in the cosmos there exists the One, which is infinite being, and a number of beings which are generated from it. Of these latter we are concentrating on those (viz. human souls) which are capable of a determined return to the source and maker. It should not be surprising, therefore, if we assert that a relationship of this kind, of the "alone with the Alone", implies a new and high valuation on the individual, or should so imply it, even if this implication is not specifically drawn by Plotinus.

Is the Plotinian concept "democratic" in the sense that we have been using in this study? Here there seem to be certain ambiguities to be found in the *Enneads*. Theoretically there is no doubt that everyone is capable of the return to the One; and certainly all souls are generated in the same way and should be, at least ultimately, of similar value. But souls are apparently subject to reincarnation, and at least during any particular cycle of birth and death, some souls (lovers, musicians, dialecticians etc.)[21] seem to be the more ready to make the "return". God is present to everyone who wishes, Plotinus says, but according to Porphyry he still paid some attention to the propaedeutic sciences of the Platonists—the mathematical sciences—which are supposed to prepare the mind for dialectic.[22] Some of this may be dismissed as pious practice, following in the footsteps of the founder of the Academy; but Plotinus presumably did feel some uncertainty as to why it is that, although the One is present to those who look, it is only a very small minority who look. We have seen something of the same problem in Plato, but Plotinus has at his disposal—though he does not necessarily use—more of the means to resolve it. For mathematical intellectual skill is not really important, despite Plato, in the Plotinian picture of man; other qualities of man, reflecting other qualities of "God", the One, are more important. To consider these we shall shortly have to consider the significance of Plotinus' challenge to Aristotle.

Before doing that, however, we should notice that in the case of Plotinus, and indeed of the Neoplatonists generally, the role of society in determining human value is nil. The world of the third century A.D. was a world in which any fundamental change in the form of government would have seemed out of the question. Politics, therefore, did not assume the role it played in classical or even in hellenistic times in the minds of the philosophers. Plotinus takes no particular interest in the political theses of Plato, either those of the *Republic* or of the *Laws*; he has nothing to say even on the notorious topic of the community of women and children. There is no trace of the notion that certain kinds of society or certain kinds of political activity are necessary for the development of virtue. Ethics has entirely replaced politics; virtue can be perfectly displayed in private life. And of course the life of the "spirit", built on a foundation of ordinary moral behaviour, is the aim of the wise.

Leaving society aside, therefore, let us consider the significance of Plotinus' break with Aristotle and the traditions which may be traced back to Aristotle about the nature of God. Indeed in breaking with the view that God is to be identified with *Nous* Plotinus is challenging current Aristotelian interpreters rather than Aristotle himself, even though he always thinks of Aristotle as the originator of the tradition.[23] For, Neopythagoreans and Epicureans apart, it had become the virtually unanimous opinion of the Schools that God is to be identified as Mind. Nothing else seemed to fit the requirements of unchanging, eternal Being.[24] Frequently, as in the thought of Alexander of Aphrodisias, this Aristotelian God was viewed in some sense as the formal and efficient, as well as the final cause, of the cosmos; and when Plotinus concerns himself with God as Mind, he is often discussing such expanded versions of the original theme. But his own account of the One contains a variety of features which derive from outside the Aristotelian tradition and which are important for two reasons: first of all because Plotinus rejects the particular *concept* of mind taught by Aristotle, which he regards as largely dualistic and therefore inadequate to express the nature of a first principle; secondly because he finds that the idea of God may be explored, and perhaps even better explored, through other concepts than the concept of mind; above all he favours thinking about love and the nature of the will.

Plotinian studies would be greatly advanced if we could identify the reasons why Plotinus wrote *Ennead* 6.8. This treatise, which begins with a kind of commentary on Aristotle's discussion of the freedom of the will in the *Nicomachean Ethics*, proceeds via an examination of human will to the problem of the nature of the will of the One. It is virtually unique in the Plotinian *corpus* in discussing God in terms of will, though there are remote Platonic precedents (of which Plotinus makes no direct use) in the *Laws* (967A), where we read of God's will (διάνοια βουλήσεως) to accomplish good, and in the *Timaeus* (29E), the famous passage in which it is said that God (the Demiurge) ordained the structure of the world because he wanted to make everything as like himself as possible. But these texts, of which the latter was popular with generations of Platonists, seem hardly an adequate catalyst for Plotinus' elaborate reflections. Perhaps more relevant may be the Aristotelian distinction—we know he uses the *Nicomachean Ethics* in this treatise, so why not other texts? —between actions which are natural and actions which are enforced;[25] and possibly also the further Aristotelian distinction between what is natural, identified perhaps in the case of eternal, circular motion with Mind and its choices, and what is merely random. All these distinctions occur in *Ennead* 6.8, though the latter seems to be directed against Epicurean or some other variety of atomism.

However, despite these possibilities, the basic inspiration of the study of will in *Ennead* 6.8 is neither Platonic nor Aristotelian. Plotinus in fact moves *away* from the *Nicomachean Ethics* and its discussion of choice to a quite un-Aristotelian treatment of the nature of God. In doing so he adopts an approach which in important respects is not Platonic either. We have observed already that he more or less neglects Plato's emphasis on mathematics, even though the idea of *grasping* or *seeing* certainly affected his view of what sort of language would be most useful for describing the mystical union. Now Plato's account of mathematical knowledge resembles Aristotle's view of knowledge in general, at least in so far as it maintains a certain "distance" between subject and object. The dichotomy between subject and object is strongly maintained; and such a dichotomy, from Plotinus' point of view, not only inhibits our understanding of the union of the soul with the One, but also fails to approach the nature of the One itself, that nature which must be the final and efficient first cause of all things in a way both unacceptable to Aristotle and genuinely non-Platonic.

In one important respect, however, Plotinus remains Aristotelian, though in the spirit of the *Nicomachean Ethics*—which he uses in *Ennead* 6.8—rather than that of the *Metaphysics*. For it is Aristotle who first deliberately emphasizes the question of choice, who isolates the phenomenon of choosing as of peculiar importance and in particular as an especial mark of the good man. By moving from the particular to the general, from the human to the divine and cosmic, as he so often does, Plotinus makes choosing, the act of will, the primary feature of God, of the One itself. Hence, of course, those who share in this faculty are peculiarly godlike—a fact which helps us understand the special position of man as our traveller in the metaphysical world.

At this point we must become rather more technical, and revert to the fact that when Plotinus rejects the Aristotelian doctrine of the identification of God as Mind, he frequently thinks of this thesis in the form presented, for example, by Alexander of Aphrodisias. But Alexander's assimilation of the Aristotelian God-Mind with the Platonic form of the Good is far from satisfactory to Plotinus and is not the source of the voluntarist approach of *Ennead* 6.8. Certainly it might be argued that

Alexander propounds some kind of emanation-theory;[26] at any rate there are similarities between his treatment of a first principle and that of a number of "Middle Platonists" such as Albinus. But Alexander's God, even though also identified with the Aristotelian Active Intellect, is far from the Plotinian God of "love" and "will" as 6.8 presents him. From Plotinus' point of view the God of Alexander is philosophically inadequate; his role as efficient as well as final and formal cause of the universe is not properly delineated.

What then is the origin of Plotinus' theory? And why does he offer it in 6.8, and to all intents and purposes, only in *Ennead* 6.8? Not necessarily because he would have repudiated it later or rejected it earlier. As we have already suggested, it is far from out of keeping with his more general proposals about God and value. There are a number of possibilities; some or even all of them may be correct. The first is that Plotinus was influenced at this point in his career by an unplatonic, unaristotelian source in his search for clarification of the first principle, dissatisfied as he was with Aristotle's view and, *de facto*, though inadvertently, with Plato's also. The second possibility is that he worked, as we have already suggested, from Aristotle's conception of the morally good man to a new position about the nature of God. Against that is the fact that in his very latest treatises, which are peculiarly ethical in tone, the new concept of God is not developed—though that is worth no more than are most other arguments *ex silentio*. The third possibility is related to the second, but would be presented in a slightly different form. Dodds has argued that Plotinus' greatest claim to philosophical importance may rest with his work in the field of psychology, and not only of philosophical psychology.[27] We have already observed that Plotinus is inclined to take psychological theories, perhaps drawn originally from Plato (as the famous "Being good is doing good" derives in some sense from the *Timaeus*), and make them into cosmic rules—and what is more natural if man is a microcosm?

Our present problems with 6.8 may be another instance of this: the starting point is the (Aristotelian) proposition that the good man is the man who regularly makes the right kind of choices. From there we move, as does Plotinus himself in the course of 6.8, from the notion of a choice between good and evil, a moral choice, to the notion that the good man is *disposed* in a particular way and will always choose the right. In Platonic-Plotinian terms such a choice of the right is to be described as having one's soul directed solely to the intelligible world, totally unattracted by matter and non-being. But in Plotinus' view such proper direction is preferably described as occurring not *by nature*, but by choice, by an act of the will. Such an act of will, directed towards the highest goal, is not entirely possible for man's empirical self; and even in the case of the "upper soul" it cannot immediately engage the highest possible object, the One itself, but only the world of Forms. In the case of the One, of course, the will attains the highest possible goal, which is itself.

Plotinus, in *Ennead* 6.8, views this specially important psychological phenomenon in two closely related ways, in terms of will (boulēsis) and in terms of Eros, that is, of a kind of desire. The highest principle of the cosmos, the One, must be seen to will its existence and to desire the highest possible object, that is, itself (6.8.15). Beings therefore which possess this combination of will and desire, even in an inferior way, are to be viewed as especially like the One; hence the importance of the soul (from which Plotinus originally drew his idea) in the Plotinian system, despite those passages where Plotinus rebukes others (Gnostics in particular) for overestimating the significance of the human subject in the vastness and complexity of the cosmos. Plotinus was probably led to believe that this way of approaching the One is Platonic—which it manifestly is not—by his use of the concept of Eros, though the notion of a self-desiring principle has no true parallel in Platonism; and it is *only formally* influenced by the Aristotelian notion of a self-knowing mind and the Platonic concept of a self-*moving* mover.

We should further recognize that Plotinus' concept of both man and God as combinations of a certain kind of will and desire, though bearing certain resemblances to the Cynic idea of the value and nature of "freedom" which we discussed in an earlier chapter, is in many obvious ways very different from the creed and spirit of Cynicism. First and most important is the fact that Plotinus has solved the Cynic problem, derived in part from the Socratic search for goodness, of a lack of content in the highest principle. Whatever the One is, that it desires and wills to be; and the One is to be identified as infinite Being, as a Being of infinite power who has created the cosmos. To say, and it is sometimes said, that in the Plotinian world the One lacks content is thus to confuse it with its utterly formless and ineffectual opposite, namely matter. In fact goodness is to be seen not only as doing good, but more precisely as willing to do good. And although it is certainly true that for Plato to know what is good entails to want to act in accordance with that goodness, the matter is brought out into the open by Plotinus in a way which goes far beyond what Plato presumably envisaged—though Plotinus doubtless thought that he was merely being Platonic. It can, of course, be argued that he is no more unplatonic in *Ennead* 6.8 than he is elsewhere when he treats in any detail of the nature of the One.

Nevertheless the shift in emphasis from Plato to Plotinus, in their conception of what it is to attain likeness to God, is of the utmost importance in considering the question of the value of human beings. For Plotinus is in a much better position than Plato to "democratize" his theory of human value. "God is always with us", he tells us, "but we are able to be with him when we put otherness away, and look towards him". The emphasis is not so much on knowing the Forms, though that certainly is required, but on turning, on reaching out, that is on choosing and desiring (ἐφίεται, 6.9.8.33 ff). Of course Plotinus would say that this is merely the proper interpretation of the Platonic doctrine of conversion, but his new emphasis guarantees that the good man is more clearly identified as the man who makes a special kind of moral determination for himself.

As we have already seen, there is certainly Aristotelian influence on the new emphasis on *Ennead* 6.8. Are we nevertheless justified in taking this treatise to represent a peculiarly Plotinian attitude towards the self and the One which its author would have always advocated? For if we are not, we cannot so readily use 6.8 to argue that Plotinus normally holds that the value of an individual depends on his *being* a certain kind of "thing", i.e., being like the One in respect of the "faculties" of desire and will. What are we to think, for example, of the remark in 6.9.8 that we are like the One when we desire it? Or is the possible coincidence of this with 6.8 merely accidental?

It is certainly possible to hold that Plotinus is carried on by the course of the argument in 6.8 to a position which cannot be identified with what we find elsewhere in the *Enneads*. This could be supported by the fact we have already observed, namely that there is virtually no reference to the notion of God as will in earlier or later parts of the *Enneads*. Thus one could perhaps say that Plotinus did not see the full implications of what he had presented in 6.8. Against this, however, can be put the counterargument that there is nothing in the rest of the *Enneads* which *conflicts* with what is to be found in *Ennead* 6.8. But that is obviously not an adequate response: 6.8 could be in accordance with the rest of the *Enneads*, while Plotinus still remained unaware of some of the more general implications to be drawn from it. The sceptic could still say that in 6.8 Plotinus is led on from point to point, in a somewhat Aristotelian manner, by his discussion of the doctrine of choice as presented in the *Nicomachean Ethics*.

In fact, unless we can make progress on the recondite question of what induced Plotinus to compose *Ennead* 6.8, we can probably advance no further with the problem of his conscious intentions. And one point in this connection is somewhat in favour of the agnostic. It is rather striking for Plotinus to take much direct interest in the *Nicomachean Ethics* at all; there is no other extended discussion of it elsewhere in our text of the *Enneads*, and Porphyry, who alluded to the use Plotinus makes of the

Metaphysics, has nothing to say of the *Ethics*.[28] Nevertheless, various themes from the *Ethics* were known to Middle Platonic writers, and Albinus at least seems to have known it at first hand.[29] We may almost certainly assume that Plotinus knew Albinus' work,[30] and therefore it is just possible that he recalled that Albinus had also talked of God's will (βούλησις).[31] Yet it is hard to think that Albinus' vague echo of the *Timaeus* was Plotinus' specific source; nor does the comment of Albinus suggest that God's will was particularly discussed, rather than occasionally mentioned, in Middle Platonism.

Furthermore, despite the commentary of Aspasius, the *Nicomachean Ethics* seems to have received comparatively little study even among Aristotelians. Perhaps, however, the discussion of choice and will is an exception to this. At least Alexander was greatly interested in it, being desirous of using it to refute Stoic determinism. But interestingly Plotinus' discussion in 6.8 does not devote much time to the refutation of Stoicism. Rather it is concerned to move from human will to divine will, to the question of the nature of God which is quite un-Aristotelian, but always central to Plotinus.

The above points seem to indicate the high probability that although Plotinus *may* have read Aspasius (or others) on the *Nicomachean Ethics*,[32] there was some particular set of circumstances which persuaded Plotinus to compose *Ennead* 6.8 when he did. *Ennead* 6.8 is number 39 in Porphyry's chronological list of Plotinus' work. The treatises immediately surrounding it are 6.7 and 2.1; and the "will of God" is mentioned twice in 2.1.1. It can be dated to approximately 265 A.D. Obviously our knowledge of the philosophical activity of this period is limited. We know of no significant treatise on the notion of the freedom of the will, or of the concept of the First Principle as Will, though such may have existed.[33] What we do know, however, is that Christian writers throughout the third century were much concerned with theories about the will of God. Pantaenus may have discussed the matter, and both Clement of Alexandria[34] and Origen in *On First Principles* (2.9.1) developed the same theme. The Christians were not imprisoned by the "Aristotelian" tradition which held that God must be identified with Mind, though they certainly held Mind to be one of his basic characteristics. They were, of course, concerned to think in the terms prescribed by *Genesis* of God's decisions.

Whether Plotinus was affected by a Christian text on the will of God we do not know. If he was, it may have been something obscure and quite unknown to us. It could have been composed in Rome, though the possibility also remains open that he was sent something from Alexandria. It seems unlikely, however, that it was a work of Origen's; for by 265 Origen had been dead for some years, and it is most unlikely that the memory of debate from his old Alexandrian days suddenly stirred Plotinus to write or speak out. The only treatise available to us which could have been written during the relevant period is the work on *Free Will* of Methodius of Olympus, now surviving only in a translation into Church Slavonic,[35] but though this is certainly "Aristotelian" in some respects, it is concerned with human rather than divine will. Its date, indeed, is unknown, but the mid-third century is possible. But Methodius apart, the possibility of Christian influence on Plotinus at this period cannot be ruled out. Plotinus need not even have had a specific treatise in mind. He could have discussed the new ideas in Rome with friends from Egypt or Syria. At least some of his circle must have known something of the developing patterns of thought in an East now rapidly becoming Christianized.

Plotinus' dynamic conception of the One, clearly developed far beyond Platonic and Aristotelian notions, and indeed beyond the limits of classical thought in general, might have encouraged him to take an interest in such new speculations; and, though it is only a matter of opinion, such a solution seems more likely than that he suddenly stumbled on the original ideas of 6.8 solely as a result of thinking about the *Nicomachean Ethics*. If he was, in fact, led to compose his strange treatise by discussions or by reading of a specific Christian text about the nature of God, we can easily understand why there is no development of such themes in later (or earlier) treatises. As we have already suggested, they were probably not fully integrated into his thought, though it is likely that what he says in 6.8 about Eros could have been assimilated more readily than the discussion of will.

In brief, we conclude that Plotinus' views on man and his value must be closely related to his theory of the One. His first principle is radically different from that of the Platonists, Aristotelians and Stoics who preceded him. As in other areas of his thought, his conception is indeed in many respects a synthesis of what went before; but it cannot be overemphasized at the same time that it is something new: a dynamic first principle whose character as efficient cause is to be viewed in terms of Eros and of will as much as of mind and knowledge. That being so, and man being a microcosm, one should expect to find—and we find in fact—a different conception of man, and, compared with Plato and Aristotle, a new intrinsic importance assigned to him. Man in Plotinus is created perfectible and valuable, but he may not live up to himself; if he does not do so, it is his own fault and neither other men nor gods should be held responsible. Above all, for Plotinus, no saviour god is required to get us out of the troubles in which we immerse ourselves through crime and folly.[36]

Finally, we should emphasize that the concept of man we have sketched can be *found* in Plotinus, rather than that it is specifically taught. It is only occasionally—perhaps in 6.8 and a few other places—on the surface of his thought. He is on the edge of expressing it and consciously reflecting upon it, but usually he does not quite do so. On the other hand it must be insisted that the theory is there, that it neither contradicts nor conflicts with what we find widely in the *Enneads*; rather it confirms and unifies Plotinus' often scattered philosophic insights: on the union with the One, on Eros, on forms of individuals and on the general application of the doctrine of man as a wanderer in the metaphysical world. With Plotinus we have come close to the view that all men have intrinsic and basic value, from which could flow a doctrine of intrinsic rights; but despite his doctrine of the self and his novel version of the theory of man as a "divine spark", which here includes a special relationship between the soul and the One, Plotinus still holds to the ancient position which asserts that value and rights must be *claimed* by mature human beings. If we neglect virtue, we neglect our value; and if we neglect our value we still lose it.

CHAPTER NINE

SOCIAL CONTRACTS

The identification of ethics as a specific field of study serves to focus attention on man, as distinct from God or Nature, especially if it is also laid down, as it is by Aristotle, that this study has particular rules and specially appropriate modes of argument. Greeks, like everyone else, made "ethical" statements from the earliest times, and various pre-Socratic philosophers, especially Heraclitus, struck ethical poses. But before the time of Socrates, as Aristotle already recognized,[1] little was done to advance philosophical *arguments* about ethical questions. What about the Sophists and Empedocles? Many of the sophists were contemporaries, rather than predecessors, of Socrates, and although they certainly produced effects on Greek morality, they taught surprisingly little of what we should call ethics. We are probably misled by Aristophanes' *Clouds*—and even that makes Socrates, not, say, Protagoras, the central character—into postulating a great deal of *formal* ethical enquiry. Perhaps we should rather say that one of the effects of the general relativism of Sophistic teaching was that Socrates and others began to *isolate* ethical problems as such. Certainly Socrates' interlocutors, including some of the greatest Sophists themselves, are depicted by Plato—and Aristotle's judgment about the role of Socrates in the history of philosophy seems to confirm this—as finding Socratic enquiry into the nature of virtue, the virtues and the "moral" care of the soul, new and strange. There is no reason to suppose these attitudes unhistorical.

In modern philosophy the question of rights is much discussed; in ancient philosophy it is not isolated as a philosophical problem. It arises *en passant* during discussion of such things as ideal constitutions, human nature or more generally the problem of justice. But by implication rights are under consideration whenever the value of human beings, the importance of human beings, or of some human beings, is in question. And such things are already in question in "Homeric times", that is, in the poems of Homer.

We must at this point avoid repeating the mistake of spending so long working out the views of Homer and his archaic successors that there is neither time nor space for a consideration of the philosophical periods which followed; a few general comments will suffice to provide the necessary background for our present problems. Briefly we may assume that peer-recognition is the source of value in the Homeric period. A member of the aristocratic class expects and receives recognition both from his peers and from those inferior in status to himself, though often only when he is able to defend his own position. People who were more important in the society enjoyed a larger number of rights, even, we should insist, of basic rights. Such patterns, of course, have continued, though overlaid by others, in many of the institutions of society down to modern times. In the Roman Republic rank always affected punishment, and in the Empire from the time of Hadrian those of "humbler" status (even among citizens), the so-called *humiliores*, were increasingly liable to more severe and more degrading punishments than the more "honourable".[2] Similar practices still survive (especially in the armed forces) in most modern states: officers are treated as deserving of more dignified treatment than "other ranks". An old joke sums it up, describing the spouses of military personnel: officers and their ladies, N.C.O.'s and their wives, private soldiers and their women.

Strictly speaking, within the aristocratic circle there already exists the idea of equality. The peers are more or less equal: the high king is regarded among the lords not so much as a master or ruler, but as *primus inter pares*. Everyone agrees, says Aristotle, that rights should be distributed equally among equals;[3] the problem is, however, what kind of equality we are dealing with. Oligarchs in the classical age advocated what they called "geometrical equality",[4] a form of equality which denied recognition of "egalitarian" political claims.

In more contemporary discussion it is generally assumed, but not always argued, that the concept of political equality is based on the observation of recognizable and important similarities between individual human beings. For example it may be claimed that the relevant similarities between blacks and whites, or Caucasians and Jews, are far more important than such apparent dissimilarities as skin pigmentation or the shape of the nose. Such obvious external differences are of no significance beside the fact that blacks and whites can interbreed, learn the same languages, understand the same moral principles, etc.

As an operating principle we may assume that by the time of Socrates the "aristocratic" notion of superiority could no longer rest solely on the claim to come from the right family; among those who thought, however, it was sometimes argued that certain excellences were more likely to be "achieved" in such families, that is, that some people are more likely to have been born with specific kinds of superior potential. Such superiority could be viewed as moral or intellectual, or both. So when an opponent of political democracy, like Plato, argued that only a few should rule, he would not simply assert that particular individuals should rule because they are born in a particular family; rather he would try, as in the

Republic, to identify those who he can argue are *naturally* better able to govern.

As Aristotle said, everyone agrees that equals should receive equal treatment. The question is: who is equal? Ancient thinkers, not easily misled by democratic cant, rarely denied the fact that some people are more intelligent than others and can perform various tasks (of administration, for example) better. They also assumed such considerations to be of paramount importance, and that the less well-endowed may *prima facie* have less claim to political rights. But they were insufficiently aware (though we have mentioned the exceptional case of Plato's *Laws*) of the fact that intelligence and training are no necessary check on the corrupting influences of power as such—which seem to be far greater and more insidious than was generally recognized by ancient theorists.

But whatever the weaknesses of ancient analyses of power may have been, the philosophers were not blind to the truth that, generally speaking, the stronger faction rules, frequently in its own interest alone. And in saying "stronger" we think of power in its crudest form: the ability to liquidate one's opponents or drive them into exile; as Göring was later to put it: my fist on your throat. Hence, under democratic forms of society, the central problem of politics was often viewed as the protection of the weak against the strong. In Callicles' language, this meant curbing the natural greatness of the strong in favour of the puny and slavish interests of the weak.

Now since, as we have seen, the traditional background to Greek society is the aristocratic view that to the few belong rights and privileges, it is natural that the function of democracies was seen as extending such rights and privileges to a larger group of citizens; and when philosophers took up the matter, they soon began to think in terms of a *contract* between individuals by means of which the advantages of a larger group could be upheld. The first version of this theory of which we have detailed knowledge is that proposed by Glaucon in the second book of the *Republic*, though Callicles in the *Gorgias* seems to suppose that in general, in "unnatural societies", agreements are made by the weak at the expense of the strong. "Slaves" band together so that "natural" rulers shall be thwarted.[5]

That such theses were widely mooted in the fourth century we take as certain, though to us they only emerge fully as the suggestions of Socratic interlocutors. Let us then make certain general observations. First of all such proposals are secularist. They depend on no theory of God's plan or God's will, nor do they require any religious or metaphysical doctrine about man or man's soul. They imply, though they do not actually state, that *per se* man is an animal among animals with no particular "rights", that rights are in fact something which may be "claimed", but that only a recognition of self-interest will encourage anyone to admit the claim of another. The claim, therefore, is not absolute; human beings can make deals of various kinds to concede various advantages to one another and to dignify these advantages under the name of rights. A right then becomes what is naturally agreed on by the parties to the agreement to be such. Where such theories originated we do not know; nor do we know whether anyone ever supposed that they are descriptions of historical events, and that such contracts have been literally made. It is more probable, however, that the contracts were not thought of as matters of historical fact, but that their genesis was described "mythologically". Indeed there are parallels to this, such as the account penned by Critias of the origin of belief in the gods: they were invented by a clever tyrant to keep people's minds in order. It seems unlikely that Critias thought he was describing an historical event: he was giving an "insight", in a purportedly historical guise—for all good mythology poses as history.

We may now notice that in Glaucon's version of the social contract there is no real recognition of human value. Value itself is a convention; it is a *device* used by the weak to protect themselves against the strong. There is no recognition in this model of a theory of justice, let us say, as fairness, no necessary awareness that because people seem basically similar they should be treated, ought to be treated, in particular ways. This notion, dear, as we have seen, to contemporary secularist thinkers, is absent from the ancient version. That version is honestly Hobbesian; it is based on expediency, on each man looking to save himself; and it seemingly would disappear if an individual or group of individuals decided that their interests were no longer served by keeping the contract. There would, apparently, be nothing *simply immoral* about a unilateral termination of the "agreement".

We should also insert at this point that the notion that a defence of morality must be conducted without any reference to what is expedient is unknown in Greece or in Greek philosophy. Greek thinkers did not have to trouble themselves with imperatives for which no justification can ultimately be produced, if expediency, advantage or the will of a divine being are declared irrelevant. There is no "simple ought" in Greek ethics, and we should least of all expect to find one in such a secularist theory as that of the contract.

It is commonly observed that the contract theories found in Plato are somehow to be understood as developments of the relativist ethics of the Sophists. It is uncertain, as we have seen, how far most of the pre-Platonic writers would have gone in their advocacy of *historical* contracts, but from the widespread Sophistic view that the conventions of individual cities lead to the laws of different cities, and provide the ultimate justification for those laws, it is a fairly short step to suppose that the conventions themselves are formally contracted. From the point of view of Sophistic relativism it is comparatively unimportant whether conventions arise by contract or merely by chance; but from the point of view of a teacher supposing—as apparently became widespread—that the basic motive for human action is simple self-interest (whether viewed crudely or in terms of "higher" satisfactions), the shift from chance to contract would be very important. While emphasizing the significance of human egoism, it would also give due weight to the "humanistic" notion of human decision-making.

In the long-run, perhaps the most important feature of ancient contract theories is that they are ultimately individualistic. It is individuals, not cities, which make the contracts, and the goal is the individual's good, to which the good of other groups of communities, large or small, is wholly subordinated. Not surprisingly, therefore, neither Plato nor Aristotle was particularly attracted to them. For both Plato and Aristotle are concerned with the individual as a member of the *polis*, the community of citizens. Both of them suppose that the individual belongs to a city not merely for protection or for cruder reasons of advantage, but for the development of the higher capacities and the attainment of happiness. Even the Stoics, who particularly in their earlier and more Cynic moments, put less weight on the importance of the city, are still generally of the opinion that man is a naturally social being, that from the most basic urge for self-preservation we can see develop a wider and wider sense of community with our fellow men, and indeed with the cosmos as a whole.[6] And the contract theory, though possibly *compatible* with the notion of man as an essentially social being, is an uneasy bedfellow. It harmonizes better with more atomistic views of men as essentially isolated creatures, living in a hostile world which by any means available to them they seek to make hospitable. Of the major thinkers of antiquity whose social and political theses we can determine with any degree of accuracy, only Epicurus provided a world-view of this type. And also the Cynics? But Cynic freedom, we recall, is freedom *from*, above all freedom from conventional restraint. Cynics do not want to make agreements with anyone. Even Alexander can do nothing for Diogenes except get out of his light.

Democritus may have taught a certain relativity of virtue, in the Sophistic manner, for he certainly held that sweet and sour are different by convention, not by nature.[7] But whatever his views on convention, it seems unlikely that he used the contract theory. Yet his atomist successors were the only important later philosophers to use it freely, to account for friendship and justice, as well as to provide a limited account of value and rights. In fact it is in the context of Epicurus' theory of friendship that we find him claiming that people obtain rights and value by agreement. Epicurus, we recall, denied that there is any "natural" link between different human beings which impels them to socialize.[8] Even friendship is a kind of treaty (*foedus*)[9]: considerations of immediate self-advantage at other people's expense are suspended in the interest of securing a certain absence of pain over a longer term, together with the relief of anxiety and the fulfillment of hope which friendship above all can bestow on us. Under the terms of such treaties, which are not entered upon lightly, and which should not be lightly broken off lest the chance of friendship in the future is lost, each party contracts to consider the other as another self, to suffer and rejoice with the other, even, in some circumstances, to die for him.

Thus for the Epicurean those with whom we have formed contracts, our friends, are credited with the same importance as we credit to ourselves. In terms of rights this may not seem very significant, for the notion of rights, even of one's own rights, is almost alien to the spirit of Epicureanism. The Epicurean values his pleasure, thinks it important; but he does not think he has a right to it in the sense of anyone else's owing it to him. He wants it and takes what he can get with safety. Friendship modifies this restriction somewhat. Friends cannot be supposed to have rights qua human beings, but we will try to get pleasure for our friends even though they have no natural right to expect help and hope from us; similarly we shall expect such returns ourselves.

Thus for Epicurus whereas any concept of intrinsic human value, or of basic human rights, is baseless in the larger world, in the world of the *polis* (just as it is in the hypothetical construction of Glaucon in the *Republic*), yet within the Epicurean community itself, which is, above all, a group of allies, rights do exist, by agreement, for all the parties who live there. These rights, based on friendship, will at least have deeper roots than any that would be derived from a mere contract for justice. Thus for the Epicurean the world is divided into two groups, those who out of "friendship" have been accorded special rights and value, and those who have not, (though some of the latter are owed something in accordance with "justice"). There are doubtless many reasons for the hostility Epicureans often showed for those outside their own group, but this way of looking at the world would certainly encourage it. "We", the Epicureans, are valuable (because they try to benefit me); "they", the outsiders, are worthless, because they have not agreed to do so.

It is important to insist that within this Epicurean scheme there is nothing remotely suitable for use as the basis for a Declaration of Human

Rights. It does not matter at all to the Epicurean whether those outside the community have "relevantly similar features" to those inside. All that matters is whether they have entered into a contract. They could do so (in some cases at least), but they have not done so. So value has nothing to do with justice as commonly understood, or fairness, or equity. In a sense we are indeed all equal, at least all similarly reducible to atoms in the void; and justice itself is a convention, an agreement not to harm one another.

Epicurus' ethics is determined to be consistent; hence his attitude towards crime is particularly revealing. If the wise man could get away with it (but perhaps he cannot), he would be a criminal if crime was pleasurable. Similarly he would tolerate the crime and "injustice" of his friends. Certainly he will take them as they come.[10] We now recognize the basis for this attitude. We start from the fact that there really are no values of any kind in the outside world, the world beyond the community, whether we think of things "out there" or of people. The vision is almost Sartrian: "Thus it is man who renders cities destructible".[11] Strictly speaking in that value-free world, beyond our own pleasure and pain, there are only arrangements of atoms in the void.

The same point is made by Epicurus in his attitude to the gods. Epicurus falls within the second class of "atheist" described by Plato in the *Laws*,[12] that is, he is a man for whom the gods certainly exist—we have a clear vision of them[13]—but who thinks that it would be too bothersome (and essentially degrading) for them to concern themselves with mankind.[14] In fact the attitude of the gods exactly reflects that of Epicurean wise men. They accord no value to men, nor indeed would they accord value even to one another were it not that they are able, by so doing, to enjoy the pleasures of friendship. And according to Philodemus wise men may be called friends of God, for they benefit from God's existence. Gods, of course, do not benefit through man's existence, so Philodemus is somewhat out of step in calling gods the friends of the wise.[15]

In saying that the gods are uninterested in human behaviour, Epicurus is, in fact, emphasizing that "wrongdoing" does not matter; if it were significant, the gods might be interested in it. As it does not, the apathy of the gods is the only correct attitude. Human beings are thus not only without value; strictly speaking—and the gods by definition "speak strictly"—there is no such thing as value at all. When Epicurus said that "virtue" is an empty name (Fr. 511 Usener), he meant virtue in the widest possible sense of the word, the old sense of the word in English. He meant anything which can be labelled "excellence"—and he "spat on" everything noble, including everything of value (Fr. 512). Even before Epicurus the word "aretē" covered a much wider spectrum than "moral virtue", and it should not be limited to the moral realm in the writings of Epicurus himself. "Valuable" for Epicurus is, therefore, a word to be applied only to what gives long-lasting pleasure; as such, it has nothing to do with the more traditional notions of excellence, whether moral or of any other kind. And indeed it was probably only the Stoics, in any case, who clearly isolated *moral* excellence from other kinds.

The contract theory of Epicurus is not "democratic" in the sense we have given to this term in our present study; it does not imply any equality of value, but only an equality of ultimate insignificance. Indeed, in general, as we have suggested, the contract theories of antiquity have to do with the origin of conventions, not with some kind of thesis about human nature. They may coexist with views about human nature of an "undemocratic" type, whether or not of the traditionally aristocratic variety, or with illiberal versions of what we have been calling "divine spark" theories. Probably such theories originated with a desire to protect the poor and weak against the strong, against the natural rulers. But in the Epicurean version, the contract is associated with the view that there are no natural rulers, no natural supermen; it is a means for sensible people (i.e. Epicureans or others thinking along Epicurean lines) to secure something pleasant or at least free of unnecessary pain.

It is instructive once again to compare Epicurus with Marcus Aurelius. Marcus, we recall, often speaks of Stoicism and Epicureanism as representative of the two most basic ways of viewing the universe, at least in metaphysical terms. But Marcus too, like Epicurus, is very inclined to consider human beings and human activities as of no value. At the philosophical level this may be explained as a reaction or counterbalance to the inflated pride of power of which he is naturally conscious. But at a psychological level it has been diagnosed (by Dodds) as the symptom of an identity-crisis in Marcus himself.[16] Certainly, as we have observed, there are striking texts in Marcus which have no true parallel in orthodox Stoicism, and which indeed conflict in important respects with the Stoic notion of man as partner with God in the rational organization of the universe. "A procession's vain pomps, plays on the stage...marionnettes dancing to strings...every man is worth just so much as the worth of what he has set his heart upon" (7.3 tr. Farquharson). In Marcus' view, human beings are like puppies squabbling over a bone or mice scurrying about aimlessly. The sentiment reminds one slightly of a sad mood of Plato's in the *Laws*,[17] where humans are compared to puppets operated on strings by the gods; and also that the doctrine of providence does not always entail an elevated view of man. But while this is a passing mood in Plato, it is a normal attitude in Marcus, and it suggests—thus bringing us to the comparison with Epicurus—that human beings are quite without value. The slaughter in the amphitheatre is grotesque, not pitiable; the victims do not matter: they are merely absurd in the way they cling to life at all costs. Human beings in this kind of vision appear as mere units, to be rationally organized like other units which happen to be inanimate. It is probably such an "atomic" view of the world itself which makes Marcus speak less harshly of Epicurus than is usually the custom among his Stoic predecessors. Where Epicurus finds that among many valueless people some of the more sensible can make a deal to look after themselves, Marcus finds that they are material to be organized.

Despite Epicurus, it must be allowed that "contract" theories are on the periphery of ancient political thought; and it is not clear that Epicurus worked out his own theory in the detail it deserves. One of the reasons for this difference between ancient and modern times is perhaps that more recent contract theories are designed, at least in part, to explain the origins of rights, whereas the concept of rights exists only in the shadows of ancient political and legal philosophy. For the ancients, contract theories are primarily offered to account for the origins of society and its conventions; they are designed to be descriptive rather than normative. It is no accident that they achieve the greatest importance in the system of Epicurus, where strictly speaking, there are no norms at all. After Epicurus they have no further philosophical history in antiquity.

CHAPTER TEN

CLAIMING ONE'S RIGHTS

At several places during the course of this study, I have alluded to the question of claiming one's rights, whatever be the metaphysical or social source of those rights. If we consider Aristotle's remarks about the "great-souled" man in the *Ethics*, we recall that it is of the essence of the great-souled man that he both deserves much and claims what he deserves (1123B). If he claims less than he deserves, he is mean-spirited and in this regard defective in his virtue. In this saying Aristotle seems to condemn not only false humility, but to a considerable extent humility as well. In the not too distant past the passage was regarded as peculiarly objectionable from the moralist's point of view, for in it Aristotle was supposed to have revealed the arrogance of his moral attitudes in a crude and unvarnished form. More recently, due to advances in the science of psychology, a new attitude has come to the forefront: Aristotle is now praised (in contrast to the "Christian" tradition) for insisting on the importance of the notion of self-respect in the sum of one's attitudes to oneself and to one's fellows.[1]

Part of the problem with which we are concerned here, between the older and the newer interpretation of the *Ethics*, is that it is easy (and has proved so historically) to confuse self-respect with selfishness, although both Plato in the *Laws* and Aristotle himself in the *Politics* show that they are already well aware of the distinction between them.[2] In fact, both earlier hostility and more recent re-evaluation of the morality of the great-souled man's attitude towards himself may derive from the fact that, unlike many contemporary writers on such topics, Aristotle perhaps assumes, but certainly never makes explicit, a theory that would connect one's attitude to oneself to one's attitude to other people. In contemporary discussions, we are often reminded that we form our attitudes to ourselves by learning in early childhood to recognize ourselves as objects in the same way as we recognize other people. We acquire a certain self-objectification—which is itself developed by learning to distinguish ourselves from our mothers and seeing ourselves as one *among* others. From this we may recognize that the attitudes we adopt towards ourselves will be reflected in our attitudes to others, and vice versa. Thus a man lacking in respect for himself will probably also lack respect for others, and hence treat them badly. Since there still exists a misguided tradition among moralists to regard one's behaviour towards others as more important than one's attitudes towards oneself, treatment of others becomes the principal danger signal. And if it is recognized as such, there follows a recognition of the need to build up the sense of self-respect. But at a time when such considerations were far from the minds of critics of Aristotle, they felt able to indulge themselves with condemnations of the megalopsych's naked "self-absorption".[3]

We may take it as axiomatic that all ancient thinkers would have agreed in principle with Aristotle's attitudes to self-respect. Men are supposed to recognize their own worth. And we may take it for granted too that such attitudes were also to be found in Greek popular morality from the earliest times. In popular morality, however, self-respect may also be connected with another supposedly desirable "possession" from which we must clearly distinguish it. For in popular morality, and probably at times in philosophical morality too, self-respect will easily be confused with the search for "honour" or "fame". Hence deprivation of honour will seem a slight to one's self-respect to which exception should be taken. From such exception deaths of others, or failing that of oneself, may follow. Hence in the earliest Greek popular morality with which we are familiar, much importance was attached to honour. Indeed in a sense, as we have already observed, honour was the root both of the value of members of the society and of their rights.[4]

But honour and self-respect are not necessarily interlocked. A man can be dishonoured and still keep his self-respect. For the source of honour is the society to which we belong; whereas self-respect is something internal, something dependent on one's own self and one's own will. Plato already made the distinction sharply in the *Gorgias* (474C ff.), where he argues that, although the good man would rather suffer injustice than practice it—and to suffer is certainly in the "world's eyes" to be dishonoured—yet he does not thereby lose his self-respect; indeed the contrary is the case: he would lose his self-respect if he acted otherwise. Similarly in the second book of the *Republic* Glaucon expounds in detail on the miseries, tortures and other acts of despite which may be inflicted on the good man (362A), but he has no success at all in persuading Socrates that such sufferings matter in comparison with the good of the soul, and the wise man's conscience, wherein lies his self-respect.

Certainly it must be admitted that not all the philosophers were as clear about the correct relationship between honour and self-respect as Plato. For in so far as anyone supposed that a man's value depended on the estimate society put on him, he might lose the ability to form a correct estimate of the role of self-respect. At times, indeed, such attitudes are to be found in the *Nicomachean Ethics*, as our earlier remarks about the role of society in human valuation in Aristotle would lead us to expect. Plato, of course, does not tie his estimate of human beings to their position in society and to society's regard for them, which also helps him form a clearer grasp of the proper relationship between honour and self-respect. And in a latter age Platonists were able to combine a traditionally Platonic attitude to honour with an interpretation of a text from the book of *Genesis* (3.21) in which we are bidden to lay aside our "coats of skins",[5] representing various false attractions of life, the last of which is glory. They were even able to misinterpret the *Theaetetus* so as to suggest that Plato himself there urged this very point. In doing so, though misinterpreting the particular dialogue, they well understood the attitude of Plato himself.

But leaving aside the question of honour, let us consider how Plato views the relationship of rights to self-respect. If a man has value in his own eyes, if, that is, he has self-respect, will he wish to claim the rights which go with that self-respect? In one sense yes, in that he will have no *necessary* reason to conceal the fact that others are treating him improperly, or denying his rights (though he may choose to do so from time to time, as we shall see). Indeed if he has rights, these rights should normally be claimed; otherwise it might be supposed that they cannot openly and avowedly be regarded as rights. For I do not lose my self-respect, as Plato saw, if I do not enjoy the rights I am heir to ; I lose it if I do not make clear in the public domain that I indeed have rights. For if I do not claim rights, I am by my silence letting it be assumed that I have none. And someone with no rights *at all* in the outside world must have no value in that world. But is there a difference between having no rights and having one's rights totally disregarded, and between having no value in society and having no value *per se*?

We may assume that despite the *Gorgias* Plato would agree with Aristotle that rights should be claimed, regardless of whether the claim is upheld. But what about the more fundamental point, the question whether if we do not claim our rights, we do not have them? Again no simple answer can be given. For clearly this question cannot be dissociated from the problem with which we have been concerned throughout, that of the *origin* of the value of each of us. For clearly the matter of claiming is different if the rights are intrinsic to man qua man, if they are guaranteed by some metaphysical situation of man, or if they are bestowed by the possession of *nous*, by society, etc. Let us therefore start with the question of intrinsic value.

If a man has certain basic, inalienable rights, regardless of what he does and of what he is—let us say, at the lowest, the right to a fair trial—then that right should be guaranteed whether he claims it or not. Such minimal rights would presumably be acceptable to Plato, Aristotle and the Stoics, though not to Epicurus. For Cynics, however, and for all the worshippers of freedom, even basic rights would not be guaranteed. For if a man is so "unfree" as not even to demand minimal justice for himself at other people's hands, then so much the worse for him. Thus for the Cynics we assume that, although everyone *can* have rights, all rights must be claimed if they are to exist at all. Once again Epicurus turns out to have a rather similar view. We have already observed that children cannot easily claim rights; that is one reason why, in an Epicurean world, there is no reason to suppose they have any except in special circumstances. For whoever enters into the basic "social contract" creates rights for himself; mere outsiders have none. The Epicurean thus recognizes a certain value, for his own reasons, for those in his own community, the friends he has made, but none for anyone else, except in so far as good sense has led him has made certain "limited treaties" about "justice" with those in a wider group.[6] Now children, in our parlance, are minors, so presumably whatever claims they have must be made for them. Epicurus, of course, would not allow anyone of necessity even such a basic right as a fair trial, and in any case "fair" is a mere word, referring to nothing with objective status in the world. But if a member of the Epicurean community had children, his membership in the community would extend to his children, who would thus be assumed, as it were by proxy, also to have rights within the community whether they actually claimed them or not for themselves. And in so far as the Epicureans thought it worthwhile to promote "justice", children outside the community might be protected in the same way.

The view of a modern defender of basic human rights (whether claimed or not) is diametrically opposed to that of the Epicureans and Cynics; and it is not difficult to determine and observe such differences. With the "intermediate" cases, Platonists, Aristotelians, Stoics, etc., the problem is more complicated; but there is an informative passage of Plotinus with which we may begin. Of all ancient thinkers Plotinus, we recall, is perhaps the one who comes closest to the view that each human being is established with certain basic rights in virtue of his "creation" by the One and as an image of his divine archetype. But the carelessness of individuals can still easily lead to a virtually complete forfeiture of these rights. Consider some of the "harsher" passages of the *Enneads*, such as the one in which Plotinus envisages a group of rich, overfed, indolent young men being beaten up by toughs on their way home. What is it worth more than a laugh?, he comments. An exaggerated statement, not to be taken too seriously, one might say; for there is no doubt that Plotinus would condemn the injustice of this sort of violence. But what about the victims? Plotinus is certainly telling us that they deserve all they get; for, he observes, the palaestra is at hand. They could exercize, keep fit and thus be able to look after themselves better. If they don't, then from one point of view what happens to them is their own fault. They have not done what they should have done to guarantee their right to safety on the streets; therefore they have lost that right. In other words, although everyone has rights potentially, they must act in the appropriate ways, and such acts constitute a claim, if they are to have rights in fact.

Mutatis mutandis, the famous passage about the folly of those who expect a god to descend from heaven to get them out of the troubles in which they are immersed through their own stupidity and wickedness points to a rather similar conclusion:[7] folly and vice deprive a man of his rights. With that we would all agree to some extent—except for the few who wish to abolish all restraints on the criminal, or at least all prisons or detention centres. But the point that Plotinus makes would go further than that; virtually all rights can be forfeited because virtuous action constitutes a kind of claim to them. But, one might say, this is a claim in a rather metaphorical sense. It differs considerably from the claim with which we began, that of the great-souled man. Here we reach the explanation of the great-souled man himself, for in Aristotle's view—and perhaps there is something to be said for it—what is wrong with the man who claims little though deserving much is that he is guilty of a kind of dishonesty. If I really deserve much, but pretend that I do not, I am lying, and guilty in exactly the same way as I would be if I disallowed rights due to someone else. For if a friend is a second self, why should a second self be treated *better* than a first self? In fairness they should have equal rights. And although it may be right to *give up* some of one's rights for the sake of others, that is a very far cry from not recognizing, and recognizing in the public domain, that we have such rights to give up.

It may add something to approach the matter from another angle, that of a famous controversy in antiquity, primarily between the followers of Aristotle and the Stoics.[8] For Aristotle, happiness requires a modicum of external goods, and these external goods may well include a proper recognition of one's rights in the form of honour, while the Stoics want to insist that the only good is virtue, which alone is sufficient for happiness. Thus the wise man will need nothing beyond the consciousness of his own virtue, and in so far as recognition by others is an "external" good, he will make no further claim. It will be of no importance to him whether rights are accorded him by the outside world or not. He will claim his rights, one must suppose, only because it is honest and just to do so in proportion to his worth, and because, at the "non-moral" level, to do so is much conducive to virtue in others; but clearly within such a framework his claim is to be viewed differently from that of the Aristotelian.

Let us pursue the question of claiming our rights. For it seems that a right *must* be worth claiming, at least on occasions, if not by the person who has it, at least by someone else on his behalf. For a right is a "fact" in the external world, and must therefore be recognizable by someone. If it is not, then its possessor cannot strictly be said to possess it, for no one, including himself, knows its value. Thus it would become a moral obligation on the possessor of rights to claim them for himself as for other people. Indeed, if there are any *basic* rights, if one does not claim them for oneself, one is in that action failing to claim them for other people as well. Therefore basic rights must be claimed both for oneself and for others.

What does this make of the so-called virtue of humility? Aristotle, as we saw, is inclined to deny it altogether, and many others in antiquity would have agreed with him. But the root of the problem was not identified by Aristotle, or perhaps by any other classical thinker. For perhaps with all varieties of abnegation, virtue resides exclusively in the reasons for which they are espoused. So, contrary to Aristotle, one might argue that to claim less than one's desert *would* be acceptable if there were good reasons to do so,[9] while agreeing with Aristotle that it is "unjust" to claim less than one's desert in normal circumstances. In "non-Aristotelian" circumstances humility would in fact become a species of generosity, thus displaying a positive quality and ceasing to be a mere denial of fact.

It might even be argued that a refusal to claim one's rights is an act of supererogation; and at the same time that the refusal to claim rights does not constitute a denial of their existence. But in the light of the argument presented so far, we have to insist that since rights are in the "public" domain, a failure to claim them altogether would imply that they cease to exist altogether as rights. In the case of humility, as we have been studying it in relation to the "great-souled" man, we should note that the ancients in general do not recognize it as virtuous; distinctions such as those just proposed about *reasons* for humility were not normally available. It was the spread of Christianity in the ancient world which made humility fashionable, but the context for its exercise was notoriously different. For even though the Christian might voluntarily refuse to claim his due for good reasons as well as for bad, his basic value in the eyes of God was in no way diminished; his rights are laid up in heaven. For it was held to be of the nature of God to allow all men made in his image to share in his value and thus to possess rights among their fellows. Indeed, as we suggested earlier, the traditional Greek gods played a weaker version of this role; we noted that strangers, for example, were supposed to have rights under the protection of Zeus. But such rights were established precariously in the popular mind, and there was certainly no body of theological writing or theorizing to help them become part of the ideological structure of society.

Once again the question of rights brings us back in antiquity to the question of power, the power in this case to enforce them. Consider the average member of an ancient community. How is he protected? In the first instance, and primarily, by his family. Hence from earliest times the catastrophe for wife and children—not to speak of elderly relations—if the husband, the bread-winning male of the family, is killed in battle. And for the old, in a world without social security of any kind, the only hope, in normal circumstances, resided in the younger members of the family. The role of the state in helping out in such situations—and the case is similar with illness—is virtually nil.[10] Whatever those outside the family circle may do must be counted an act of generosity, not to be expected, and for which "thanks" (*charis*) in kind may reasonably be assumed. In these respects even the city-state is atomized; and it is this atomization which many political theorists, especially Plato, wished to overcome. For what it means is that the weak, the sick and in general the disadvantaged lose their rights—and that this is accepted as the norm—if they have not the power of enforcement.

Such a brutally realistic view can find no philosophical objection in Epicurus; the Christians, on the other hand, seem to have rejected it outright, at least among themselves and to some extent in a wider circle as well, for they considered themselves bound to help the sick and the afflicted.[11] God is still concerned with such, even if they have lost the power to claim their rights. Here then is the basic issue about claiming one's rights, that in ancient thinking (as also more recently) it was widely assumed that "claiming" had no meaning unless there was some means of enforcing the "claim". What do the philosophers in general make of such "realism"?

The answer is "everything and nothing". For certainly, with the exception of Cynics and Epicureans, they all call upon us to be generous, to recognize and help people in trouble, that is, to recognize that for some reason they are "worth" helping. But the lack of suggestions for improvement at the institutional level (with some obvious exceptions) is probably connected with a failure to ask the basic questions we have raised here: are there rights which all human beings possess regardless of their virtue, position in society, intellectual capacity, etc? Are there inalienable rights which any just man would respect and which all men *should* respect?

We have touched on a possible approach to this already: namely what rights does the most corrupt and vicious man possess in the ideal societies which the philosophers offer us? Certainly he has no inalienable right to life, probably he has no right to be free of suffering degrading or brutal punishments. His minimum right, which is guaranteed by justice and would be respected, as we observed, by Plato, Aristotle, Plotinus and the Stoics, though not necessarily by Epicurus or the Cynics, is the right to a fair trial; and he should have that right whether he claims it or not. But even this "right" may not be a right in the strict sense. He obtains it not because of his own intrinsic value, but because to deny it would be an act of injustice on the part of those who deny it. It is not a matter of his merit or desert, but of their virtue.

The criminal awaiting a fair trial is an interesting example from another point of view too. He is wholly powerless: it makes no difference whether he claims rights or not; whether he is accorded any depends entirely on others, so at least from the ancient point of view his claiming them is to no purpose. Indeed since in the extreme case he may be totally without value, there is no rationale to be found behind his claiming anything. But with the great-souled man, and to a lesser degree with all men possessed of a certain virtue, there is some rationale. For so far as they are virtuous, they may possess a measure of justice. And in so far as they are just, they must claim what is their due. In this respect at least the philosophical position, if we may call it that, has risen well above the "popular" level. For it is not based simply on considerations of power, but on considerations of justice. And, as we saw earlier, it is above all the aim of many philosophers, and perhaps particularly of Plato, to maintain that society, though of course needing power, is not simply a power-structure. It is to be a structure based on justice. In the suffering of the just man, deliberately accepted in preference to unjust behaviour, we see the explicit rejection of the worship of power in favour of the worship of virtue.

Power and justice: the two rivals may be observed again in relation to claims to rights and value. In a "power" society no rights are recognized which cannot be enforced. In origin Greek society (perhaps all society) was of that kind, and many of its features survived into historical times. In a "just society" rights are recognized when it is just to recognize them.

In antiquity all questions about the recognition of rights boil down to the problem of someone else's good. The good ruler rules for himself *and* others;[12] the bad ruler for himself at the expense of others. The good ruler *avoids* power if it is just to do so; the bad ruler acquires as much power as he can. The good ruler lays down laws to restrict abuses of power by both others and himself. The bad ruler avoids law in the desire to exploit others according to his whims. But this very antithesis shows that the ancients do not identify the concept of rights in the same way as we do. For them the issue is basically the relationship between power and justice; the philosophers condemned the poets because they sang of the gods as careless of justice in their immoral treatment of one another and of men. It would be almost true to say that the ancients approached the issue the opposite way from ourselves. Instead of starting with a consideration of human rights, or of basic rights, they start with theories of power and of how power shall be tempered by justice. As their thought proceeds, they come to recognize that certain types of people, for various reasons, are in fact possessed of rights. That brings them also to the question of claiming, for, as we have seen, in Greek popular morality claiming is an activity in which the powerful, those able to do so, may engage. For the philosophers, however, it is not now merely a matter of power; rights should be claimed in the interests of honesty and of justice, including justice to oneself, although they did not put it in those terms.

We recall at this point that neither Plato, nor Aristotle, nor the Stoics, nor Plotinus is particularly enamoured of democracy, though Aristotle accords it a higher value than the others. For in much non-totalitarian democratic theory it is held that government should be minimal, sufficient only to equalize justice and protect the weak and disadvantaged against the strong. The emphasis here is on protection; whereas in ancient times it is usually on the question of who is fit to rule, to exercize authority, and what are the criteria of such fitness. Hence the moral problem is not viewed in terms of enlarging or protecting the rights of the weak, but of controlling and rationalizing the power of the strong. Clearly in such a perspective—and it is again a "realistic" one—the question of claiming rights assumes only minor importance.

Which brings us to the final point: if we consider a society from the point of view of the problem of power rather than that of rights, we are liable to view the "receiving end" of any power-structure impersonally. Such impersonality has come up many times in our study and must at some point be faced directly. We have frequently spoken of difficulties with the ancient philosophers' "rejection" of individuals. What about the question of the special kind of individual which is a person? But before coming to grips with this problem, there is a methodological question to be resolved in the area of the sociology of Greek metaphysical statements.

CHAPTER ELEVEN

METAPHYSICS OR SOCIOLOGY?

At earlier stages of this enquiry, I declined to consider the motivation of ancient philosophers when examining their particular views of the value of human beings. I dealt with theories as presented, together with the reasons offered in support of them, thus leaving aside whether individual thinkers were really governed by certain other factors, openly acknowledged or operating in secret. I did suggest, however, especially in the case of Aristotle, that we can identify assumptions about what is valuable which cannot be readily understood in terms of his openly avowed philosophical argument.

It is now appropriate, however, to broach the question of motivation, fortified as we are by the results of our metaphysical and ethical analysis. *Prima facie* it might be supposed that the motivations with which we are concerned are purely metaphysical. Plato, we observed, determines the value of man by his degree of characterization by Form, Aristotle usually thinks of the type of mind or intellect the individual possesses, Plotinus considers the awareness of the intelligible or the "conversion" of the soul to the One, others think of freedom or of the possession by man of some kind of "divine spark". All these proposals look straightforwardly metaphysical, and metaphysical (or physical) explanations of them are offered.

We pass away from purely metaphysical ground, though metaphysics is not left entirely behind, when we come to the proposal, also present in Aristotle, that it is in so far as he succeeds in being a good member of his society that a man obtains "value" and hence rights. But this view is itself part of a more general thesis, still largely metaphysical in nature, that the individual *grows* into something of greater value as he matures or, in Aristotelian terms, as he realizes his potentiality. A somewhat similar view was identified in the statement of Plotinus that although the One is always present with us, we can be present with Him if we wish; in other words that we can make certain kinds of moral choices which will enable us to develop our potential, or rather perhaps, for Plotinus, exhibit what we really are. Again in Stoicism we find something similar: we can learn to live harmoniously with the divine reason which is in us, but we can only do so when we are mature, that is, for the Stoics, at least fourteen years old.

Theories of this sort tend to presuppose, and some state explicitly, that the adult male human being is the member of the species which alone attains or can attain the perfect form. All others are approximations of various types to this perfect example, or potentialities which we hope will develop into it. Hence those who are not adult males cannot be as valuable as adult males, cannot have similar rights to adult males, and must be valued in proportion to their degree of proximity to this possibly mature specimen. At first sight such a conclusion, however, unwelcome or unacceptable we may find it, might seem merely the logical result of a metaphysic which we may hence infer to be defective. But a look below the surface will reveal that there are other, quite extraneous factors which have come into play. It may well turn out, in fact, that although the metaphysic will permit such conclusions, it does not necessitate them. I propose therefore to return briefly to the problems posed by women, children and slaves.

II

The evidence about women, which we have already discussed in part, points to the influence of extra-metaphysical factors more strongly in Plato because in his writings we can detect two levels of treatment. We can see what he says about the nature of women in an ideal society and then contrast this with the assumptions he draws from his own society. In the *Republic* it is clear that the position of women in the Guardian class is what Plato supposed was possible in an ideal social situation, while among the other classes the ordinary assumptions of fifth and fourth century Athens probably remain more or less unchanged. Socrates argues in the *Republic*—and expects the argument to be not easily accepted—that the female members of the Guardian class are to be given all the rights and responsibilities of their male counterparts in so far as their inferior physical strength will allow.[1] They are to be educated in a similar way, both physically and culturally, and are to be freed from the burdens of bringing up children in a conventional setting in order that they can devote themselves to administration and government. But even in this account a number of anomalies arise. Plato seems to think that it will be harder to find female Guardians, and that generally the most able women will be less able than the most able men. Secondly when he speaks of the rewards apportioned to the virtuous, he tells us that the male Guardians who distinguish themselves will have greater sexual access to women; he does not say that the successful women will have greater access to men—at least until they have passed the "official" child-bearing age. And the general sexual arrangements are called a "community of women and children"; Plato does not speak of a community of men. In other words the society is looked upon primarily from the male point of view.

Plato has not entirely succeeded in extricating himself from conventional assumptions even in the course of sketching the society of the Guardians—though his proposals, particularly concerning the abolition of the family, were indeed revolutionary and retained their power to shock for many centuries.[2]

It is not surprising, therefore, that when Plato turns aside from the special society of the Guardians, or perhaps when he is caught off guard in respect to the capabilities of women, he reverts to a much more conventional position. In the *Timaeus* (41D, 91A), we hear that those men who live badly will be reincarnated as women. In the *Symposium* the statement that it is an inferior love of men which turns to women is never explicitly rejected, though the creation and role of the presumably fictitious figure Diotima obviously rules out any idea that women are incapable of philosophy. In all this two questions call for an answer. Where did Plato get the view that women are generally less intelligent? Where did Plato get the view that women are generally less virtuous? Neither of these views is necessitated by his own metaphysics. We find them recurring elsewhere in ancient philosophy, but we may begin by observing that Plato may have thought that there are philosophical reasons for supposing a connection *between* the two alleged defects. For the highest virtue presupposes a specifically godlike quality of intelligence; if that is missing, the Forms cannot be recognized and genuine morality is impossible.

It might be argued, of course, that in reconstructing the relationships between male and female Guardians Plato showed an awareness that the family as it existed in Greek society was a major cause of female incapacity and inferiority; and that he therefore wished to destroy the family in order to give women the educational and social advantages which as Guardians they would need, and which would otherwise be denied them. There may be some truth in that explanation, but against it we should observe that the reason Plato actually mentions it is that he wants to avoid subversive jealousies among the ruling group. To secure this is the purpose both of the "community of women and children" and of the Guardians' common ownership of property. This interpretation of the legislation seems also to be that of Aristotle when he criticizes Plato's proposals in the *Politics*.

Conventional prejudices are likely to be the most enduring in matters concerned with sex, marriage and the institution of the family. Plato probably had some awareness of this, and in his sweeping proposals for change we detect the whole-hearted attitudes of the genuinely revolutionary mind. It will hardly surprise us, therefore, if we find that Aristotle, who is more deeply suspicious of extreme modifications of society, exhibits the same two prejudices about women, namely that they are less intelligent and less virtuous. And just as for Plato these defects mean that women are less *likely* to be characterized by goodness and hence to possess value, so a similar view is to be found in Aristotle.

Aristotle tells us directly in the *Nicomachean Ethics* (1160B34) that a husband should rule his wife because of his greater worth. At *Metaphysics* 1058A29ff., the "thought" behind this is revealed. It is not that men are of a different species from women—the species is the same—but that in the case of women the form has mastered the matter less well. How does this relate to the claim that the husband has greater value? Clearly because, value being related to mind or intellect, women are supposed to be less formed, less well endowed in that regard. They are incomplete, as the *Generation of Animals* tells us (737A227, 767B8, 775A15); and incomplete certainly refers in some way to the mental capabilities which primarily distinguish men from animals and which are themselves primarily valuable. But again, as in Plato, there is nothing in the theory of Aristotle to *necessitate* this result, except perhaps the view that in the act of conception it is the male who through the semen provides the form or programme (*logos*) which is to become the individual. In other words in Aristotle's thesis about the nature of conception we can observe a desire to assimilate the biological process to wider theories about the relation of form and matter. By itself that need not give us our undesirable result; the trouble arises because Aristotle wants to allot each parent a particular role. One must provide the *entire* form, the other must provide the entire matter. Without that additional proposition, the general theory of form and matter need not give the results that Aristotle comes up with. We may observe that if we knew more about Plato's biological theories, we might find that he too subscribed to something similar. Perhaps everyone did. And yet Plato, if he did subscribe to it—or to something like it—would look illogical and inconsistent in supposing that being a good Guardian is possible even for a limited number of women! They would all have to be inferior.

So it seems that Aristotle's view of women is to some extent due to his acceptance of a particular thesis about the nature of conception and the different roles of the parents. It is interesting to note, however, that he seems remarkably unimpressed by Plato's proposals in the *Republic* for changing the social situation of women by giving those able to benefit the special education of the Guardian class. In fact, he seems to have thought Plato mistaken in making such proposals. Having decided that the existence of female Guardians is of no help in promoting the unity of the state, he appears to lose interest in them. So that although we conclude that his metaphysical theories of form and matter do not necessitate any particular view of the roles of men and women, we may also observe that he was quite content to find them compatible with a thesis of male superiority; for he accepted a version of the popular opinion in believing that a temperamental instability in women affects their decisionmaking capacities, and such capacities are the peculiarly important mark of human beings.

The fact that conventional beliefs about the inferiority of women could so clearly affect a man like Aristotle, fully aware though he was of Plato's attempt to abandon them, cannot be lightly dismissed. In the face of such evidence it is appropriate to look for unrecognized motivating factors. These cannot, of course, be entirely unearthed, but a degree of understanding seems possible. First let us consider the word *andreia*, which we often translate "courage", but which has originally a much wider range of meaning, approximating more to our notion of "manliness" of "the virtue of a man". Thus to say that a woman has *andreia* is to suggest that she has some of the characteristics of a man (anēr). *Andreia* in fact looks in earlier Greek almost like aretē (virtue in general), and in particular often seems to symbolize the *active* rather than the cooperative virtues, to borrow the fashionable terminology.[3] Plato addresses the problems in the *Politicus*: *andreia* (the typically masculine virtue tending to reduce to "courage") is hard to harmonize with *sophrosyne* (moderation, self-control, etc.), which when free from association with conservative politics, is often regarded as a virtue peculiar to women.[4]

Let us notice an ancient debate which may seem almost academic: the discussion as to whether all the virtues are one. The Socratic-Platonic position seems to have been that since all the virtues, if they are real virtues based on knowledge rather than merely on true opinion, involve knowledge of the Good, then he who possesses one of them will possess them all[5]—somewhat analogously to the way in which at the end of the *Symposium* Socrates is found arguing that a real poet should be able to write both tragedies and comedies. We notice, by contrast, that interlocutors of Socrates may opt for different virtues for different types of people, and in particular that in the *Meno* Meno himself mentions as examples of this the different virtues of men and women. Woman's virtue, as he expounds it, is traditional (71E).[6]

Aristotle's view is nearer to Meno's than to that of the Socrates who develops the theme of female Guardians. For although differences in biology and physical strength ensure that for Plato the roles of male and female Guardians will not be entirely identical, they overlap in a large number of areas; indeed in many areas they are identical. The lower value of women in Aristotle (and in the traditional account) seems tied to the fact that the roles (and therefore the virtue or excellence) of men and women in society are held to be almost entirely dissimilar. Hence it can be formulated as an axiom that insofar as ancient philosophers urge that men and women can do the same things (purely biological matters apart), to that degree they will also attribute to them a similar value. Perhaps a certain significance should be attached to the fact that it is precisely at the gymnasium, the traditional centre of male culture in a Greek city, that Plato anticipates there will be the most hostility to the coeducation of male and female Guardians. Will it not be absurd for women, even older ones, to wrestle naked among the men? But Socrates argues that the apparent absurdity must be faced down if the best city is to be developed.

That the gymnasium (and the palaestra or wrestling-school) symbolized much of traditional society and its conventions was recognized by others beside Plato. In the *Republic* of Zeno, a work in the Cynic manner, as we recall, public buildings are to be abolished: gymnasia are specifically singled out.[7] Furthermore in this *Republic* men and women are to wear identical clothes, and there is to be no "mystery" about female genitals; they are to be as visible as male, so that artificially and conventionally different ways of living for the two sexes may be abolished.[8] And in his "Stoic" period, Zeno (followed by his school as a whole) taught an even stronger version of the thesis that virtue is one than that of Plato and the Platonic Socrates. The Stoics are explicit that it is impossible to possess any single virtue without possessing them all.[9] Hence the virtue of the wise woman will be in all essentials identical with that of the wise man, though it should again be noted that in more informal assumption, as opposed to strict theory, the Stoics still normally thought of the sage as male.

Again we may ask why this should be so; and probably the answer is that the Stoics, like most ancients as well as moderns, believed that women are more conventional than men, and therefore less able to take the bold steps forward to the radically new life of virtue. In particular it was supposed, and in terms of the conventions of Greek society rightly supposed, that women are unable to free themselves of sexual "prejudices". The story of the Cynic wedding of Crates and Hipparchia brings these assumptions to the light of day. Crates tries to dissuade Hipparchia from her wish to marry him by saying that if she did so, she would have to commit herself to the Cynic life; and after the marriage was consummated (apparently in public), they lived together publicly and went out to dinners together—the latter also an example of the breaking of a convention.[10] Men might be sexually gratified at dinner-parties, but certainly—in aristocratic circles at least—not by their wives. If a woman can live the Cynic life in the way a man does, she is a member of the community of the wise, but even the Cynics seem to have supposed it more difficult for women to be "virtuous" in this way than for men.

Nevertheless, as far as we can see, in the Stoic versions of the Cynic ideal state, the Platonic view that women, or at least some of them, can be freed from their servitude to convention is maintained. Musonius Rufus specifically urges that women should study philosophy (fr. 3). Indeed the Stoics probably went beyond Plato in regard to the *number* of women who, in theory at least, could be emancipated. For the divine spark is present in both men and women alike, all of them, not merely in a select group suitable for membership in an élite Guardian class.

Before leaving this topic, and distinctly relevant also to the question of the origin of the notion that women are *morally*, as distinct from *intellectually* inferior to men, we refer again to the testimony of the late Stoic Musonius Rufus. Musonius upbraids his fellows for expecting a higher standard of women than of men in the matter of marital fidelity and chastity. No one worries, he observes, about the master having intercourse with his slave-girl, but similar licence is strictly forbidden to the mistress of the house; and that despite the fact that it is generally assumed that women are morally weaker than men.[11] Though weaker, by repute, a higher standard is expected of them, which is a manifest absurdity.

We can now proceed to identify several factors which led to the assumption, from which Plato almost broke loose, but which still influenced Aristotle, of the moral and intellectual inferiority of females, hence of their defectiveness and corresponding lack of value and of rights. First of all, and perhaps most important, they are physically weaker and supposedly therefore less courageous, less able to endure the battle-line, the standard and inadequate test of courage. Secondly they lack the strength to arrange the society in their interest, but also, obviously, because child-bearing at an early age rendered education less likely, and sexual taboos kept them from those institutions in the society where education in adulthood and adolescence was available. It is worth noticing that both Plato and Aristotle, in the interest of extending the education of girls as well as for eugenic reasons, made arrangements in their ideal societies for women to marry later than was customary in Athens, Plato proposing twenty as an appropriate age for marriage for women of the Guardian class, and Aristotle insisting that the minimum age should be about eighteen.[12]

There can be little doubt that inadequate education for women and the consequent underdevelopment of women's minds in antiquity was a function of the nature of society itself. Originally, of course, the man tilled the land and drove off the enemies while the wife stayed at home with the children, who were born to her early. In classical Athens the men tended to live in public, in the lawcourts, assemblies and gymnasia if "at home", and in the army or navy if abroad, thus preserving the pattern of the earlier society with its distinctive and separate roles for husband and wife. Tending the home, looking after one's private affairs was basically the responsibility of the wife, looking after public matters was the concern of the husband. Hence each of them seemed to require the kind of education or training which would fit them for their respective duties. Clearly in such a situation a wider knowledge would seem appropriate to the father, especially if the family was of the governing class, for it would be beneficial in understanding foreigners and alien customs.

The same result will be reached if we approach the problem from a slightly different angle. There are traditionally different virtues for men and women. Above all the female virtue is *sophrosynē* (moderation), and we have already noticed that *andreia* (manliness, courage) is, even by its name, traditionally male. Let us now consider the virtue which deals, at least originally, with all the different relations between families and individuals (in practice, of course, usually between men). Just as piety (*eusebeia*) concerns the relations between man and god, so justice deals broadly with the relations between man and man. It is no accident that both Plato and Aristotle accord justice much longer treatment than any other virtue; the whole of the *Republic*, at least nominally, is given over to justice, as is the whole of book five of the *Nicomachean Ethics*. But justice, a matter of relationships outside the family circle, is primarily a male concern (despite tragic heroines like Electra and Antigone), not only because it was normally men who operated in the wider world, but also because justice is inextricably tied up with public authority and government. In the first book of the *Republic* it is no mere accident of the progress of a particular conversation that discussion shifts from the more obvious questions of paying back what one owes to problems of who shall rule, what kinds of laws are passed in what kind of states, and the idea, beloved both of Thrasymachus and of Socrates, of the real ruler and his modes of operation. In other words discussion of justice leads immediately to questions of power; and it was precisely because of their lack of power that women were in a subordinate position in Greek society even when that society was democratic. "Democracy" meant equality before the courts and participation in government for all free males over a specified age; although women were counted as citizens, they did not have all the rights and responsibilities of male citizens: quite specifically they did not serve as jurors and they did not vote in the Assembly.

Perhaps the most fundamental principle behind all forms of government is that those worthy of power, in some sense of worthiness, are the ones who should exercize it. Thus in Greek terms aristocrats judged a class deserving of authority, democrats held that power is properly shared between all adult males. Both in Plato and in Aristotle good and bad forms of government are distinguished by the touchstone of whether the governing group, be it large or small, concerns itself exclusively with its own interests, or whether it also seems to promote the interests of the governed. But when dealing with general questions of interest and government, Greek thinkers, as we have already observed, tend not to notice what is regarded today as a peculiarly salient feature of the topic, namely that power is sought not only for the rewards it brings, wealth, ability to do what one likes, access to women and boys, adulation etc., but that it is psychologically attractive in and for itself, almost like a noxious drug. It would be an overstatement to say that this aspect of the phenomenon of power was wholly hidden from ancient thinkers, but its importance was largely unnoticed and uncommented. The comparatively frequent, Stalin-like, phenomenon of the "ascetic" tyrant seems little known, and perhaps was rarely to be found, in antiquity.

Different attitudes to power in ancient political thought may help us to explain something of the origin of the notion of female inferiority: women were less fitted, through mere lack of strength, to take power; and the uses of the power of which the ancient writers speak are to a marked extent "male" uses of power: access to women and boys is of primary significance among the abuses. And even among "honourable" forms of government the question of strength matters. One of the primary purposes of government was and is to protect the state, to preserve its constitution and the lives of its members. In ancient terms this meant, above all, the ability to fight when necessary. Physical weakness and pregnancy inhibited that. From such elemental facts conventions and norms arise.

Before leaving the question of whether metaphysical or sociological explanations should be sought for the view that women are intellectually and morally inferior, let us call in a particularly perceptive writer. It is appropriate that it was Augustine, at the end of what we conventionally call the Ancient World, who was the first to realize, or to assert, that Power was basically the religion, the way of life, of the ancients. The traditional religions are merely disguises for that basic phenomenon, power as such, which was worshipped. That being so, we need not be surprised that in so far as it was men who were the possessors of that power, they should "disvalue" those who were without it, that is, women, and also children, slaves, and others such as resident foreigners (metics) who were in a city but not of it.

Finally, Epicurus. Again it seems no accident that the only Hellenistic philosopher specifically to teach withdrawal from public life, to argue that public life is almost always both painful and therefore undesirable, should have been the most attractive to women and slaves, that is to the most unpolitical, or politically excluded classes. Power is anathema to

Epicurus; it is always a source of pain.[13] And with the renunciation of power and politics, and the return to a higher evaluation of a very specific kind of private life, we are free of the obsession with conventional power-structures and social structures. Even the family, or some kind of extra-familial, Platonic-style arrangement for the generating of children, ceases to be necessary for the Epicurean sage; and an attempt is made to build up a new ethic on wholly different principles, not on virtue understood, as the ancients understood it, primarily as an epiphenomenon of the world of affairs, but as based on the search for pleasure and the avoidance of pain. In a sense it is a return of men to what the ancients thought of as a woman's domain. But in that domain there is no reason for the superiority or inferiority of either males or females.

III

Children

For children we have in some ways even less detailed evidence than for women. And the problem is different at a theoretical level; for although children may have rights and gradually responsibilities, these rights are not all identical with those of adults, and the responsibilities are quite different. It would be hard to disagree entirely with any ancient thinker who said that children have to be helped to mature, to grow, to move from some kind of potentiality to the fulfillment of their capacities. But even in this area there are real differences of opinion: it appears that Aristotle,[14] and perhaps many others, thought that at some stage before birth the fetus could not be described as an individual at all, and that even after birth he is in a number of important respects to be listed merely among the animals, the creatures of sensation but not of reason. That is not to say that Aristotle held that a child is worth no more than an animal because it cannot *yet* use its reason properly to moderate its instincts. For he knew well enough that the *yet* is important, that children *will* (as a rule) learn to moderate their instincts, and that to some degree they are always capable of doing so. But it is certainly true, on the other hand, that when considering children Aristotle always thinks of what they will become. As we have seen already, he held that since they are not yet developed, not yet possessors of a mature intelligence, they are less valuable than adults, who are. Here again we must take note of what seems to be a marked influence of the conventions and customs of Greek society.

It was almost universally held in antiquity that a child has no intrinsic right to life in virtue of being born.[15] What mattered was being adopted into a family or some other institution of the society. Both Plato and

Aristotle, as well as the Stoics, Epicurus, and presumably Plotinus, accept the morality of the exposure of infants, and presumably also abortion, on eugenic or sometimes on purely economic grounds.[16] Certainly they would have rejected abortion purely on the request of the woman—as would almost any moralist in antiquity—but rejection would be on the grounds of injury to the husband rather than because of the value of the child. We see here further clear evidence of the ancient view that somehow value is acquired, either by the development of intelligence or by the acceptance into society. There is no reason to think that the philosophers made substantial advances on the assumptions of the general public in this regard.

Children, in fact, are valued in so far as they can be turned into adults. With the exception of a few late Stoics, there is little appreciation in the writings of the philosophers that childhood has any value of its own, that it might be judged on its own terms.[17] The distinction between "childish" and "childlike" can be made in Greek, easily enough, but it is far from the forefront of thought. Perhaps the saying "Unless ye become as little children" is a great deal more revolutionary in the context of ancient philosophy than it may seem to us, accustomed as we are to the notions of "child-centered" education and respect for the spontaneity of the young. Indeed if values are seen in terms of attributes which can be found fully-developed only in male adults, there is no reason to attribute particular value to children as such. It is a case of women and children last!

Do we see any difference in the views of Epicurus? Yes and no. Or perhaps the evidence is too meagre to enable us to make a clear judgment. Certainly the child is not valued as such. We have already noticed the advice to expose. And the wise man will not normally have children; they are the cause of too much trouble. But Epicurus cannot take the view, common to almost all other ancient philosophers, that it is what we grow into that counts, or that it is our success in attaining virtue. These things are unimportant; pleasure is what matters, and that may be equally available for the child as for the man. Indeed in one sense—and the Stoics took a similar view—the child is especially admirable, for he is not yet corrupted by false opinions, and his natural desire for pleasure and aversion to pain is not yet inhibited, even in part, by bogus and misleading talk of virtue. Here indeed the child is godlike, though he has not the means to ensure satisfaction which are necessarily available to the gods. But although Epicurus was fond at least of some of the children of his friends,[18] and perhaps also less inclined to regard them as mini-adults or potential adults than most of his contemporaries and philosophical predecessors, we must repeat that there is no evidence that he accorded them any particular value or rights, except, at times, as "adjuncts" of their parents. For Epicurus rights are to be claimed, and children as such do not make claims which we have good reason to recognize.

IV

Slaves

We have already considered the position of slaves in Aristotle. Little more need be said here, for Aristotle was not alone in thinking slavery both natural and unavoidable. For Aristotle, as we have seen, *if* machines could work automatically,[19] perhaps slaves would be unnecessary; but that is an absurd sort of conditional, and we should be in no doubt that if the city is to survive, if the best life is to be possible for those capable of it, many others must be enslaved. In any case, there are many for whom slavery is a good. Slavery in fact was an institution in ancient society, and, to an even greater degree than the institution of marriage and the family, its necessity was universally assumed, even by philosophers. Critics of slavery as an institution were rare and virtually unnoticed;[20] even Epictetus, himself an ex-slave, finds only the brutality of the slave-owner unacceptable, not the existence of slavery itself.

Despite the very few who criticized slavery as such as contrary to nature, the Aristotelian argument from need must normally have seemed irrefutable. If the good life could not exist without slaves, then substantial disagreement must be only about whom it is appropriate to enslave. Furthermore many philosophers, especially those, like Aristotle, who were suspicious of revolutionary change, were prepared to give explicit formulation to beliefs which were in any case widely held: that the basic institutions necessary for the good life would not change with the passing of time; and that history is worked out exclusively by the choices and behaviour of individuals. Hence with some exceptions (such as debt-bondage) criticism of institutions, rather than of the behaviour of the individuals working within those institutions, is more limited than the radicalism of a Plato or a Diogenes might lead us to expect. It is difficult for us, living since the eighteenth century in a period of ever-increasing change, to imagine that the way of life of the vast masses of people over the thousand years or so which comprised the Greco-Roman world varied very little in broad outline. Certainly there might be plagues, famines or wars, but customary rhythms of life continued, almost unchallenged; the utopian proposals of a *few* philosophers made no difference to that.

V

What then can we conclude about the relative importance of metaphysics or of institutions and conventions in affecting the value of individuals in the ideas of the ancient philosophers we have considered? That of the institutions slavery was by and large the most immune to criticism, because it seemed necessary, and therefore natural. As with power more generally, so with slavery in particular, the ancient moralists preferred to concentrate on abuses, rather than on the nature of the institution itself. As for other institutions, such as marriage and the family, they exercize considerable influence, as traditionally conceived, on the more conservative Aristotle; and the same may be said of traditional views of the different roles of men and women in the processes of reproduction. Against that, however, should be set the fact that the Platonists, the Cynics, the Stoics and the Epicureans make revolutionary proposals for institutional change despite the vast weight of tradition in a number of sensitive areas.

It might seem that we could conclude from this that in a surprisingly large number of instances, metaphysics has triumphed over traditions, conventions and prejudices. Such a conclusion would bear eloquent testimony that we should take with the utmost seriousness the claims made by the philosophers that they were prepared to follow reason wherever it led, and that they consistently upheld the Socratic claim that the unexamined life is not worth living. A word of caution, however, should be inserted. Although many Greek philosophers, as we have seen, felt free to attack some of the basic institutions and conventions of their society, the justifications they offered for their new proposals were not always free from the traditional assumptions of the institutions they criticized. Hence Plato can still, at times, think of women as inferior and the Cynics can still find it hard for women to be Cynics. The case of Aristotle, however, is the most instructive, for he often allows traditional ideas to impose interpretations of a metaphysical thesis which are permitted but not necessitated by the thesis itself. And with slavery such attitudes are almost universal.

We must conclude, with regard to matters of human value, not that the theories of particular philosophers were necessarily vitiated by a residue of traditional belief, but that where philosophical proposals were open to a traditional "interpretation" or "justification", that fact should not be overlooked. In other words the problem lies not so much with the logic of philosophical deductions but sometimes rather with their axioms. As Newman once said: Ten years later I found myself in another place; paper logic is but the record of it". So we must not forget the nature of the justifications offered by ancient philosophers in their attacks on venerable institutions, while still retaining our admiration for the spirit of boldness and intended disinterestedness in which they were frequently advanced.

CHAPTER TWELVE

INDIVIDUALS AND PERSONS

We began with the concept of rights and the Declaration of Human Rights, and asked ourselves on what basis we could approach the question of human rights in the ancient world. It seemed best to consider the evaluation of the human person and what basis such an evaluation might have. We did not approach the question through a lexicographical scrutiny of Greek words for value, for although such words exist (axiōma, axia), they are little help to us. We may now observe that these words have not come up in the course of our enquiry itself, for although *axiōma* means "reputation", what is thought of one, this meaning has no special significance or emphasis in philosophical texts; and although *axia* is a technical term in Stoicism, it is only used to describe a sub-group of phenomena which are neither virtues nor vices, but which are said to have worth (*axia*) in so far as they may lead us towards virtue and away from vice.

But although the word "value" in our sense appears lacking in philosophical Greek—*axiō*, however, gives some of the right sort of connotations—that is no reason for despondency. The same kind of problem would have arisen if we had considered the concept of "rights" merely from the point of view of the existence of philosophical terminology. Obviously the word "rights" can be translated, though perhaps not by a single word, into Greek. There is, indeed, even a single word *atimia* which is used for the deprivation of civil rights, of the rights of a citizen; but that is not a broad enough notion for our present purposes. For we should not assume, at least in classical Greece, that if a man loses his citizen rights, he becomes an outlaw, possessed of no rights at all, who may be maltreated or killed with complete impunity. Even if he is not protected by civil or criminal law, he is still to some extent under the protection of the gods.

Nevertheless, although we should not be unduly impressed by the fact that there are no Greek words corresponding very closely to the notions of "value" and "rights", and that philosophical investigation did not lead to their introduction, the non-existence of the terms is not wholly without significance. When a concept is identified as such, it tends to be given a new name; or a name which previously had some more limited or different purpose is given a new function. In the history of Greek philosophy we can frequently observe such developments: Aristotle seems to have thought that his pre-Socratic predecessors could deploy the concepts of quality and matter, hence that when a philosopher claimed that all was composed of air or fire, he was using the term "matter" in the way Aristotle could himself accept. But that is not the case; Greek philosophers did not start with the concepts of form and matter, substance and quality, cause and effect. By philosophizing, they came to analyze the world and to recognize such categories within it. The history of ethics shows a similar development. As any Socratic dialogue makes plain, the Greeks did not have a precise concept even of individual virtues, though that did not stop them talking about virtues or people being virtuous.

The point needs to be laboured, since it seems to have caused much unnecessary confusion, particularly in discussions of the Homeric and archaic periods of Greece. A concept can, of course, be in use before it is isolated and discussed philosophically; but it is paradoxical to suppose that isolation and philosophical discussion leaves usage unaffected, at least the usage of sophisticated people. There is no reason to suppose that the Greeks always thought in the same categories as we do, even when they used terms, for example ethical terms, which are apparently equivalent to ours. Consider once again the word "courage". In the whole discussion of that term in the *Nicomachean Ethics* of Aristotle—and it is a long discussion (1115A6-1117B23)—no single instance of what we should call "moral courage" is considered. The Greeks seem to have thought of courage in irredeemably physical, active and indeed warlike terms. Aristotle will not even allow the man facing death by disease to be called courageous (1115A30). Similarly with the notion of "happiness"; the Greeks seem to have found it difficult to imagine that a man could be "happy" unless he is physically well-sized and well-shaped: Epicurus still makes the point about the bodies of the gods.[1] Yet we are often inclined to think that *eudaimonia* in ancient texts more or less corresponds with what we normally understand by the word "happiness". There are, of course, many other more important differences (such as the role of the will) between *eudaimonia* and happiness, but the matter of physical "excellence" perhaps demonstrates their non-correspondence most startlingly.

In the course of this investigation, we have found not only no adequate terms, but no explicit theory of human rights and only traces of a generalized theory of human value. Doctrines which *emphasize* men's "divine spark" seem to offer a better opportunity for the development of such ideas than do the teachings of Plato, who bases value on characterization by goodness, or of Aristotle, who prefers to laud the possession of certain qualities of intellect. But in the Stoic version of the "divine spark"—and it is the most developed—the pantheistic nature of the system as a whole prevents any development along modern lines. For within such a system it is difficult to distinguish the individual at all as a unitary person possessing rights.

But reflection on pantheism helps to identify the root of the more basic problem. For it seems that the primary reason for the lack of a theory of rights is the unclear status of the individual and the tendency to regard marks of individuality as degrees of imperfection, of failure to reach the ideal or paradigm case. In the case of Plato we have endorsed, with certain limitations, the view that individuality is something to outgrow. Only in the *Phaedrus* do we get the modification that there is a plurality of perfect types, but even there we assume that, though perfect of its kind, the Apollonian individual is inferior to the Zeus-like. Similarly in Aristotle, there is almost no discussion of individuality; and one is left to thresh out the question of whether it depends on form or on matter, perhaps to come to the conclusion that it is the particular "informed" matter which is the individuating cause within the species which form represents. For although Aristotle argues that individuals are "real" and substantial, and although, after an early "semi-platonizing" period, represented by the *Categories*, he rejects the view that secondary substances (genera and species) are also real existents, he still thinks that philosophy can deal with individuals only in so far as they are members of classes, and that it has nothing to say about their individuality as such. Such an attitude at least *suggests* that although individuals exist, their individuality itself has no importance.

With the Stoics one might expect something different and more "hopeful", for two reasons: the Cynic roots of much of Stoic ethics, and the metaphysical theory of common and individual qualities which the Stoics teach, and in which so much more emphasis seems to be placed on the individual qualities. But Cynicism in this matter gets us nowhere. For although Cynic freedom emphasizes the individual, the emphasis does not lead to concern for his value or rights as such. The ideal individual is free from the conventions of the city and of social life. In that regard he is "different" from his fellows. But the lack of detail in the Cynic characterization of the sage, the tendency to speak of him as a member of a class whose only interesting feature is the ability to parade his release from subservience to convention offers nothing. Indeed far from the Cynics advocating any general theory of rights or of value, they exaggerate the élitist tendencies inherent in all ancient ideas of freedom; they emphasize contempt for the unfree and complete unconcern with the miseries to which the "servile" masses of humanity are surrendered through their own vice or folly.

Again the Stoic theory of common qualities might have been used to encourage respect for man as such; and historically it may have been a factor in the formulation, by certain Platonists, of the theory that individuals too exist in the intelligible world—a theory which must be viewed in context as a daring attempt to overcome the problem of individuality which Platonism generally ignored or dismissed. But although in Stoicism each individual man is differentiated by his common *and* his individual qualities, the doctrine that the ruling part of each of us is itself a segment or fragment of the divine Reason nullifies the possible advantages. For in their purified form these fragments are simply rationality, and as such qualitatively, though not numerically, equal and identical. Although the Stoic sages—those like Socrates and Cato who were recognized by the school as models of virtue—were obviously not qualitatively identical in fact, the theory had to maintain that they are; at least in so far as they are moral, and at least as regards their ruling part.

This question needs to be pursued further, for the idea of two identical persons seems paradoxical. If we think of a person, we think not of an identical but of a unique individual, not of a substitutable unit, but of a special case.

For human behaviour and human action are in obvious ways (which are admittedly often difficult to formulate) distinct from the behaviour of inanimate objects—which are subject to more easily identifiable laws of cause and effect; and significantly different too from the behaviour of animals. That being so, then the subject which performs so differently, the decision-making human subject which itself behaves and acts so distinctively, must also be distinguished from all non-human individual units. Yet there is no clear-cut discussion in antiquity of the peculiarity qua individual of that special kind of unit which is the human person.[2] It seems to be assumed that a general theory about individuals will do for human individuals as well; and, as we have seen, even such general theories are themselves only to be found in traces here and there. Human individuals, like other items, are discussed in terms of possessing various *types* of value-producing qualities.

The philosophy of Epicurus bears striking witness to the lack of concern about "personal" individuality, for in Epicurus' world it seems that there are even gods who are numerically different but qualitatively identical. Yet Epicurus aside there are in other ancient thinkers interesting discussions of what it is to be human, which yet leave out the question of uniqueness. We must now consider this fact, and try to determine a possible explanation.

In both Plato and Aristotle it is in virtue of his possession of certain mental powers that man is distinguished from animals. Aristotle proclaims this clearly when he recognizes in man a particular faculty (*dianoia*) which no animals possess. Hence man is able, in the moral area, to control his instincts rather than be led by them. But in Plato and Aristotle this very faculty (if we may call it that in both cases) is almost viewed as though it were a computer. The mind can work out or decide rationally what to do, and then proceed to act. It is true that Plato in particular does not always speak in such terms: in the ninth book of the *Republic*, as well as in the myth of the *Phaedrus*, the rational part of the soul (*logistikon*) is endowed with emotional powers and experiences appropriate pleasures. But a more characteristic attitude still appears in the late dialogue *Philebus*, where a life of pure intellect is specifically contrasted with a life of pleasure. The human subject can experience intellectual activity *and* pleasure—indeed some intellectual activities produce pure pleasure—but, it seems, as two separate phenomena. Intellectual activity qua intellectual activity—as with the gods—is not pleasurable; it is the whole "person" engaging in it who feels pleasure. But far from this leading to a higher estimation of the "person" as a special type of individual, it leads to a devaluation of the "person" in comparison with a special kind of unit, namely the mind. One might indeed suppose that Plato, who associates human *worth* with qualification by goodness, would be more likely to identify human individuals as unique than would Aristotle, who thinks about value exclusively in terms of the functions of an intellect which distinguishes men from animals; that is, more directly on the "computer-style" model. But he does not do so; perhaps because of the influence of the model of form stamping matter as a seal-ring marks wax. If the Platonic form is all-important, and if it is successfully deployed, it will turn out identical models on the material mold. Only so far as it fails to achieve perfect instantiation, will its individual products be qualitatively distinct. In Aristotle the process is different, but the result is the same. Here the individual minds (and perhaps above all the individual active intellects) which seem to be the sources of the worth of each individual, are either qualitatively identical or desirably so.[3] No value can be found in their being unique.

A comparison may clarify the theory to which Plato and Aristotle assent. It seems as though they think of the highest mind as like an ideal language. This language can contain and express all the nuances of actual languages, so that no "untranslateable" differences remain. Thus the words and phrases in the ideal language are perfect and all variations will be comparatively impoverished.

Let us also notice that in Plato and Aristotle there is no discussion of the special features of different "classes" of unities (inanimate unities, animal unities, human unities) insofar as these may affect each individual member of a class qua individual. Indeed from Plato's remarks about "monads" and "henads" in the *Philebus* (15AB) it would seem that all unities are simply envisaged as similar qua unity. With the Stoics, there is some discussion of the principle of unity at different levels of being; and different terms are employed for the various unifying factors in different types of individuals (*hexis, psychē*, etc.). But the Stoics, so far as we know, did not pursue this point in the direction of seeing grounds for a high evaluation of individuality *within* a particular group as related to the specific nature of the group to which the individual belonged. The opportunity was there, but was not taken; perhaps, as we suggested, because the Stoics were distracted from concentration on the peculiarly human which their psychosomatic theories of human action might have made possible by the pantheistic nature of their cosmos as a whole: and indeed not only by the pantheism of their cosmos, but by its finitude, for in Stoicism, as with Plato and Aristotle, perfect being is finite being, and a theory which could associate perfection with individual uniqueness might seem to compromise that principle of finitude.

Now with Plotinus greater opportunities for development are available, for the One, the source of value, is infinite. And it may be no accident, as we have already suggested, that it is in Plotinus too where there seem to be Forms not of all individuals, but of all individual *persons*, such as Socrates. This indeed suggests that Plotinus distinguished in a non-trivial sense between human individuals and other kinds of particular units. For these other units do not apparently require a Form of the individual to explain their being.

At the very least it should be noted that even if, in Plotinus' final analysis, there are no Forms of individuals, the mere fact that he raises the question particularly about human beings shows that he is fighting his way towards identifying the problem of human uniqueness. We should also note, however, that although he is apparently aware of the Stoic distinctions between types of unities, he makes no more use of them than the Stoics in treating of the problem of differences in value between different types of individuals. Furthermore there is no more evidence in Plotinus than in the other major ancient thinkers which points to a clear, conscious and deliberate identification of that difference between inanimate and animate, human and non-human particulars with which every Greek and Roman must have been to some degree unconsciously familiar—and which we met in the passage from Cicero's *De Amicitia* (14, 13) quoted at the beginning of this study: "What is so absurd as to delight in empty things...and not to delight a little in a sentient being?" The philosophers seem to overlook the obvious importance of the question for the sake of generalizations about particulars as a whole. We can perhaps identify the single most important factor in this oversight. But first a final point about Plotinus' near miss.

It is certainly with Plotinus that the problem of the recognition of human individuality presents itself in its most striking and interesting form. Since scholarly study of the *Enneads* was renewed in the early years of the present century, the nature of the union of the self with the One has been a subject of frequent disagreement; and the problem of "mysticism" has been linked with further dispute about the degree of "personality" to be attributed to the One itself. It is inappropriate to discuss the latter issue now, but we may assume that there are in Plotinus' concept of the One a number of "personal" characteristics. In general, the One is viewed more in the personal light of a God of religion than as an Absolute of metaphysics.

Our present concern is with the problem of the individual man and his uniqueness. In the Plotinian union with the One there is reason to believe that the individuality of the self is not wholly lost.[4] Difference, seemingly viewed as qualitative difference, between the One and the elevated soul, is suspended at the moment of ecstasy, but will always return insofar as we are never identified with or as the One, but rather united with it for more or less brief periods of time. The self on these occasions seems to be suspended, as one's being is entirely "concentrated" on one's source; but in Plotinus we recall that each individual soul, indeed any individual being, has been left "outside" the One at its "creation".[5] It is a different creature. Here lies a most important difference from Stoicism. Were Plotinus' system pantheistic, each being would lose its individuality, or rather would abandon the semblance of individuality which it appeared to possess, at the moment of union with the One. But although Plotinus' system is neither pantheist nor "panenhenic"—a religious thesis in which the soul is identified not with the universe but with the source and cause of the universe as a kind of Absolute Self[6]—his language and probably his thought is imprecise on the individuality he must necessarily accept for the human soul. This itself arises in part because he has not raised the problem of individuality *formally*. As we have already observed, we can use concepts—indeed we do so constantly—without examining them as concepts in themselves; but when we do so examine them, we find that not only are "earlier" problems clarified, but that the way is open for the investigation of fresh ones.

We have argued that for a number of reasons, the thought of Plotinus is, of all ancient systems considered here, the most suited for the development of a theory of rights, because it comes nearest to recognizing the individual person and hence the individual person's value. But although Plotinus comes closest, he does not get there; and since in the study of the history of philosophy it is important to observe both what a philosopher says and what he does not say on any particular topic, I have tried to show something of *why* he does not get there.

What is it that makes the final step so difficult? Is there some particular feature of Plotinus' thought, a feature which he shares with his predecessors, which would have to be abandoned before the final step could be taken? There is only one particularly striking candidate. The problem lies, as we have several times hinted, with a particular thesis about perfection. So long as perfect being was associated with finite being, then the notion of being perfect carried with it the notion of an identifiable and precise characterization. Now although the One in Plotinus is not finite (it is the world of Forms which is finite), the ethical implications of this development are not worked out; the new theory served a metaphysical, not an ethical purpose. In Plotinus' under-developed ethics the older Platonic way of thinking of perfection—leading to the postulating of a set of perfectly identical beings—still casts its shadow. It seems that nothing could have been done to reformulate the ancient notions of individuality until a number of assumptions about perfection and perfectability had been cleared away. And to make such a change would have required (and did require in Augustine) a much greater emphasis on the *difference* between what ultimately creates (whether temporally or extra-temporally) and what is created, between God and the perfect soul.[7]

That is not to say that a theory of human value must *always* be transcendental—it is not the place to raise that question here; it is to say that historically, in the Ancient World, a theory of God which marked the gap between creature and creator more clearly was needed before a fuller and better account of the individual person and his value could be developed. The Cynic, Stoic and Aristotelian roads to this in antiquity were dead ends; the Platonic road was opened up but not developed fully in pagan Neoplatonism. Aliens—barbarians, according to Porphyry[8]—had more success.

CHAPTER THIRTEEN

A NEW PERSPECTIVE?

The problem of the impact of Christianity on ancient society may take many forms. We can consider the "classical" question of whether or in what sense Christianity contributed to the downfall of the Roman Empire, in what ways it changed Roman law and institutions, and its effects on art and literature. But frequently it has been asserted that the impact of the conquering religion was more fundamental: that it presented new themes and new insight into the nature of man of such a kind as to deserve the title revolutionary in the context of ancient society. So Nietzsche spoke of the transvaluation of all ancient values, thus agreeing in his diagnosis, if not in his appreciation, with Luther. Most of these sweeping theses have proved attractive and deceptive: Christian "love" is not entirely opposed to the Platonic version, though many of its emphases may be different. But the Christian doctrine that "salvation" is by faith (whether or not "formed" by love) must be recognized as affording hope to Jew and Greek, slave and free, male and female.

But we may say, surely Epictetus, for example, offers as much: what matters is virtue; sex, class, race, or social position are matters wholly indifferent. All have the opportunity, and the capacity for virtue and hence for value. But herein rests the problem. We have identified various theories about human value as being, in comparison with others in antiquity, more "democratic". But in developing these "democratic" features, even a writer like Plotinus, who we thought came closest to a theory of the basic and inalienable residual value and rights of all human beings, is still inclined to think entirely in terms of capacity and achievement, to propose not that at a certain basic level all are equal in a non-trivial sense, and therefore possessed of certain inalienable rights, but that all are made equal by a metaphysical process which can, however, be reversed by human choices: and reversed in so radical a fashion that with the total failure to achieve excellence goes a total loss of even minimal value. Thus in general we may identify only *two* basic types of position in the non-Christian thought of antiquity: one which simply asserts or argues that for whatever reason (e.g. lack of *nous*) men are born unequally valuable in some ultimate sense of "valuable"; the other, the more "democratic", which urges that men are born potentially or in capacity of equal value (and with equal rights), but also that such rights are alienable, sometimes *in toto*, and that thus it could turn out that some people get themselves into a position of having no rights at all.

The case of Plotinus (and of other Neoplatonists) is particularly interesting in that they make a clear and necessary connection at the metaphysical level between "being" (existence) and goodness, that is, they argue that each existent, qua existent, is possessed of a certain measure of goodness and "excellence". But this "metaphysical" excellence seems not to imply the necessary possession of value, however paradoxical such a position may seem to be. Presumably Plotinus and the others are so concerned to emphasize human choices that they are blind to the oddity of holding both that something (someone) is good, and that it has lost all value. And that too despite the greater emphasis on the individual person in the Neoplatonic systems.

II

In concluding a study of ancient philosophical ideas about the value of man, I cannot attempt to treat the Patristic period systematically, or to consider more than a fragment of the material available to us. Hence I have chosen to comment on one or two of the earlier Christian writers whose knowledge of non-Christian thought is such that they may exhibit in their own persons the clash between the older attitudes we have been considering and a thesis of which we can find traces in early Christianity, namely that all men are created equal in the sight of God and remain possessed of residual value and rights whatever they do and regardless of how they behave.

Love thy neighbour as thyself. Judge not that ye be not judged. Certainly these two texts are fundamental to Christianity and, despite much egregious exegesis, their basic meaning is not difficult to discern. The second emphasizes that it is God and not man who is the judge of man, that at the moral (as distinct from the legal) level man's powers of judgment are inadequate, for we find it easy to make (insecurely based) judgments about other people while largely lacking the moral integrity required for an honest appraisal of ourselves. But this text of the New Testament does not bring us to the sort of problem with which we are presently concerned. For although it says that we are not to condemn, let alone find anyone utterly worthless, it has, on the surface at least, nothing to say on the more basic "metaphysical" and "theological" problem of whether in fact (in God's eyes, etc.) there are such worthless human beings, potentially or actually. Perhaps "love thy neighbour" takes us further, for it certainly implies that as a rule we ourselves are lovable and so are our neighbours. For it seems absurd to be told to "love" someone who is in no way lovable. And if our neighbours are all, to some extent and in some respects, lovable, presumably they must all to some extent be good.

That certainly is the most natural interpretation of the text, but many problems still remain. For it might be argued that some at least of our neighbours were lovable once, but that this claim has now been forfeited. All men are at some stage good, saveable, lovable, etc., but in the course of time many of them have lost their excellence and, although we do not know it—for we cannot judge—all claim to value as well. Such an interpretation could not be ruled out on the grounds of its contradicting scriptural texts like "God wishes all men to be saved", for He could so wish, while human perversity might prevent His will from being achieved. In theological terms, it will therefore be helpful to return to the series of texts, as treated by patristic writers, which deal with the creation of man in the image and likeness of God, for if that image and likeness is always in man, then some goodness, some value, should remain in him, while if it is at times totally deformed or destroyed, men would seem, as in the non-Christian writers, to be possessed of a divine spark which can somehow or other be completely extinguished by vice and thus reduced to the non-being from which it sprang. As has been observed regularly by those who have treated these topics,[1] the exegesis of the text of *Genesis* (1.26) dealing with the creation of man in the image and likeness of God is inextricably entangled in the patristic writers with the interpretation of those Platonic texts which assert that likeness to God is the goal of human striving.[2]

A second theme with which we should have to concern ourselves in a full study of Patristic writers, is that of the ontological relationship between goodness and existence, that is, how far Christian thinkers argue from the continuing existence of a person to his necessary continuing excellence—or at least to his necessary continuing potential excellence, for, as in the case of Origen's view of the restoration even of Satan to grace,[3] there is further opportunity here for potentiality to creep in. Perhaps some people, while being totally vicious, yet retain the capacity (given God's grace) for improvement. This may look like having one's cake and eating it, but it is a variant on our theme which is not without significance. It does not occur before Origen, however, and will therefore be left out of our present treatment.

Before looking at a few particular thinkers, we should return to the distinction between person and thing around which we observed that so many difficulties in the non-Christian writers revolve. In Christian terms, men are created by God in his image, by a definite act of will, and God is concerned with their well-being as such. This thesis in so clear and unambiguous a form does not exist in the non-Christian philosophers of antiquity. Certainly Socrates may have thought of himself, if the *Apology* is to be trusted, as sent on a kind of mission by Apollo to his fellow Athenians; and certainly Plato thinks that the gods are providentially concerned with what human beings do; but they do not create human beings as destined for any particular end. And in Stoicism and Neoplatonism the "creation" of man is the result of a process of metaphysical evolution in which the concern of the highest being for mankind, though it may not be entirely absent, is certainly not prominent. So we may wonder whether such concern of God's is prominent, and how prominent it is, in the earlier Christian writers, and whether it leads to anything like a doctrine of inalienable value or inalienable rights. Or perhaps the value is there, but the dimension of immortality, the view that this life is only morally important, has overshadowed, or actually destroyed the possibility of a theory of rights. Yet perhaps it should not have done so, for however brief it may be, this life is a proving ground, and the doctrine of purgatory was not sufficiently developed to allow this proving ground to seem any less important.[4] We shall therefore consider some of the following questions in Irenaeus, Tertullian and Clement of Alexandria, pausing only to note that philosophical thought in the Apostolic Fathers, the Apologists and even in Justin is still too limited in its achievements to enable us to make even the restricted type of enquiry that is to follow:

1. Does the author consider the theory of man as created in the image and likeness of God?

2. Does he hold that this image can be completely destroyed?

3. Does the theory of image and likeness guarantee rights and value in this world?

4. Is the question of value to be separated from the question of rights, since the rights can, as it were, be restored on the larger context of immortality?

5. How far does the radical egalitarianism of "neither Jew nor Greek, slave nor free, male nor female" become watered down by the influence of non-Christian practices and institutions? Is the radicalism to be envisaged only on a "heavenly" rather than an "earthly" plane, even by the philosophically minded?

6. Finally, we come to the question of whether the Christian writers are consciously aware of the pagan traditions about human value and whether they are prepared to react consciously against them.

Consideration of the earliest Christian attempts to deal with some of these questions is a large undertaking. The sketch which follows is to be regarded neither as an appendix to our studies of pagan antiquity nor as a complete treatment in its own right. Its goal is limited: to show something of the contrast between Christian and non-Christian thought in antiquity, while pointing out sufficient similarities between them to encourage scholars to treat the body of ancient philosophy as a whole.

II

Irenaeus

In a surprising number of ways Irenaeus is closer to the Apostolic Fathers and the Apologists than to Clement and the more sophisticated Christianity of the third century, though admiration for his master Polycarp and through him for the ancient tradition of the churches of Asia makes this fact more comprehensible. Thus as with the Apologists, so with Irenaeus, we do not find a great deal of material to help us at present: Irenaeus is not a philosopher, but a preacher and Scriptural exegete. Just occasionally, however, particularly in the last book of his *Adversus Haereseis*, we find relevant material. Especially in chapters six and sixteen there is extended comment on the text of Genesis (1.26) which says that man is made in the image and likeness of God. Irenaeus' interpretation, which he buttressed particularly with the authority of St. Paul, is that on his original creation in the person of Adam man conformed both to the divine image and to God's likeness, but that as a result of Adam's sin, the likeness has been lost. Thus, each of us, when we are born, is formed in God's image; and by obedience to God and progress in the moral and spiritual life we are able to restore the original likeness. We are composed, all of us, of three parts, when we are perfected: body, soul and spirit; but as result of Adam's sin of disobedience, the spirit is lacking while we remain imperfect. The Gospel provides us with the means of welcoming it back. In our life in the world, therefore, in our progress towards perfection, we are all formed in the image of God, and this image is to be viewed primarily in terms of our possession of free will. Irenaeus' account of this in the *Adversus Haereseis* (4.37.4) is somewhat unclear; it seems that "unfallen" man possessed free will which contributed both to his being an image and to his being a likeness of God, and that after the Fall we still retain enough of it, qua image alone, to be able to choose for or against the good life.

All men and women, therefore, after Adam, are equally capable of perfection—and, we should notice, this perfection seems to be viewed rather in terms of the freedom of the will than in terms of likeness to God as "mind". From this it follows that we are born equally valuable in God's eyes; and the new Christian doctrine of humility de-emphasizes the importance of claiming our value, without, of course, limiting our right to worship God as we choose. However Irenaeus' somewhat naive treatment of free will leaves him liable to assume that those who choose wrongly, and thus fail in their search for perfection, will lose their value, or perhaps throw it away. They will be justly disinherited by God; flesh and blood shall not inherit (*Adv. Haer.* 5.10). They have failed to reach the level of perfect humanity, that restoration (ἀποκατάστασις) and unity (ἕνωσις) of flesh, soul and spirit which is within our grasp. Hence eternal punishment (5.27). They are punished because they choose to be incomplete, because they fail to lay hands on the good offered them. They are worthy of evil, and must therefore be assumed to be worthless. We perhaps should reiterate at this point that Irenaeus is not a philosopher; unlike Clement of Alexandria he has not confronted philosophical reflection on the notion of likeness to God, except perhaps in its bastardized Gnostic form. Hence, after all, he offers little to help us with our theme of the interrelation of Christian and Greco-Roman motifs.

Finally it should be noted that Irenaeus has nothing to say about whether women, children, slaves, etc. are less valuable than men. Perhaps we can conclude, however, that in God's eyes they are all identical; it is choices that matter, and choices alone. Irenaeus is still sufficiently wedded to the idea that the Church is a people apart not to be much influenced in the direction of a "pagan" hierarchy of humanity either by philosophical theories or social conventions. He is still lucky enough not to need to face the problem of the integration of Christian and non-Christian thought. He is still occupied enough extracting the Christian flock from a pagan, or in his eyes neo-pagan (Gnostic) background.

III

Tertullian

For slightly different reasons the case of Tertullian must be pronounced to be similar. His Christianity, even in his Catholic period, is that of the expanding ghetto, the growing but embattled circle of Christians surrounded by the vicious and the persecutors. Tertullian's attitude towards those outside the Christian group is often merciless. Persecutors will be tortured in the afterlife, and the good Christian will rejoice at it.[5] The world around is divided into the elect and the rest, and the rest fully deserve what they are going to get.

Yet traces of a wider sympathy remain. Tertullian follows the already traditional view in his condemnation of abortion and the exposure of infants, and his hostility to bloodshed in the arena is not to be attributed only to the fact that Christians were among the victims.[6] Beyond that, indeed, Tertullian's rejection of the forms of Roman life cannot be put down entirely to any merely theoretical juxtaposition of Christian and pagan, of Athens and Jerusalem. It is normally wrong to hold office: it is not the part of a Christian to judge, and to kill, let alone to torture.[7] How does one square this with post-mortem rejoicing over the damned?

Because the judgment is that of God, not of men. Tertullian's outlook on man is dominated by the concept of the Christian God, and where his attitude to ancient views of man clashes with the Graeco-Roman past, the changes, in whatever direction, depend on the new concept of the deity. Yet although Tertullian quotes the text of *Genesis* about man being the image of God,[8] he makes little theoretical use of it. He is too close to the practical problem of the survival of his community to find the leisure, even had he wished it, for more abstract reflections on the possibility of human dignity. The nearness of the next world probably overshadows such "details" about this one. The only right with which Tertullian is concerned is the right to freedom of worship, which he claims to be a natural and universal right[9]—a novel enough claim indeed.

On slaves and children, even among the elect, he has virtually nothing to tell us; on women nothing particularly unusual for his times: they are the gate of hell, at least in the person of Eve, who destroyed God's image[10]; yet they can live a Christian, even a martyred life, like men. The two principal followers of Montanus were women.

IV

Clement of Alexandria

The last Christian thinker to be treated here, Clement of Alexandria, is in a different world from both Irenaeus and Tertullian. Irenaeus hardly notices society around him except in so far as it impinges on the Christian community. Tertullian strives with increasing bitterness to reject the "temptation" to find a *modus vivendi* with the external world that seems more and more necessary as the number (and education) of Christian believers increases. Clement, on the other hand, being well-versed in Greek literature and philosophy, neither wishes to live in isolation from the better features of Graeco-Roman thought nor to be submerged in its invitations to vice and its concomitant vices. Indeed his sympathies were strong enough and well enough known to incur suspicion bordering on hostility among the "simple" believers of Alexandria.

Like most of the Greek-speaking Christian writers who were to follow him, Clement is particularly concerned with the return of man to God—which helps him to link his Christianity with Platonism. Now offering a detailed exegesis of *Genesis* 1.26, and bringing it into line with Plato's remarks in the *Theaetetus* (176AB), Clement claims that man was originally formed in God's image and that, if he progresses in holiness, he will obtain a likeness to that of which he is born the image. Thus we all have the aptitude and capacity for virtue, and the "Gnostic", the perfected believer, has the thing itself (*Strom.* 6.12). This idea should ensure that for Clement there is always something valuable in man, since we cannot avoid the sign of our creation in God's image. The image seems not to be totally blotted out. But before looking at more detail, let us consider the nature of the progression of the good man from image to likeness: it is a progress by which we approximate to God as a "simple" and above all a rational being. As we progress, we become more like God qua rational. Hence, we may suppose, and the tests bear out this supposition, we eliminate as far as possible the "non-rational" elements of our person. Thus Clement, involving himself in the dispute between Aristotelians and Stoicizers about whether the "passions" should be extirpated, comes down for the more extreme position. *Apatheia* is the ideal; it is a form of love, not merely, as the Stoics would have it, a "emotionally rational state" (εὐπάθεια); and it is closely linked to likeness to God.[11] In passing we cannot avoid noticing how this increasing "rationalization" of the progress of the soul takes us in the direction of Greek philosophical enquiry in a way which seems alien to the simpler beliefs about the Christian God and his people we noted in Irenaeus.

Let us now look at a few implications of the new approach:

1. Since all human beings are created equal qua human beings we should even love our enemies,[12] qua men, as works of God (*Strom.* 1.6; 4.13)[13]; but we are apparently unequal in capacity and natural predisposition to virtue.

2. By themselves men are equal and equally lovable (*Paed.* 1.3; 1.6); but a degree of inequality is introduced by the distinction between male and female, though women too are capable of perfection if they become "unfeminine", and "manly" (*Strom.* 4.19; 6.12; 6.100.3). In discussing this thesis, we must take into account that Clement is influenced at this point not only, and perhaps even not primarily, by the Greco-Roman tradition, but by the Judaism of Philo of Alexandria,[14] to whose exegesis of the Old Testament he is constantly indebted, and by the *Gospel to the Egyptians*.[15] Males (vis-à-vis females) are superior—the beard is a sign of it (*Paed.* 3.3), and as a female progresses she becomes male. As in Philo the concept of maleness seems to have two forms: at a "lower", sexual level male is opposed as a partner to female; at a higher level male seems to mean asexual or, in this special sense, virgin.

We find in Clement, as a result, a strange ambivalence both about marriage, which is good though virginity is better (*Strom.* 4.147-9), and about the good life for women. Clement is quite clear that women must philosophize and seek virtue—do we see here something of the overemphasized influence of Musonius Rufus?—and that their virtue is one and the same with the virtue of men; but they are naturally weaker morally as well as physically (*Paed.* 2.33.2; 2.117.1), despite the fact that

Clement, following earlier Christian teaching, allows them equal opportunity to achieve the highest crown of martyrdom (*Strom.* 4.8). The idea of the perfect human being as in a special sense "male" probably accounts too for the inordinate emphasis, even by strict patristic standards, on sexual morality within the area of morality in general to be found in the *Paedagogus*[16]—and particularly for the emphasis on sexual morality for women who, as we have seen, are weaker and therefore, particularly in this area, more liable to sin (*Paed.* 2.11). Thus although virtue is common to men and women, women are to be veiled except at home; while allowed to exercize they are not to wrestle, but only to spin, weave, supervise the cooking and perform other household chores (*Paed.* 3.10). Yet even if subconsciously thinking primarily of the male, Clement regards marriage as a good in so far as it is directed to the birth of children; and man is an image of God in part at least in so far as he is generating the species in co-operation with his Maker.

But if masculinity and femininity, particularly the latter, are marks of inferiority,[17] they are also marks of individuality. Hence when we progress beyond them to the state of being "neither male nor female" (or hyper-male), one of our individualizing features is to be removed. Do we see evidence in this area of a persistence of the ancient view that individuality is something to outgrow? The notion of likeness to the *simpleness* of God might seem to reinforce that suspicion.

3. The process of growth from image of God to likeness to God—Ye shall be as gods (Ps. 81.6)—might suggest that the more advanced we are, the more valuable we become, though not that we have more rights, for the notion of man's rights before God would have seemed absurd to Clement. And indeed this is the case; the perfect believer, and therefore member of the Elect, or Gnostic, is a friend of God and more honoured by Him. The same attitude carries over into the way in which we are supposed to treat our neighbours. We should give to all who need, but we should give "justly", that is, in accordance with desert.

4. We are born in the image of God; but can that image be totally destroyed? If it cannot, it would seem that, contrary to the views of the classical philosophers, man's value cannot be entirely lost: existence, at least in the case of man, is then radically tied to value. A test of Clement's view may be provided by his attitude to God's punishments. Unless some of us are incurable, and thus wholly ungodlike, punishment should be—and Clement says it is—not only expiative and deterrent (*Strom.* 4.24) but purificatory. Clement does not talk about purgatory as such, but he thinks of post-mortem punishments as purgatorial (*Strom.* 6.14). Yet there are some who are incurable (*Strom.* 7.16.102), presumably consigned to hell; and these people must be suffering after death

in a non-purgatorial way, for it would seem paradoxical even for God to try to cure the incurable. In fact Clement tells us that fornicators are dead to God, corpses, abandoned by God (*Paed.* 2.100.1) and quite overcome by sin; they are beasts (*Paed.* 1.13). So again there seems to be a minimal group who lose all value; they are candidates for hell where, it seems, no degrading punishments will be spared them; rather they will seem appropriate. Yet Clement's thought in this area may be merely confused, for when dealing with the restoration of all things (ἀποκατάστασις) he seems to think differently (*Strom.* 7.56). Origen's more logical mind was to resolve the confusion, but heretically.

In brief then, we may conclude that Clement's doctrine of our being created in the image and likeness of God might have provided him with a theory that all human beings are possessed of basic and irreducible rights at least before their fellows. It does not do that in certain cases; and we can only assume that traditional beliefs and attitudes of the Greco-Roman world, combined in some cases with a new Philonic or more generally Alexandrian theory of inequality, succeeded in watering down what seems to be the potentiality of a new and radical approach. In particular in the case of the status of women Clement manages to graft a *de facto* superiority of men on to texts which preach that in Christ there is neither male nor female. As for bond and free, Jew and Greek, Clement certainly regarded Jews as inferior to Christians (as refusers of belief), though without the vigour of Tertullian in the matter; and he is as uninterested in the institutional relationships between bond and free as are any of his pagan predecessors. Real freedom is moral; those under sin are slaves (*Strom.* 4.3); being a slave affords as much scope for moral freedom as being a slave-owner. Although Clement is very conscious of the corrupting influence of the Roman theatre and arena, and of much else, he apparently sees nothing inherently corrupting in the institution of slavery itself, aware though he obviously was of the degrading acts which many slaves were regularly obliged to perform. For Clement it is enough that a slave can choose martyrdom (*Strom.* 4.8).

We should, however, note one area of morality in which the belief that we are formed in God's image is used as an argument for a well-established Christian view we have already observed to be sharply in conflict with standard ancient practice: abortion and exposure are sinful as unlawful forms of killing (*Paed.* 3.4). Such an attitude is in effect an extension into a new area of some kind of basic human right. And we note that in Clement the justification for the new strictness is not so much an appeal to justice but, presumably and interestingly enough, to the belief that in such cases at least the divine image cannot have been defaced.

Finally, if man is created in God's image, what he is depends on what God is.[18] Clement thought of God primarily as a superior Mind, at least when he philosophized rather than expounded the New Testament. Hence he put value on mind; hence in so far as he valued man as rational only, the fault, if such it be, lies with his doctrine of God. His God was still too much the God of the philosophers to allow him further change (or to be content with the simpler world of Irenaeus). Plotinus too, as we have seen, found that an inadequate view of the first principle involved not only problems in metaphysics but also in ethics and above all in philosophical anthropology.

At this point we bring our sketch of the complicated relationships between early Christian thought about human value and classical philosophy to a close. Enough has been said to indicate how much needs to be done in just a few of the more fruitful areas of enquiry. Complete evaluation of the Christian evidence can only be achieved, of course, when some measure of agreement has been reached about the non-Christian philosophers; and when it is more generally recognized that the Christians must be viewed against much of same background as their pagan rivals.

NOTES TO INTRODUCTION

[1] ἀντιφίλησις is perhaps first mentioned by Aristotle, *N.E.* 1155B28. You are not friends with a bottle of wine! Cf. *E.E.* 1236B3 ff.

[2] Of course Athenian lack of concern for human life, especially *foreign* life, had frequently appeared during the Peloponnesian War. Recall especially the arguments about whether or not to exterminate the Mytilenaeans (Thuc., 3.36-50).

[3] *Tusc.Disp.* 2.41. Cicero admits that others were more positively hostile; cf. M. Marius, *ad Fam.* 7.1. Seneca, who calls men a *sacra res* (*Ep.* 95.33) finds these shows vicious; cf. *Ep.* 7; *de Tranq. An.* 2.13. Cf also Pliny (*Ep.* 4.22), but in *Pan.* 33 Pliny argues, with Cicero, that they promote courage.

[4] K. J. Dover, *Greek Popular Morality* (Oxford 1974).

[5] J. M. Rist, *Eros and Psyche* (Toronto 1964).

NOTES TO CHAPTER ONE

[1] Note the presentation of Protagoras in Plato's dialogue (*Prot.* 320 D ff.).

[2] B 11 (DK) = Sext. Emp., *adv. Math.* 9.193.

[3] Cf. A. R. Hands, *Charities and Social Aid in Greece and Rome* (London 1968) 78.

[4] Plato still wishes him well and urges respect for him at *Laws* 879E.

[5] Aristophanes, *Clouds* 1078; cf Euripides, ap. Men., *Epitrep.* 765 f with E. R. Dodds, *The Greeks and the Irrational* (Berkeley 1951) 187.

[6] *Rep.* 379 B15-16.

[7] Cf. B. Williams, *Morality* (N.Y. 1972) 68-78.

[8] Cf. *N.E.* 1178B, though elsewhere (1179A25 ff.). Aristotle follows a more "popular" view of providence; cf. 1134B27 ff.

[9] Cf. J. M. Rist, *Epicurus: An Introduction* (Cambridge 1972) 140-163. For a different version of this indistinguishability see D. Lemke, *Die Theologie Epikurs* (Munich 1973).

[10] Though not, of course, among ordinary people; cf. A.-J. Festugière, *Personal Religion Among the Greeks* (Berkeley and Los Angeles 1960) and A. D. Nock, *Conversion* (Oxford paperback 1961).

NOTES TO CHAPTER TWO

[1] SVF 2.295.

NOTES TO CHAPTER THREE

[1] Cf. R. Robinson, *Plato's Earlier Dialectic* (Oxford 1948) 55; J. M. Rist, "Plato's Earlier Theory of Forms", *Phoenix* 29 (1975) 336-357.

[2] Note that Plato does not say that "being" entails "being good" or "doing good".

[3] Cf. G. Vlastos, "The Paradox of Socrates" in the *Philosophy of Socrates* (N.Y. 1971) 21.

[4] Cf. *Phaedo* 99D.

[5] G. Vlastos, "The Individual as an Object of Love in Plato", *Platonic Studies* (Princeton 1973) 6-11.

[6] *Lysis* 215B.C. If there is no need, there is no ἀγάπη or φιλία. All love is thus connected with utility, cf. Vlastos, "The Individual", 8-9. Note that in the *Lysis* passage Plato uses not the noun ἀγάπη but the cognate verb.
[7] L. A. Kosman ("Platonic Love" in *Facets of Plato's Philosophy*, ed. W. H. Werkmeister (Assen/Amsterdam 1976) 53-69) tries (to my mind unsuccessfully) to meet this point.
[8] Cf. J. M. Rist, "Plato's Earlier Theory of Forms", 336 ff.
[9] Fr. B25 DK.
[10] If I perceive, I perceive something (τινὸς) (*Theaet.* 160B); perception is of what exists, i.e. that which exists (*Theaet.* 152C).
[11] J. M. Rist, *Plotinus: The Road to Reality* (Cambridge 1967) 22.
[12] G. Vlastos, "Creation in the *Timaeus*: Is it a fiction?", *Studies in Plato's Metaphysics*, ed. R. E. Allen (London 1965) 401-419; J. Whittaker, "The Eternity of the Platonic Forms", *Phronesis* 13 (1968) 138 ff.
[13] R. Hackforth, *Plato's Phaedo* (Cambridge 1955) 85-86.
[14] After death souls continue to exist in space and time, in Hades (*Phaedo* 71E2); cf. J. Whittaker, *op. cit.* 138 ff.
[15] Rightly G. Vlastos, "Does Slavery Exist on Plato's *Republic*", *CP* 63 (1968) 291-5 = *Platonic Studies*, 140-6.
[16] *Rep.* 469C4-5; *Laws* 776C ff, 757A1, "Slaves and masters can never be friends".
[17] Cf. *Rep.* 470A-E; *Phil.* 18B7; *Laws* 799A, 819A.
[18] *Rep.* 592 B.
[19] At *Polit.* 262C-E Plato criticizes as bad logic the division of mankind into Greeks and barbarians. But that is only because barbarians differ among themselves as much as they differ from Greeks. Barbarians are probably still "generally" inferior to Greeks. On the whole topic, see the interesting remarks of R. Schlaifer, "Greek Theories of Slavery from Homer to Aristotle", in *Slavery in Classical Antiquity*, ed. M. I. Finley (Cambridge 1969) 168 (96).
[20] Cf. *Laws* 781B. Women are naturally (i.e. normally) inferior to men in "excellence"; *Rep.* 455D 1-5; cf. W. W. Fortenbaugh, "On Plato's Feminism in *Republic* V", *Apeiron* 9 (1975) 1-4.
[21] *Rep.* 461C.
[22] Fear of pregnancy may be a factor here.
[23] *Tim.* 42B, 91A. For much more similar material see D. Wender, "Plato: Misogynist, Paedophile and Feminist", *Arethusa* 6 (1973) 80-82.
[24] *Laws* 854DE, 855C ff.
[25] "Degrading" penalties are to be avoided, however, for free men, because they encourage resentment—which presumably matters less in the unfree (*Laws* 777A, 793E, cf. 854D, for branding of slaves and foreigners).
[26] *Theaet.* 176B, 176C-177E; *Rep.* 472CD, 613B.
[27] *Rep.* 469A8, 540C1-2.
[28] *Phaedr.* 252C, 256D.
[29] *Phaedr.* 249C.
[30] P. Merlan, *Studies in Epicurus and Aristotle* (Wiesbaden 1960) 66 ff.
[31] See Chapter one, note 9 above.
[32] G. M. A. Grube, *Plato's Thought* (Boston 1958) 148.
[33] *Theaet.* 157 BC, 209C7; cf. Porph., *in Isag.* 7.22 Busse.
[34] See p. 21.
[35] Arist., *Met* 990B16ff.
[36] See below p. 114 and Cf. R. Schlaifer, "Greek Theories of Slavery", 180 (108).
[37] J. M. Rist, *Eros and Psyche* 44-47.
[38] G. E. L. Owen, "The Place of the *Timaeus* in Plato's Dialogues", *CQ* 3 (1953) 79-95.
[39] H. Cherniss, "The Relation of the *Timaeus* to Plato's Later Dialogues", *AJP* 78 (1957) 225-266; J. M. Rist, "The Order of the Later Dialogues of Plato", *Phoenix* 14 (1960) 207-221.

⁴⁰ Cf. *Tim.* 27D.
⁴¹ πράττειν τὰ ἑαυτοῦ *Rep.* 435B5.
⁴² Arist., *Met.* 990B, 1079A, etc.
⁴³ *Met.* 1091B13-15.
⁴⁴ Cf. Proclus, *in Parm.* pp. 38, 31 ff; Iamb., *De Comm. Math.* 15, 5-18, 12 Festa with (recently) J. Dillon, *The Middle Platonists* (London and Ithaca 1977) 14.
⁴⁵ *N.E.* 1152Bff.
⁴⁶ Dillon, *op. cit.* 18.
⁴⁷ D.L. 6.3.
⁴⁸ Arist., *Met.* 1076A1.
⁴⁹ Arist., *De An.* 404B30.
⁵⁰ D.L. 4.16.
⁵¹ See above p. 25.
⁵² περιστροφή, *Rep.* 521C5.

NOTES TO CHAPTER FOUR

¹ See the generally sensible survey by C. J. de Vogel, "Did Aristotle Accept Plato's Transcendent Ideas", *Archiv. für Geschichte der Phil.* 47 (1965) 261-298.
² See in general W. J. Oates, *Aristotle and the Problem of Value* (Princeton 1963).
³ Cf. *N.E.* 1160B34; a husband rules his wife because he is said to be more worthy.
⁴ *De Gen. An.* 736B24.
⁵ Cf. Appendix B in A. L. Peck's Loeb. edition of *De Gen. An.*
⁶ J. M. Rist, "Notes on Aristotle *De Anima* 3.5" in *Essays in Ancient Greek Philosophy*, ed. J. P. Anton and G. L. Kustas (Albany 1971) 506-7.
⁷ J. M. Rist, *ibid.* 507.
⁸ *N.E.* 1134B18-35; *Rhet.* 1368B7ff., 1373B4ff.
⁹ *Pol.* 1253A2, 1278B12; cf. *N.E.* 1169B20. Many of the questions treated below are examined in more detail in my "Aristotle: The value of Man and the origin of Morality", *Can. Journal of Philosophy* 4 (1974) 1-21.
¹⁰ *Gen. An.* 736B3; 740A24.
¹¹ They also resemble slaves in that they may *respond* to reasoned admonition (*N.E.* 1102B34). Cf. W. W. Fortenbaugh, "Aristotle on Slaves and Women", in *Articles on Aristotle 2. Ethics and Politics* (ed. J. Barnes, etc., London 1977) 137.
¹² *N.E.* 1160B34.
¹³ Fortenbaugh (*op. cit.* 138) is right to observe that the inferiority of women is due not to their lack of reasoning powers, but to the fact that their reason is ἄκυρον, easily swamped by emotion (*Pol.* 1260A6ff.).
¹⁴ *Pol.* 1275Aff.
¹⁵ *N.E.* 1166A16ff., 1168B35ff., 1178A1ff. The point is already made in the *Protrepticus* (Fr. 6, p. 35, 11-12 Ross).
¹⁶ Cf. J. M. Rist, "The One of Plotinus and the God of Aristotle", *Review of Metaphysics* 27 (1973) 75-87.
¹⁷ The account that follows does not take account of the rather different ideals which Aristotle advocates in the *Eudemian Ethics*. If A. Kenny (*The Aristotelian Ethics* (Oxford 1978)) is correct in arguing that the *Eudemian Ethics* is later than the *Nicomachean*, we should have to allow that Aristotle had broadened his concept of superiority.
¹⁸ Fr. 5 Ross.
¹⁹ Cf. P. Merlan, *Studies in Epicurus and Aristotle* 19-20.
²⁰ J. M. Cooper, *Reason and Human Good in Aristotle* (Cambridge, Mass. 1975) 157-60, followed by Kenny, *op. cit.* 209.
²¹ Aristotle is aware in the *Nicomachean Ethics* (1169B3) that friendship is the greatest of external goods. But he is not thinking of contemplatives here; he observes that friendship affords the opportunity for beneficence.

NOTES TO CHAPTER FIVE

[1] Though not always, cf. G. Vlastos, "The Individual as the Object of Love", 16; Thuc. 2.37, 2-3; Arist., *Pol.* 1275A22-3.
[2] Plato, *Rep.* 557B, *Cf.* Thuc., 7.69.2.
[3] D.L. 6.35.
[4] Cf. E. R. Dodds, *The Greeks and the Irrational* 187-8.
[5] *Laws* 713C. At 691C Plato still seems to be saying only that the *young* will always be seduced by power. There is still apparently some hope for the old. At 875A-D he hopes that maybe one day someone superior to the temptation may arise—but he is not optimistic.
[6] Xenocrates, fr. 6 Heinze; cf. *Rep.* 597C, though this raises problems about forms of manmade objects which cannot be discussed here.
[7] D.L. 3.35.
[8] D.L. 6.11.
[9] See above p. 37.
[10] D.L. 6.24.
[11] D.L. 6.3.
[12] See below p. 65.
[13] Cf. Cic., *de Orat.* 3.67.
[14] *Meno* 93C ff; *Gorg.* 515E ff.; *Rep.* 488B ff.
[15] *Phaedo* 99C.
[16] Cf. G. Vlastos, "The Paradox of Socrates", in *The Philosophy of Socrates* (N.Y. 1971) 1-21.
[17] Cf. *Rep.* 487B ff.
[18] For Demonax, See D. R. Dudley, *A History of Cynicism* (Hildesheim reprint 1967) 158-162.
[19] D.L. 7.17.
[20] J. M. Rist, *Stoic Philosophy* (Cambridge 1969) 54-80.
[21] D.L. 7.4.
[22] Cf. J. M. Rist, "Zeno and Stoic Consistency", *Phronesis* 22 (1977) 170-171.
[23] Cf. especially Epictetus, *Disc.* 3.22.
[24] D.L. 7.160.
[25] SVF 1.409-421.
[26] Epict., *Disc.* 1.29.16; cf. J. M. Rist, *Stoic Philosophy* 228-231.
[27] M. Pohlenz, *Philosophie und Erlebnis in Senecas Dialogen NAG*, phil. hist. Kl. I 4.3 (1941) 55-108 and *Die Stoa* 2 (Göttingen 1964) 140.
[28] *Disc.*, 2.17.34; cf. 1.4.6; 2.23.44.
[29] D.L. 6.63; 6.72.
[30] The discussion of G. R. Stanton, ("The cosmopolitan Ideas of Epictetus and Marcus Aurelius", *Phronesis* 13 (1968) 183-195) is limited, but draws a few important distinctions.

NOTES TO CHAPTER SIX

[1] W. J. Verdenius, *Parmenides* (Groningen 1942) 29-30; S. M. L. Darcus, *The Notion of Self in Xenophanes and Heraclitus* (Ph.D. thesis, Univ. of Toronto) chapter 7.
[2] Fr. 115 DK.
[3] *N.E.* 1175B.
[4] See W. Burkert, *Lore and Science in Ancient Pythagoreanism* (tr. E. Minar, Harvard 1972) 192-208.
[5] *Rep.* 540C2.
[6] *Symp.* 202E, 215B.
[7] *Tim.* 90A.

[8] *Rep.* 617E.
[9] W. K. C. Guthrie, "Plato's Views on the Immortality of the Soul", *Entretiens pour l'Antiquité classique* 3 (Vandoeuvres-Geneva 1955) 11-12.
[10] Cf. Arist., *Met.* 1076A1.
[11] Cf. Tatian, *Orat. ad Graecos* 1.13.
[12] SVF. 1.65.
[13] SVF. 3.456 etc.
[14] Sext. Emp., *adv. Math.* 11.8 (SVF 2.224).
[15] J. M. Rist, "Zeno and Stoic Consistency", esp. 167-174.
[16] H. Merki, ὉΜΟΙΩΣΙΣ ΘΕΩΙ (Freiburg, Switzerland 1952) 7.
[17] D.L. 7.125 (SVF 3.237).
[18] Cf. Epictetus' views on the unimportance of slavery, *Disc.* 3.24.66 etc.
[19] In general see A. A. Long, "The Stoic Concept of Evil", *Philosophical Quarterly* 18 (1968) 329-343.
[20] *N.E.* 1177AB.
[21] Plot., *Enn.* 6.8.5.
[22] Hipp., *Phil.* 21 (SVF 2.975).
[23] S. G. Pembroke, "Οἰκείωσις", in *Problems in Stoicism*, ed. A. A. Long (London 1971) 114-149; G. Kerferd, "The Search for Personal Identity in Greek Thought", *Bull. of J. Rylands Library* 55 (Univ. of Manchester 1971) 177-196.
[24] Galen, *de plac. Hipp. et Plat.* 8.652 (Fr. 32 Edelstein-Kidd).
[25] 4.32; 8.31; 8.37.
[26] Here perhaps we should follow J. L. Talman (*The Origins of Totalitarian Democracy* (London 1965)) in distinguishing "liberal" from "totalitarian" democracy.
[27] D.L. 7.4.
[28] Plato takes this cosmic view at times also, as in *Laws* 903C.
[29] For a corrective see primarily L. Edelstein, "The Philosophical System of Posidonius", *AJP* 57 (1936) 286-325.
[30] Fr. 83, 84 Van Straaten. Panaetius' novelties are (unconvincingly) denied by R. Hoven, *Stoicisme et Stoiciens face au problème de l'au-delà* (Bull. Univ. de Liège 1971) 51-57. In general, D.L. 7.15 (SVF 1.522; 2.811).
[31] 4.23; cf. 4.4, 4.29 etc.
[32] 6.10; 4.27 etc.
[33] 11.3.
[34] 1.17.7.
[35] 7.3.

NOTES TO CHAPTER SEVEN

[1] Cf. *Laws* 630BC, 770C-E.
[2] The "noble lie" (414B) is not an exception, for even distorting the truth may also be necessary in private life.
[3] *Rep.* 406E, 460C4, cf. 461E.
[4] *Rep.* 600B2.
[5] If virtue cannot be recognized, value is lacking. Hence presumably the justification for abortion and exposure.
[6] *Pol.* 301C6-E4; for the *Laws* see p. 60.
[7] *Rep.* 520A.
[8] *N.E.* 1177A30ff.
[9] *N.E.* 1099A.
[10] J. M. Rist, "Aristotle: The Value of Man", 1-21.
[11] *Laws* 630BC, 770C-E.
[12] *Rep.* 352-3.
[13] *Apol.* 30D-31B.

¹⁴ Admittedly *Laws* 10 indicates that providence does not necessarily elevate man (cf. p. 121.
¹⁵ *Laws* 716C.
¹⁶ D.L. 6.21; D. R. Dudley, *A History of Cynicism* (reprint Hildesheim 1967) 54-5.
¹⁷ D.L. 6.38.
¹⁸ SVF 1.264-6, 268 (D.L. 7.33); cf. H. C. Baldry, "Zeno's Ideal State", *JHS* 79 (1959) 3-15.
¹⁹ J. M. Rist, *Stoic Philosophy* 68.
²⁰ Cf. Sen., *Ep.* 73.12 etc.
²¹ Ath., 12.547A (512 Usener).
²² *B.D.* 31-38.
²³ Cic., *De Amic.* 37.
²⁴ For artificial bonds see *De fin.* 1.20.70; Lucr., *De Rer. Nat.* 5.1019, 1025; V. Goldschmidt, "Le fondement naturel du droit positif selon Epicure, *Arch. de Phil. du Droit* 21 (1976) 184.
²⁵ Hostility persisted as late as the second century A.D. See Lucian, *Alex.* 38.
²⁶ Cic., *de Fin.* 1.70; cf. J. M. Rist, "Epicurus on Friendship", *C.P.* 75 (1980) 121-129.
²⁷ D.L. 10.119.
²⁸ Epict., *Disc.* 1.23.7-10.
²⁹ A new fragment of Diogenes of Oenoanda suggests that later Epicureans were "heretically" Utopian. Justice and love of one another will be universal. (NF 21, in M. F. Smith, *Thirteen New Fragments of Diogenes of Oenoanda* (Vienna, *Ost. Akad. d. Wiss. Phil.-Hist. Kl.* 117, 1974).
³⁰ See above p. 82.
³¹ 7.3.
³² Cf. the studies of F. Millar, *The Emperor in the Roman World* (London 1977).
³³ In general see R. Mellor, *ΘΕΑ ΡΩΜΗ: The Worship of the Goddess Roma in the Greek World*, (*Hyp.* 44, Göttingen 1975); *Le Culte des Souverains dans l'Empire Romain* (Entretiens Hardt 19, Vandoeuvres-Geneva 1973).
³⁴ *Pol.* 2.3.

NOTES TO CHAPTER EIGHT

¹ *Enn.* 5.1.8; cf. 4.4.22.12; 4.8.1.27 etc.
² W. R. Inge, *The Philosophy of Plotinus* I (London 1921) 203.
³ For general questions of Plotinus' psychology see H. J. Blumenthal, *Plotinus' Psychology* (The Hague 1971).
⁴ *Enn.* 3.4.3; cf. 1.1.8.
⁵ *Enn.* 4.8.8.8 ff.
⁶ *Enn.* 3.4.6.
⁷ For "inner" and "outer" man see *Enn.* 1.4.8.3, 5.1.10.10, 6.4.14-15, 3.2.15; cf. Plato, *Rep.* 589A7 ff.
⁸ *Enn.* 5.1.1.1.
⁹ Cf. J. M. Rist, *Eros and Psyche* 107.
¹⁰ For discussion see especially J. M. Rist, "Forms of Individuals in Plotinus", *CQ* 13 (1963) 223-231 and "Ideas of Individuals in Plotinus", *Rev. Int. de Phil.* 92 (1970) 298-303; *contra* H. J. Blumenthal, "Did Plotinus believe in Ideas of Individuals?", *Phronesis* 11 (1966) 61-80.
¹¹ J. M. Rist, *Plotinus* 56, 195. *Contra* P. Hadot in *Annuaire, Ecole Prat. des Hautes Etudes V⁰ Section* 78 (1970-1) 279, who thinks (I cannot agree) of the Active Intellect. See also D. O'Meara, "L'Expérience mystique de Plotin", *Mnem.* 27 (1974) 238-244.
¹² J. M. Rist, *Plotinus* chapter 16.
¹³ *Enn.* 4.8.1; 6.9.11.

[14] J. M. Rist, *Plotinus* 116.
[15] *Enn.* 3.8.1.
[16] See above p. 38.
[17] Fr. B2, 6, 8 etc. DK.
[18] *Enn.* 5.5.12.57; 6.8.19.18.
[19] For Pythagoreanism see Porph., *V.P.* 20.
[20] Cf. J. M. Rist, *Plotinus* 29-36.
[21] *Enn.* 1.3.
[22] Porph., *V.P.* 14.
[23] *Enn.* 6.7.37, 6.9.6, 5.5.9-10 etc.
[24] Note the phrase νοῦν ἢ θεόν at *Enn.* 6.9.6.12; and for Middle Platonism see Dillon, *The Middle Platonists*.
[25] Cf. *De Caelo* 2.8-9 etc.
[26] Cf. J. M. Rist, "The Indefinite Dyad and Intelligible Matter", *CQ* 12 (1962) 103, with *Enn.* 6.7.37, for the assimilation of Aristotelianism and Platonism.
[27] In *Les Sources de Plotin* (Entretiens Hardt 5, Vandoeuvres-Geneva 1960) 385.
[28] Porph., *V.P.* 4.
[29] Cf. J. Dillon, *op. cit.* esp. p. 303.
[30] Cf. A. H. Armstrong, "The Background of the Doctrine that the Intelligibles are not Outside the Intellect", *Entretiens Hardt* 5 (Vandoeuvres-Geneva 1960) 405.
[31] Albinus, *Did.* 10, cf. Ps.-Plut., *De Fato* 573B.
[32] Porph., *V.P.* 14.
[33] Cf. H. Langerbeck, "The Philosophy of Ammonius Saccas", *JHS* 77 (1957) 71-72.
[34] Fr. 7, p. 214. 11ff Koetschau; cf. J. Dillon, *The Middle Platonists* 284, n. 2.
[35] For a concise summary of the evidence on the chronology of Methodius see H. Musurillo's edition of the *Symposium* (*ACW*, Washington 1958) 3-5.
[36] *Enn.* 3.2.9.

NOTES TO CHAPTER NINE

[1] *Met.* 1078B27ff.
[2] See P. Garnsey, *Status and Legal Privilege in the Roman Empire* (Oxford 1970).
[3] Arist., *Pol.* 3.9; 3.12; 5.1.12 etc.
[4] Cf. Plato, *Gorg.* 507A6, *Laws* 757BC.
[5] Cf. generally W. K. C. Guthrie, *A History of Greek Philosophy* 3 (Cambridge 1969) 135-147.
[6] Cf. the doctrine of οἰκείωσις for which see Pembroke, *op. cit.*; in general also p. 78 above.
[7] Fr. B9 DK (= Sext. Emp., *adv. math.* 7.135).
[8] Epict., *Disc.* 1.23.3.
[9] Cic., *De fin.* 1.70.
[10] Epicurus, *V.S.* 35; *BD* 31-38.
[11] J. P. Sartre, *Being and Nothingness* (tr. H. Barnes, N.Y. 1966) 10.
[12] *Laws* 899D-905D.
[13] D.L. 10.123.
[14] D.L. 10.81; Lucr., *De Rer. Nat.* 4.823-857.
[15] *De dis* 3, col. 1, 14, p. 16 Diels.
[16] E. R. Dodds, *Pagan and Christian in an Age of Anxiety* (Cambridge 1965) 29, n. 1.
[17] 644 E, 803C.

NOTES TO CHAPTER TEN

[1] Cf. E. Fromm, *Escape from Freedom* (N.Y. 1941), chapter 3.
[2] *Laws* 731D-732B; cf. Aristotle, *Pol.* 1263B.

[3] W. D. Ross, *Aristotle* (London 1949) 208.
[4] Cf. especially Dodds, *The Greeks and the Irrational* and A. Adkins, *Merit and Responsibility* (Oxford 1960) e.g. 63 ff.
[5] Cf. Philo, *Leg. All.* 3.15 f, and for other references E. R. Dodds, *Proclus, The Elements of Theology* (Oxford² 1963) 307-8.
[6] D.L. 10.132. Justice, of course, is to be understood in Epicurus' special sense.
[7] *Enn.* 3.2.9.
[8] *N.E.* 1011A15ff.
[9] There may be some awareness of this in Aristotle's comments (*N.E.* 1138A1) on the merit of not insisting on the letter of legal justice.
[10] In general, on these questions see A. R. Hands, *Charities and Social Aid in Greece and Rome* (London 1968).
[11] E. R. Dodds, *Pagan and Christian* 136ff.
[12] Plato, *Laws* 630BC, 770 C-E.

NOTES TO CHAPTER ELEVEN

[1] See above pp. 27-28.
[2] Cf. Lucian, *Philosophies for Sale* 17.
[3] Cf. *Adkins, op. cit.* e.g. 37ff.
[4] Cf. H. North, *Sophrosyne* (Ithaca 1966).
[5] Problems in this area have been much discussed. See recently C. H. Kahn, "Plato on the Unity of the Virtues", in *Facets of Plato's Philosophy* (ed. W. H. Werkmeister, Assen-Amsterdam 1976) 21-39.
[6] *Rep.* 452A10ff.
[7] D.L. 7.33 (= SVF 1.267).
[8] D.L. 7.33 (= SVF 1.257).
[9] SVF 1.200-220.
[10] D.L. 6.97.
[11] Musonius fr. 12 (C. Lutz, *YCS* 10 (1947)). For Seneca see the remarks of C. E. Manning, "Seneca and the Stoics on the Equality of the Sexes", *Mnemosyne* s. 4, 26 (1973) 170-7, esp. p. 171. But not too much weight should be put on the pejorative use of *muliebris* (e.g. at *ad Helv.* 12A). We probably have here something of the same tendency we noticed in Plato to "lapse" into the "sexist" phrases of everyday speech. See above pp. 27-28.
[12] *Rep.* 460E. In the *Laws* Plato says 16 to 20 for marriage at 785B, 18 and up at 893 D For Aristotle, *Pol.* 1335A28.
[13] J. M. Rist, *Epicurus* 139.
[14] *Pol.* 1325B23 ff.
[15] Cf Arist *H A* 588A. If death occurs in the first week, no name is given.
[16] Aristotle is hesitant about economic grounds (*Pol.* 1375B2ff.): custom is against it. For Plato see *Theaet.* 151C, *Rep.* 459DE, 460C ff. (with Adam's note and Appendix IV in *The Republic of Plato* (Cambridge 1963)). For Epicurus see Epictetus, *Disc.* 1.23.7-10. Musonius, as usual more humanitarian than many Stoics, condemned exposure (fr. 15).
[17] For the exceptions (Antipater, Musonius, Hierocles) see F. H. Sandbach, *The Stoics* (London 1975) 117-118, 163, 171; SVF III 62.3 (Antipater).
[18] D.L. 10.19-21.
[19] *Pol.* 1253B35 ff.
[20] Only Alcidamas was famed in this regard. See *Pol.* 1253B20 and scholiast to *Rhet.* 1373B. Cf. Guthrie, *A History of Greek Philosophy* 3, 159-160. More generally R. Schlaifer, "Greek Theories of Slavery".

NOTES TO CHAPTER TWELVE

[1] Cf. Aug., *Ep.* 118-25; Sext.Emp., *adv. math.* 9.25.
[2] It is, of course, pointed out that he has different faculties from animals or stones, but that is no more than a beginning. And usually when humans are distinguished from animals (e.g. by the thesis that they can attain likeness to God), they are distinguished *as a group*.
[3] J. M. Rist, "Notes on *De Anima* 3.5", *CP* 61 (1966) 8-20, reprinted in J. Anton and G. L. Kustas ed., *Essays in Ancient Greek Philosophy* (Albany 1971) 505-521.
[4] J. M. Rist, *Plotinus* 222-230.
[5] *Enn.* 6.8.19.18.
[6] The term is taken from R. C. Zaehner, *Mysticism: Sacred and Profane* (Oxford paperback 1961) 28-29.
[7] Cf. J. M. Rist, "Plotinus and Augustine on Evil", *Plotino e il Neoplatonismo in Oriente e in Occidente* (Rome 1974) 507-508.
[8] *Cf.* Eus., *H.E.* 6.19.

NOTES TO CHAPTER THIRTEEN

[1] For the most convenient general study see H. Merki, ΟΜΟΙΩΣΙΣ ΘΕΩΙ. *Von der platonischen Angleichung an Gott zur Gottähnlichkeit bei Gregor von Nyssa* (Freiburg, Switzerland 1952).
[2] *Theaet.* 176AB etc.
[3] On this "heretical" notion see *De Principiis* 3.6.5.
[4] On a possible source for the doctrine of purgatory see Tertullian, *De Anima* 58.8 with the comments of J. H. Waszink, *ad loc.*
[5] *De Spect.* 30. Cf. R. Joly, "La contemplation des supplices inférieux" in *Christianisme et Philosophie* (Brussels 1973) 171-182.
[6] *Apol.* 1.27 (exposure); *Ad Ux.* 5 (abortion); cf. *Virg. Vel.* 14, *De Anima* 25. Cf. *Didache* 2 (abortion); 5 (infanticide); *Ad Diog.* 5 (exposure).
[7] *De Spect.* 19: the innocent find no pleasure in another's sufferings; *De Idol.* 17 (against torture and setting in judgment); *De Cor. Mil.*; warfare is inappropriate to Christians.
[8] *Adv. Prax.* 12; *Exh. Cast.* 1.
[9] *Ad Scap.* 2.1: humani iuris et naturalis potestatis est unicuique quod putaverit colere. Is this the language of the *Constitutio Antoniniana*?
[10] *De Cultu Fem.* 1.1. Tertullian refers to Gen. 1.26 here, but does not develop it; cf. *Adv. Prax.* 12.1.
[11] Cf. S. R. C. Lilla, *Clement of Alexandria: A study in Christian Platonism and Gnosticism* (Oxford 1971) 15, 108 etc.
[12] Noted also, but hardly practised by Tertullian (*ad Scap.* 1.1.).
[13] Indeed we can become "gods" or as gods. Note the exegesis of Ps. 81.6 (*Strom.* 7.13.1; 7.51.3; 7.56.6); cf. Lilla, *op. cit.* 187; E. F. Osborn, *Ethical Patterns in Christian Doctrine* (Cambridge, 1976) 66; W. E. G. Floyd, *Clement of Alexandria's Treatment of the Problem of Evil* (Oxford 1971) 85-86.
[14] Cf. R. A. Baer, *Philo's Use of the Categories Male and Female* (Leiden 1970) esp. 37-44.
[15] Cf. J. P. Broudéhoux, *Mariage et Famille chez Clément d'Alexandrie* (Paris 1970) 54-55.
[16] Note, however, that for Clement sexual activity is not the first sin. Sin arises from disobedience to God and hence a precipitate rush to marriage: cf. Floyd, *op. cit.* 52; *Strom.* 3.94.3, 3.81.
[17] Note that if males are sexually penetrated, i.e. become physically "female", they are adjudged more vicious than female sinners.
[18] In early Christianity the importance of the question of the nature of the *Deus Christianorum* cannot be overemphasized. Thus a detailed enquiry into philosophical views of man in the Patristic period must start with theology.

SELECT BIBLIOGRAPHY

Adkins, A. *Merit and Responsibility*, Oxford 1960.
Armstrong, A. H. "The Background of the Doctrine that the Intelligibles are not Outside the Intellect", *Entretiens Hardt* 5, *Les Sources de Plotin* (Geneva 1960) 393-425.
Blumenthal, H. J. *Plotinus' Psychology*, The Hague 1971.
Blumenthal, H. J. "Did Plotinus believe in Ideas of Individuals?", *Phronesis* 11 (1966) 61-80.
Cooper, J. M. *Reason and Human Good in Aristotle*, Cambridge, Mass. 1975.
Dillon, J. M. *The Middle Platonists*, London/Ithaca 1977.
Dodds, E. R. *The Greeks and the Irrational*, Berkeley 1951.
Dodds, E. R. *Pagan and Christian in an Age of Anxiety*, Cambridge 1965.
Dudley, D. R. *A History of Cynicism*, Hildesheim 1967.
Festugière, A.-J. *Personal Religion among the Greeks*, Berkeley 1960.
Fortenbaugh, W. W. "On Plato's Feminism in Republic V", *Apeiron* 9 (1975) 1-4.
Fortenbaugh, W. W. "Aristotle on Slaves and Women", in *Articles on Aristotle* 2 ed. J. Barnes et al. (London 1977) 135-139.
Garnsey, P. *Status and Legal Privilege in the Roman Empire*, Oxford 1970.
Goldschmidt, V. "Le fondement naturel du droit positif selon Epicure", *Arch. de Phil. du Droit* 21 (1976).
Hands, A. R. *Charities and Social Aid in Greece and Rome*, London 1968.
Kenny, A. *The Aristotelian Ethics*, Oxford 1978.
Kerferd, G. "The Search for Personal Identity in Greek Thought", *Bull. of the John Rylands Library* (University of Manchester 1971) 177-196.
Long, A. A. "The Stoic Theory of Evil", *PQ* 18 (1968) 329-343.
Merki, H. *ΟΜΟΙΩΣΙΣ ΘΕΩΙ*, Freiburg, Switzerland 1952.
Oates, W. J. *Aristotle and the Problem of Value*, Princeton 1963.
Pohlenz, M. "Philosophie und Erlebnis in Senecas Dialogen", *NAG* Phil.-Hist. Kl. 1.4.3 (1941) 55-108.
Pohlenz, M. *Die Stoa*, Göttingen 1964.
Pembroke, S. G. "ΟΙΚΕΙΩΣΙΣ" in *Problems in Stoicism*, ed. A. A. Long (London 1971) 115-159.
Rist, J. M. *Plotinus: The Road to Reality*, Cambridge 1967.
Rist, J. M. "The One of Plotinus and the God of Aristotle", *Rev. of Met.* 27 (1973) 75-87.
Rist, J. M. *Epicurus, An Introduction*, Cambridge 1972.
Rist, J. M. "Aristotle: The Value of Man and the Origin of Morality", *Can. Journal of Phil.* 4 (1974) 1-21.
Schlaifer, R. "Greek Theories of Slavery from Homer to Aristotle", in *Slavery in Classical Antiquity* (ed. M. I. Finley) Cambridge 1969.
Stinton, G. R. "The cosmopolitan ideas of Epictetus and Marcus Aurelius", *Phronesis* 13 (1968) 183-195.
Vlastos, G. "Creation in the *Timaeus*: Is it a fiction?", in *Studies in Plato's Metaphysics* (ed. R. E. Allen) London 1963.
Vlastos, G. "The Paradox of Socrates", in *The Philosophy of Socrates* N.Y. 1971.
Vlastos, G. *Platonic Studies*, Princeton 1973.
Wender, D. "Plato: Misogynist, Paedophile and Feminist", *Arethusa* 6 (1973).
Whittaker, J. "The Eternity of the Platonic Forms", *Phronesis* 13 (1968) 131-144.

INDEX

Active Intellect, 43-44, 53, 100
Albinus, 108, 111
Alexander of Aphrodisias, 107, 108
apatheia, 37, 62
Aristotle, 2, 8, 26, 33-35, 39, 42-58, 59, 67, 77, 89, 90, 98, 106, 107, 123, 127, 135, 136, 146
Aspasius, 111
Augustine, 140
banausos, 28, 40, 47
"barbarians", 27
children, 28, 46, 141-143
Christians, 4, 98, 111, 128, 153, 163
Chrysippus, 67, 78, 79
Cicero, 1, 67, 94, 150
Clement of Alexandria, 111, 159-163
contemplation, 54
Crates, 65, 137
criminals, 3, 29, 47, 98, 130
Critias, 22, 60, 116
Cynicism, Cynics, 37, 62, 63-66, 68-70, 79, 80, 91-94, 118, 137, 147
daimòn, 50, 72, 73, 74
Declaration of Human Rights, 1, 119
Demiurge, 8, 16, 38, 41, 50, 73
Diogenes, 62, 64, 71, 92
Empedocles, 71
Epictetus, 67, 71, 74, 79, 80
Epicurus, 8, 82, 94, 95, 96, 98, 118-122, 126, 140-1, 142
evil, 7, 37, 78
exposure, 95, 142
foreigners, 1, 40
freedom, 59-70
friendship, 20, 56, 57, 94, 119
Gnostics, 2, 102, 159
God(s), 5-10, 21, 29, 38, 47, 56, 105, 106-109
good (good for, good at, etc.), 11, 12, 17, 18, 20, 23, 24, 25, 29, 34, 35, 36, 38, 41, 58, 73, 103
guardians, 27, 28, 39, 50, 84, 86, 134
hēgemonikon, 77
Heraclitus, 71
intrinsic value, 31, 76, 125
Irenaeus, 157-8
Marcus Aurelius, 3, 79, 80, 81, 82, 96, 121, 122

Methodius of Olympus, 112
mind (*nous, noēsis*), 43, 47, 48, 49, 57, 73, 80, 83, 137, 149, 153
Musonius Rufus, 138, 160
nature, natural, etc. 21, 44, 66, 78, 86, 93
One, 9, 36, 99, 103, 104, 105, 109, 112, 151
Origen, 111, 155
persons, 1, 34, 36, 145-152
Plato, 1, 8, 13, 14, 15, 16-41, 49, 50, 51, 56, 57, 59, 60, 84, 85, 86, 87, 89, 90, 117, 124, 133-4, 149
pleasure, 36, 37
Pliny, 77
Plotinus, 2, 9, 10, 99-113, 126, 150, 151, 152
Porphyry, 105, 110, 152
Posidonius, 79, 81
power, 97, 116, 129, 139, 140
Prime Mover, 50, 51
prohairesis, 67, 68
Protagoras, 21, 43
providence, 9, 15, 56, 76, 90
practical wisdom, 55
punishment, 3, 40, 115
rights, 31, 32, 80, 114, 116, 123-131, 145, 146
self-respect, 124-5
Seneca, 79, 82, 83
slaves, 2, 13, 26, 40, 143, 162
social contract, 114-122
Socrates, 2, 16, 17, 18, 19-22, 38, 51, 61, 64, 72, 87, 91
sophists, 18, 114
Speusippus, 35, 36
spiritual direction, 83
Stoics, 9, 66, 67, 74, 75, 76, 77, 81, 83, 104, 126, 127, 137, 147
subhumans, 45
Thrasymachus, 22
torture, 77
true opinion, true belief, 17, 149
usefulness, 11, 12
women, 14, 27-28, 47, 133, 134, 135, 137, 138-9, 162
Xenocrates, 37-37
Zeno (the Stoic), 62, 65, 66, 79, 81, 92
Zeus Xenios, 7

Philosophia Antiqua

A series of monographs on ancient philosophy

Edited by

W. J. VERDENIUS and J. C. M. van WINDEN

1. **Verdenius, W. J.** and **J. H. Waszink.** Aristotle on coming-to-be and passing-away. Some comments. Repr. of the 2nd (1966) ed. 1968. (vi, 79 p.) [01718 6] Gld. 48.—
3. **Verdenius, W. J.** Mimesis. Plato's doctrine of artistic imitation and its meaning to us. 3rd impr. 1972. Sm. 8vo. (vi, 50 p.) [03556 7] Gld. 8.—
7. **Saffrey, H. D.** Le περὶ φιλοσοφίας d'Aristote et la théorie platonicienne des idées nombres. 2ème éd. revue et accompagnée du compte-rendu critique par H. CHERNISS. 1971. (xiv, 93 p.) [01720 8] Gld. 44.—
9. **Winden, J. C. M. van.** Calcidius on matter. His doctrine and sources. A chapter in the history of Platonism. Photomech. repr. 1965. (viii, 268 p.) (D) [01721 6] Gld. 68.—
10. **Dreizehnter, A.** Untersuchungen zur Textgeschichte der aristotelischen Politik. 1962. (xvi, 81 p.) (D) [01722 4] Gld. 28.—
12. **Waszink, J. H.** Studien zum Timaioskommentar des Calcidius. 1. Die erste Hälfte des Kommentars (mit Ausnahme der Kapitel über die Weltseele). 1964. (vii, 87 p.) [01724 0] Gld. 32.—
13. **Nicolaus Damascenus** on the philosophy of Aristotle. Fragments of the first five books, translated from the Syriac with an introduction and commentary by J. H. DROSSAART LULOFS. Repr. of the 1st (1965) ed. 1969. (xiv, 178 [16 Syriac t.] p., 1 table) [01725 9] Gld. 64.—
14. **Edelstein, L.** Plato's Seventh Letter. 1966. (x, 171 p.) [01726 7] Gld. 72.—
15. **Porphyrios.** Πρὸς Μαρκέλλαν. Griechischer Text, herausgegeben, übersetzt, eingeleitet und erklärt von W. PÖTSCHER. 1969. (x, 142 [17 Gr. t.] p., 1 facs.) [01727 5] Gld. 72.—
16. **Elferink, M. A.** La descente de l'âme d'après Macrobe. Avec une notice biographique sur l'auteur par J. H. WASZINK. 1968. (viii, 69 p.) [01728 3] Gld. 32.—
17. **Gould, J. B.** The philosophy of Chrysippus. Repr. 1971. (viii, 222 p.) [01729 1] Gld. 48.—
18. **Boeft, J. den.** Calcidius on fate. His doctrine and sources. 1970. (vi, 149 p.) (D) [01730 5] Gld. 48.—

19. **Pötscher, W.** Strukturprobleme der aristotelischen und theophrastischen Gottesvorstellung. 1970. (xiv, 150 p.) [01731 3]
Gld. 72.—
20. **Bertier, J.** Mnésithée et Dieuchès. 1972. (xvi, 280 p., frontisp.) [03468 4]
Gld. 96.—
21. **Timaios Lokros.** Über die Natur des Kosmos und der Seele. Kommentiert von M. BALTES. 1972. (xii, 252 p.) (D) [03344 0]
Gld. 68.—
22. **Graeser, A.** Plotinus and the stoics. A preliminary study. 1972. (xvi, 145 p.) [03345 9]
Gld. 60.—
23. **Iamblichus Chalcidensis.** In Platonis dialogos commentariorum fragmenta. Edited with translation and commentary by J. M. DILLON. 1973. (viii, 450 p.) [03578 8]
Gld. 152.—
24. **Timaeus Locrus.** De natura mundi et animae. Überlieferung, Testimonia, Text und Übersetzung von W. MARG. *Editio maior.* 1972. (x, 151 p.) [03505 2]
Gld. 76.—
25. **Konstan, D.** Some aspects of Epicurean psychology. 1973. (x, 84 p.) [03653 9]
Gld. 36.—
26. **Gersh, S. E.** Κίνησις ἀκίνητος. A study of spiritual motion in the philosophy of Proclus. 1973. (viii, 143 p.) [03784 5]
Gld. 60.—
27. **O'Meara, D.** Structures hiérarchiques dans la pensée de Plotin. Étude historique et interprétative. 1975. (viii, 137 p.) [04372 1]
Gld. 68.—
28. **Todd, R. B.** Alexander of Aphrodisias on Stoic physics. A study of the *De Mixtione* with preliminary essays, text, translation and commentary. 1976. (xiv, 272 p.) [04402 7]
Gld. 96.—
29. **Scheffel, W.** Aspekte der platonischen Kosmologie. Untersuchungen zum Dialog 'Timaios'. 1976. (xvi, 146 p.) [04509 0]
Gld. 48.—
30. **Baltes, M.** Die Weltentstehung des platonischen Timaios nach den antiken Interpreten. Teil 1. 1976. (xvi, 247 p.) [04720 4]
Gld. 45.—
31. **Edlow, R. B.** Galen on language and ambiguity. An English translation of Galen's *'De Captionibus* (On Fallacies)', with introduction, text and commentary. 1977. (xiv, 143 p.) [04869 3]
Gld. 44.—
32. **Welllver, W.** Character, plot and thought in Plato's Timaeus and Critias. 1977. (viii, 65 p., frontisp.) [04870 7]
Gld. 20.—
33. **Boeft, J. den.** Calcidius on demons (Commentarius Ch. 127-136). 1977. (x, 70 p.) [05283 6]
Gld. 30.—
34. **Epiktet.** Vom Kynismus. Herausgegeben und übersetzt mit einem Kommentar von M. BILLERBECK. 1978. (xvi, 188 p.) [05770 6]
Gld. 64.—
35. **Baltes, M.** Die Weltenstehung des platonischen Timaios nach den antiken Interpreten. Teil 2. 1979. (x, 175 p.) [05799 4]   Gld. 48.—

36. Billerbeck, M. Der Kyniker Demetrius. Ein Beitrag zur Geschichte der frühkaiserzeitlichen Popularphilosophie. 1979. (x, 69 p.) [06032 4] Gld. 24.—

37. O'Brien, D. Theories of weight in the ancient world. Four essays on Democritus, Plato and Aristotle. A study in the development of ideas. 1. Democritus: Weight and size. An exercise in the reconstruction of early Greek philosophy. 1981. (xxi, 419 p.) [06134 7] Gld. 120.—

38. O'Brien, D. Pour interpréter Empédocle. 1981. (ix, 138 p.) [06249 1] Gld. 48.—

39. Tarán, L. Speusippus of Athens. A critical study with a collection of the related texts and commentary. 1982. (xxvii, 521 p.) [06505 9] Gld. 244.—

40. Rist, J. M. Human value. A study in ancient philosophical ethics. 1982.

1982. Prices may be changed without notice.

E. J. Brill — P.O.B. 9000 — 2300 PA Leiden — The Netherlands

MEDE VERKRIJGBAAR DOOR BEMIDDELING VAN DE BOEKHANDEL